Microsoft® Office 365 in Business

Microsoft® Office 365 in Business

David Kroenke
Donald E. Nilson

WILEY

Wiley Publishing, Inc.

Microsoft® Office 365 in Business

Published by
Wiley Publishing, Inc.
10475 Crosspoint Boulevard
Indianapolis, IN 46256
www.wiley.com

Copyright © 2011 by Wiley Publishing, Inc., Indianapolis, Indiana

Published simultaneously in Canada

ISBN: 978-1-118-10504-7
ISBN: 978-1-118-15034-4 (ebk)
ISBN: 978-1-118-15033-7 (ebk)
ISBN: 978-1-118-15032-0 (ebk)

Manufactured in the United States of America

10 9 8 7 6 5 4 3 2 1

For general information on our other products and services please contact our Customer Care Department within the United States at (877) 762-2974, outside the United States at (317) 572-3993 or fax (317) 572-4002.

Wiley also publishes its books in a variety of electronic formats and by print-on-demand. Not all content that is available in standard print versions of this book may appear or be packaged in all book formats. If you have purchased a version of this book that did not include media that is referenced by or accompanies a standard print version, you may request this media by visiting http://booksupport.wiley.com. For more information about Wiley products, visit us at www.wiley.com.

Library of Congress Control Number: 2011930124

About the Authors

DAVID KROENKE is the author of many books on the use of information technology in business. Known for his easy-to-read, understandable, and humorous text, he's worked in the industry and academics, and been twice selected as Educator of the Year in the United States.

DONALD NILSON is a Certified Public Accountant and worked as a program manager for Microsoft for 10 years. Don currently works for a small company where he is planning the implementation of Office 365 to address the need for online collaboration among employees. He has been a pioneer in the accounting profession and in computer information systems for 40 years.

About the Technical Editor

DREW RUDEBUSCH is currently a Vendor Manager at Zulily, Inc., managing purchasing, fulfillment, and logistics for the rapidly growing, private-sale retail website. In this fast pace start-up environment, he has contributed to a wide variety of process and technology improvements throughout the organization. He has been active in the Seattle entrepreneurship community working with multiple start-ups, non-profit organizations, and university programs. His previous experience includes work in sales and account management, internet marketing, as well as a variety freelance projects in educational and technology publishing. Drew completed his undergraduate degree in Marketing and Entrepreneurship, with a Sales Certificate, from the Michael G. Foster School of Business at the University of Washington.

Credits

ACQUISITIONS EDITOR
Paul Reese

PROJECT EDITOR
Maureen Spears

TECHNICAL EDITOR
Drew Rudebusch

PRODUCTION EDITOR
Kathleen Wisor

COPY EDITOR
Paula Lowell

EDITORIAL DIRECTOR
Robyn B. Siesky

EDITORIAL MANAGER
Mary Beth Wakefield

FREELANCER EDITORIAL MANAGER
Rosemarie Graham

ASSOCIATE DIRECTOR OF MARKETING
David Mayhew

PRODUCTION MANAGER
Tim Tate

VICE PRESIDENT AND EXECUTIVE GROUP PUBLISHER
Richard Swadley

VICE PRESIDENT AND EXECUTIVE PUBLISHER
Barry Pruett

ASSOCIATE PUBLISHER
Jim Minatel

PROJECT COORDINATOR, COVER
Katie Crocker

COMPOSITOR
Chris Gillespie,
Happenstance Type-O-Rama

PROOFREADER
James Saturnio, Word One

INDEXER
Johnna VanHoose Dinse

COVER IMAGE
© iStock / Mlenny Photography
© iStock / Slawomir Fajer
© iStock / Clerkenwell_Images

COVER DESIGNER
LeAndra Young

Acknowledgments

A HUGE THANKS to Steve Fox at Microsoft, who enabled us to have access to one of the first Office 365 tenancies in the beta program. Steve is an evangelist's evangelist and a great guy! Another huge thanks to Rob Howard, also of Microsoft, for answering numerous low level and probably trivial SharePoint questions. Rob played key roles on the development side of SharePoint Designer, SharePoint 2010, and now Office 365. He's also a patient and terrific explainer!

We thank Paul Reese, acquisitions editor at Wiley, for his willingness to publish a low-level, benefit-oriented book rather than the more sophisticated, technical books that he normally publishes. Special thanks also goes to hardworking Drew Rudebusch, who checked all the technical details in this book and to Kathleen Wisor, who helped with the production issues.

We sincerely hope this book will help you use Office 365 to improve your collaborations. Have fun!

And we appreciate your business.

—DAVID KROENKE
SEATTLE, WASHINGTON

—DON NILSON
BELLEVUE, WASHINGTON

Contents at a Glance

Contents

Introduction

THE PURPOSE OF THIS BOOK is to teach non-technical business professionals the *why*, *what*, and *how* of using Office 365 for teams. Chapter 1 addresses the *why* by discussing the nature of cooperation and collaboration and some of the reasons that effective collaboration is so difficult. It then explains why the authors believe Office 365 can offer a strong helping hand for teams and team leaders.

Chapter 2 addresses the *what*. What are the four major components of Office 365? How do they relate? How does cloud-based hosting help teams in small and large organizations? Chapter 2 discusses the advantages of Office 365 and then summarizes what the risks and potential problems. Office 365 is not for every team, but nearly so.

Chapters 3–12 then address the *how*. Each of these chapters begins with a business scenario entitled, "Of Course, This Would Never Happen in Your Business." Even though these problems wouldn't happen in your business, they (or something quite similar) did in the authors' businesses. These scenarios will help you understand what Office 365 might do for you. You then learn how to use components of Office 365 to avoid the problems presented in the beginning scenario. Chapters 3–12 are roughly in order of increasing complexity, and you'll most likely find reading them in sequence to be the best strategy. However, don't be afraid to skip around. Use the index or glossary if you skip a chapter and don't know the meaning of a word.

Who Should Read This Book?

This book is written for business professionals who want to learn how to use Office 365 for teams and teamwork. It is not intended for technical people who want to know about Office 365 administration, customizing SharePoint with SharePoint Designer, programming SharePoint, or any such technical topic.

The only prerequisite to understanding this book is the ability to use a web browser such as Internet Explorer and to have a beginner's knowledge of an Office application such as Word, PowerPoint, or Excel. Having a beginner's knowledge of Outlook would also be helpful, but that knowledge is not essential to understanding this book.

This book is not an explanation of Office 365 *features*. It is neither complete nor comprehensive, and the authors make no attempt at explaining all the options of anything. You will not learn here, for example, the 27 different kinds of data you can store in a SharePoint list.

Instead, this book is about the *benefits* of Office 365 to professional teams. The teams can be small businesses; they can be teams located within medium to large businesses and other organizations; and they can be virtual teams that are federations of independent professionals, businesses, and organizations.

As stated, the authors' goal is to describe and illustrate Office 365 benefits. In the process, you will learn much about how to use Office 365. In fact, you will learn all the skills you need to succeed as a team member on any team that uses Office 365. You will not be an expert, not by a long shot, but you will know enough to contribute effectively to teams that use Office 365. You will also know enough to learn more advanced Office 365 features and functions on your own.

In short, this should be the first book a non-technical business professional reads about Office 365.

Our Website

The authors maintain a website at `www.Office365InBusiness.com`. (That's the title of this book with the words run together, followed by *.com*.) Please check out the site for late-breaking news, corrections, new ideas, and other topics that you might find of interest.

Conventions Used in this Book

To help you get the most from the text and keep track of what's happening, a number of conventions are used throughout the book.

Of Course, This Would Never Happen in <u>Your</u> Business...

These "hypothetical" business scenarios introduce a common collaboration problem that a normal business person might experience in the course of a regular day. They show you the problem that is the reason behind the rest of a chapter's content.

We say "hypothetical" because, of course, this could never happen in your business. Right?

But, with Office 365...

It Doesn't Have to Be That Way...

The note icon indicates special notes from the authors that help you understand the subject under discussion further.

Tips are sage pieces of advice—tips and tricks, if you will—that can help save you frustration as you work through Office 365.

Warnings indicate actions you should avoid so as not to lose data, precious time, or your mind.

PAUSE AND REFLECT

The authors like to consider these the book's moments of Zen—little tidbits and interesting information that give you further explanation on a subject under discussion.

As for styles in the text:

- We *highlight* new terms and important words when we introduce them.
- We show keyboard strokes like this: Ctrl+A.

Introduction to Office 365 in Business

Of Course, This Would Never Happen in <u>Your</u> Business...

A group of employees, meeting somewhere, just yesterday:

"No, Ringo! Not again! We decide something one meeting and then go over it again the next. You're driving me nuts!"

"Katherine, I just think it's important we get this right."

"If that's the case, why don't you come to the meetings?"

"I just missed a couple."

"Including last week's, when we met for two hours and decided to improve the way we're using Twitter."

"But Katherine, Twitter's so old school. Really. We need to foster a community on foursquare. It's so cool, and if ..." Katherine cuts him off.

"Ringo! We discussed foursquare last week and decided that until we can handle Twitter better, there's no need to go off on another tangent. We talked about this!"

"Not to me."

"But you weren't here! Come on, we'll never make progress like this."

"Ringo, Katherine is right," Adam jumps in to the conversation to reduce the tension, "We did talk about this. Did you get the email?"

"What email?"

"The meeting summary email that Laura sends out each week."

"I got the email but I couldn't download the attachment. Something weird about a virus checker couldn't access a gizmo or something like that... "

In response, the entire team falls silent.

"Look, you guys," Ringo, says, defensively, "I'll be honest. This meeting happens at 9:30 for you but that's 7:30 for me and it's way too early! I understand we discuss important things but I've got kids to get ready for school and a busy-lawyer wife. Sometimes, I just can't do it."

"Yeah, we get that, but we need your input. What are we gonna do?"

It Doesn't Have to Be that Way...

Why Consider Office 365?

THE WORLD DOESN'T NEED ANOTHER version of Microsoft Office. At last count, Word has over 20 toolbars; most of us use 2 or 3. The same goes for Excel and PowerPoint and the rest of the Office programs. Few of us need new versions of Office.

If Office 365 were only that... if it were just another set of 'improved' Office programs, then you could get on with your day, giving Office 365 peripheral attention, at most.

But, it isn't.

Office 365 does contain Office, but it also contains powerful communications and sharing facilities, all hosted by Microsoft in the cloud. We believe this suite of capability can help teams achieve greater success, and dramatically so.

However, if you're if you're not thinking about working in groups, put this book down. You don't need Office 365; use your current version of Office instead.

What Makes Teams Successful?

Because we claim Office 365 can help you make your teams more successful, a good place to start is with the question "What makes for team success?"

Richard Hackman, professor at Harvard, studied teamwork for many years, and his book *Leading Teams*[1] contains many useful concepts and management tips. Hackman says there are three primary criteria for judging team success. We can state them as follows:

- Successful outcome

- Growth in team capability

- Meaningful and satisfying experience

As business professionals, we all strive to achieve the first criteria. A successful outcome means that our team accomplished its goal whether it's solving a problem, making a decision, or creating some work product. Whatever the objective is, we ask "Did we get the job done?" as well as, "Was the success within our time and monetary budgets?"

The other two criteria may surprise you, but read on to see how they make sense.

Growth in Team Capability

Over time, did your team get better? If you're a football fan, you've undoubtedly heard coaches say, "We really improved as the season progressed." (If your team had two wins and 12 losses, you probably didn't hear this.) However, football teams last only a season. For a permanent team—say, a team of customer support personnel—the benefits of team growth are more desirable. Over time, if a team gets better, it is more efficient and thus provides better service for a given cost, or the same service for less cost.

But how does a team get better? For one, it develops better work processes. Activities are combined or eliminated. Linkages are established so that "the left hand knows what the right hand is doing," needs, or can provide. Teams also get better as individuals improve at their tasks. Part of that improvement is due to a learning curve; as someone does something over and over, they get better at it. However, team members also teach task skills and give knowledge to one another. Team members also provide perspectives that other team members need.

Among software developers, for example, it is well-known that a great way to surmount a difficult problem is to describe it to another developer. Often, just the act of describing the problem will provide the perspective needed to solve it.

[1] Richard Hackman. *Leading Teams.* Harvard Press, 2002, p. 30.

Team growth requires team communication. As Hackman points out, effective communication not only involves the communication skills of team members, but also requires that that team members have easy and appropriate access to one another. If I know that Maureen can show me how to hide markup in Word, but if I don't have easy access to her, then her knowledge won't benefit me. Easy access, by the way, means that she can *show me*, even if we're not in the same room. Equally important, I need appropriate access. I don't want to bother her with my question in the middle of her annual review, nor do I want to pester Maureen if she's identified someone else on the team to answer questions like mine.

As you'll learn throughout this book, the integration of Microsoft Lync with Office, SharePoint, and Exchange provides unprecedented ease of team member access, in appropriate contexts.

Meaningful and Satisfying Experience

The third element of team success is that team members have a meaningful and satisfying experience. Of course, the nature of team goals is a major factor in making work meaningful. But few of us have the opportunity to develop a life-saving cancer vaccine or safely land a stricken airliner in the middle of the Hudson River in winter. For most of us, it's a matter of making the product, creating the shipment, accounting for the payment, or finding the prospects, etc.

So, in the more mundane world in which most of us live, what makes work meaningful? Hackman cites numerous studies in his book and one common thread is that the work is perceived as meaningful by the team. Keeping prices up-to-date in the product database may not be the most exciting work, but if that task is perceived by the team as important, it will become meaningful.

Well, not quite. If it is perceived as important, and if the person doing that work is known to have done it, then it will be perceived as meaningful. Recognition for work well done is vitally important for a meaningful work experience.

Another aspect of team satisfaction is that illusive feeling of camaraderie. The feeling that one is part of a group of chums; each person doing their own thing, but combining it all to achieve something together, and having fun in the process.

As you'll learn, Office 365 has many features for team communication: Online meetings, whiteboards, team surveys, picture and video libraries, a place for announcements, and much more.

Which brings us to another consideration, what kind of a team is it?

What Kind of a Team Do You Have?

In the olden days—the days of *Mad Men*—everyone worked at the same location at the same time. Meetings were always face-to-face. People came to the office at the same time, took lunch at the same time, and went home more or less at the same time. If you wanted to meet with someone, you walked down the hall to find them, or called them on the office intercom. Clients traveled to their vendors' sites or vice versa.

Not anymore—or at least, not for most of us anymore. In this flat world, many teams are distributed, international, and multi-cultural. Also, a team of five people can represent five different companies or organizations. In addition, teams can be transitory, or perhaps the team lasts over time, but the composition of team members changes continually; when the project finishes, there is no one left on the team who started 24 months ago.

Table 1-1 shows varieties of ways that teams meet today. In spite of the flat world phenomenon, some teams still work at a single location. But, they may not work at the same time. We use the term *synchronous* to refer to teams that meet and work at the same time; asynchronous means teams work at different times. The traditional, *Mad Men* world is represented in the upper left cell of the table: single-site / synchronous.

TABLE 1-1: Types of Team Meetings Today

	Synchronous	Asynchronous
Single Site	Face-to-face	Virtual meeting, same time zone
	Virtual meetings increasing in popularity	
Multi-site	Virtual meeting required	Virtual meeting, different time zones

Even in this first category, work is changing. While face-to-face meetings are possible with everyone gathered in one place at the same time, they're not always desirable. Bring all the key players together, maybe requiring expensive, time-consuming travel, and what happens? Start the meeting and the cell phones ring and texting is underway. You can hear the fingers on the keypads. You've got everyone in the same room, each listening with one ear while they text their office, solving the burning issue back home. In this setting, of what value is a face-to-face meeting? Besides, as one busy manager put it, "When we meet virtually, using video conferencing, I can work on my budget when the meeting drags." OK, meetings aren't supposed to drag, but sin isn't supposed to happen, either.

So, today, even when everyone works at the same site, at more or less the same time, virtual meetings using audio and video conferencing are becoming more common, and popular.

Of course, if people don't meet face-to-face, virtual meetings are mandatory.

PAUSE AND REFLECT: WHAT IS A *VIRTUAL MEETING*?

A *virtual meeting* is a meeting in which people do not meet in the same room, at the same time. Virtual meetings require, at least, a conference audio call. Also, increasingly, we mean a video conference, one with a shared presentation, shared applications, shared desktops, and a common whiteboard. One in which the virtual audience can be polled.

Virtual meetings don't have to be synchronous, either. Video presentations and meetings can be saved and played to the audience, at the audience's convenience. And, when you think about, a discussion forum is a form of virtual meeting; it's just asynchronous. In this book, we will illustrate numerous ways of using Office 365 to conduct many types of virtual meeting.

Now consider the asynchronous column of Table 1-1. If the meeting is asynchronous, it really doesn't matter where people are. They can all reside on the same floor of the same building, or they can reside on all the continents of the world. They're not meeting at the same time, so location isn't important.

One factor that does vary is time zone. With a multi-site meeting, it's possible that meeting attendees have the advantage of working in different time zones. Given this, asynchronous meetings can develop a circadian rhythm. Those in Asia participate in, say, a discussion group, followed by those in Europe, followed by those in North America. The conversation continues with the sun around the world.

So, what's required for effective virtual meetings? Shared audio, shared video, shared resources—all capabilities that are part of Lync, one of the major components of Office 365. Read on to learn how Office 365 can help.

What's the Difference between Cooperation and Collaboration?

Cooperation and collaboration are not the same thing, even though they are sometimes used that way. To better understand why you might want to use Office 365, consider the difference in these terms.

What is Cooperation?

Cooperation involves multiple people working together to accomplish a common goal. Four painters who split a painting job into four pieces, each painting, say, one room wall, are cooperating. They are performing essentially the same work, but they're coordinating their tasks.

Cooperation is effective for reducing the elapsed time required to accomplish a job. However, the result of cooperation is not necessarily better. A room painted by four painters is neither better nor worse than a room done by one painter working alone.

Collaboration, at least as used in this book, is different from cooperation. For us, *collaboration* is a process of group work that involves *feedback* and *iteration*. Someone produces something—say the draft of a report—and other team members review that draft and make comments on it. The original author, or someone else, makes changes to the first draft to produce a second draft. Team members provide feedback on that second draft, and someone produces a third, and so forth. The document moves forward in this sequence of feedback and iteration until the team is satisfied with it.

Collaboration offers the possibility of creating a work product that is better than anyone could do working alone. If the feedback and iteration loops are productive, then the result can far surpass the result of a single individual. One of the great benefits of Office 365, and in particular the SharePoint OnLine component, is that it provides numerous features and functions for improving group feedback and iteration.

> **ADVICE**   By the way, this is not to say that Office 365 isn't useful to cooperating teams. In Chapter 6, we show a potential application for a painting company, in fact. It's just that we think Office 365 truly shines in a collaborative setting.

What Makes for a *Successful* Collaborator?

However, and it's a **big** however, what makes for *successful* collaborator (and therefore successful collaboration and, hopefully, a more successful team)? Studies and surveys indicate that it has nothing to do with being party-manners nice. Nor is it being particularly popular, or experienced, or even well-organized.

The qualities that define a successful collaborator are:

- The ability to give and receive critical feedback
- The ability to express an unpopular opinion
- The willingness to take a reasoned and principled stance

As Darwin John, the world's first CIO once put it, "If two of you have the exact same opinion, then we have no need for one of you."

This situation explains why effective collaboration is so incredibly difficult. We want team members to give and receive critical feedback, to express ideas with which others disagree, perhaps vehemently—while creating a successful outcome, helping the team to gain in capability, and for team members to have a rich and satisfying experience.

Let's see: I want an investment that is guaranteed to provide a 25 percent return, is tax-free, and has no risk. Hello???

But there it is.

Just because the qualities necessary for becoming a successful collaborator are hard to apply, doesn't mean they're not valid and important. This tall order means we need to take every helping hand we can get. Which leads us to:

How Can Office 365 Help?

Office 365 has four major components and dozens of features that facilitate collaboration. The next chapter explains those major components and the ten chapters that follow explore the use of many of the collaboration features. However, without getting into those details, what's the bottom line? How can you use Office 365 to get the job done better, improve your team, create a rich and rewarding experience, and facilitate critical feedback and effective iteration? We think the bottom line comes down to two critical facts:

- Office 365 makes it easier to communicate, both synchronously and asynchronously
- Office 365 makes it easy to share

> **PAUSE AND REFLECT: WHO NEEDS ANOTHER VERSION OF OFFICE?**
>
> When we said at the beginning of this chapter that nobody needs a new version of Office, we may not have been fair. While writing this chapter, one author was writing this section while the other author was editing it for typos. The same copy. Both of us at the same time. Seamlessly.
>
> The Office programs in Office 365, particularly Word, Excel, PowerPoint, and OneNote, include new features and functions to support multi-user, concurrent editing. We overlooked these new features because they don't require anything from us. They just happen.

Easy to Communicate

With Office 365, you can do email, you can do texting, you can make audio calls, and you can make video calls. You can call via the telephone system or via the Internet. You can determine who's available now.

Just a few possibilities: See a task that's overdue? Click the little green square next to the person's name. Voilà, there they are! Find out why the task is late. See a phone number in an email or document? You can click it, and you're on the phone with them.

Maybe you were a little too harsh with your criticism on a particular plan? You can click the green square next to the document and communicate with the plan's author. Want to tell someone their document is the best thing you've ever read? Send them a text with one click! Do you want to integrate team tasks with your personal calendar in Outlook? Easily done.

Easy to Share

You can't give feedback and iteration without sharing.

Ever share documents via email? Of course. What happens when you want to find the version before Don made the change to the first quarter numbers, but after Katherine put in the project justification? Where is that document? To which email is that version attached? Do you still have that email?

Instead of relying on email, you can place your documents in a SharePoint library, part of Office 365, and let it track the versions as well as record version comments and fall back to earlier versions, when needed. Everyone on the team knows where to find the current and past versions.

Want to record who's going to do what and by when? You can put tasks onto the team calendar. Need to make sure that everyone knows about the task scheduling changes? Set an alert on the task list and let Office 365 send an email about the change to everyone on the team—automatically, when the change occurs.

Want to ensure that everyone sees the pictures of the launch party? Or the video of the team award? Put them on the team site.

In short, we believe Office 365 will help teams be more successful, improve their team, and create a positive experience—all the while supporting critical feedback and iteration.

Back to the Meeting...

So there's hope for the group in the meeting that started this chapter. They don't have to meet face-to-face. If it helps, Ringo can meet at home, while he gets the kids ready for school.

They don't even have to meet at the same time. They can create discussion boards, leave notes, conduct surveys, or use many different facilities for meeting asynchronously. That group should be using Office 365!

What's Next?

This chapter describes why the authors think Office 365 can help teams. The next chapter describes the components that make up Office 365 and discusses the importance of cloud-based hosting. After that, Chapters 3 through 12 show you how to use specific Office 365 features to solve common team problems.

Enjoy!

Of Course, This Would Never Happen in <u>Your</u> Business...

Joe Schumpeter, project manager at Larsen Painting, is talking on the phone with Adam Smith, senior accountant.

"Adam, emails aren't getting through to me. Jeremy just told me he'd sent me an email yesterday... Katherine is reporting the same thing."

"Let me check, Joe. Why don't you send me a test email?"

"OK. Hey, I can't send emails, either. I can write them, but they're just going to my Outbox." Joe's voice is blaming Adam.

"Same thing is happening here." Adam says, puzzled.

"My Outbox! It's jammed. Nothing out. I better call those people at Glacier Peak. I told them I'd send..." Joe is starting to panic.

"Joe, easy, I don't know what's going on. I just tried to connect to Exchange Server and—nothing." "Let me check the machine closet."

"OK, call me back will you?" Adam's not happy.

Joe hurries down the hall and opens the door to the closet that has the server machines running Exchange. "Good grief!" he says.

Joe calls Adam back. "Well, Adam, you're not going to like this...You know that room on the other side of the wall?"

"You mean the one we're turning into a conference room?

"Yeah, that one. It looks like yesterday, when the construction crew was installing the new electrical, somebody got carried away."

"What?"

"When they were drilling a hole into the post that's in the middle of that wall, the drill bit came straight through the post and went into the server and actually came out the other side. I think we're lucky there wasn't a fire."

"So, how long until I can send email?"

"I have no idea."

It Doesn't Have to Be That Way...

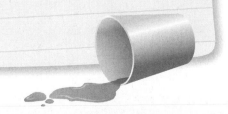

What is Office 365?

OFFICE 365 IS THE MOST COMPELLING Microsoft product offering since Windows 3.0 for three reasons:

- Each of the Office 365 products (Office Professional Plus, Exchange Online, Lync Online, and SharePoint Online) is feature-rich with tremendous utility in its own right.

- This tremendous utility is greatly enhanced by the second reason Office 365 is so compelling: deep integration. With just a few clicks, users can integrate SharePoint calendars and lists into Outlook. Also, with a single click, a manager can use Lync to initiate a video conference with an employee who owns an over-due task. Unlike earlier versions of SharePoint, with Office 365, the integration of documents between SharePoint and Office is seamless and transparent.

- The most significant reason Office 365 is so compelling is that Microsoft hosts Exchange, Lync, and SharePoint. Such hosting saves organizations the management time, cost, and risk of supporting these server applications in-house. To a large organization with in-house IT staff, such hosting offers an easy and affordable outsourcing alternative; an alternative that results in substantial cost savings and higher quality of service and reliability.

To the small business, such hosting provides a capability that has never before been possible. No small business (Microsoft defines a small business as one having 25 or fewer employees) can afford the in-house expertise needed to install and run these products. Even if it could, no small business has the expertise to provide proper security and reliability. Most rely on small hosting companies that may or may not provide appropriate security. Couple these reasons with the low price—a small business can begin with Office 365 for professionals and small businesses for $6 per month per user—and you have the biggest bargain ever! Given all of these reasons, Office 365 may very well be the best thing for business since the copy machine.

The rest of this chapter offers a closer look at:

- What's in Microsoft Office 365
- Disadvantages of Microsoft Office 365
- What you can do with Microsoft Office 365
- What Microsoft Office 365 costs

What's In Microsoft Office 365?

In a nutshell, Microsoft Office 365 is a service offered on a monthly subscription basis for businesses of all sizes that includes Exchange Online, Lync Online, and SharePoint Online plus, if you subscribe to the E3 level of Office 365 Plan E family for midsize businesses and enterprises, the latest version of Microsoft's Desktop office suite. Microsoft also plans to offer versions for educational institutions. The following sections detail the various Office 365 features.

Exchange Online

Exchange Online is based on Exchange Server 2010, which is the latest version of Microsoft's messaging platform. Exchange Online allows users to manage their email, maintain appointment calendars, store contact information, and manage their daily task lists. In addition, Exchange Online provides support for mobile and web-based access to this information. Integration with Exchange provides presence information in SharePoint and Lync, all of which make possible immediate and direct connections among people in your organization.

Lync Online

Microsoft Lync Server 2010 is designed to provide a virtual connection between you and the people you work with. You can use Lync Online, the version provided as part of Office 365, for instant messaging, audio/video calling, conducting audio and video meetings, sharing your computer desktop and applications, sharing whiteboards, conducting online polls, and working together in real time from practically anywhere.

SharePoint Online

SharePoint Online is the online version of Microsoft's SharePoint Server 2010. With Share-Point Online, you can create sites to collaborate with colleagues, partners, and customers. SharePoint is a rich, web-based platform with many capabilities. With SharePoint Online, you can:

- Manage and share personal documents and sites with colleagues using MySites
- Keep teams in sync with shared documents libraries, task lists, and calendars with Team Sites
- Set library and document-level permissions to protect sensitive content
- Stay up to date on company news, events, and business updates with Intranet Sites
- Share documents and insights securely with partners and customers using Extranet Sites
- Market your business with a simple and professional public-facing website
- Create Office documents and save them directly to SharePoint Online

Office Professional Plus

In addition to Exchange Online, Lync Online and SharePoint Online, Office 365 for mid-size businesses and enterprises includes Office Professional Plus, the top-of-the-line edition of Microsoft Office, which includes the applications shown in Table 2-1.

TABLE 2-1: Office 365 Applications

Application	Use
Outlook 2010	Manage business and personal email, calendars, contacts, and tasks.
Word 2010	Create and edit documents.
Excel 2010	Create and edit electronic spreadsheets.
PowerPoint 2010	Create and edit presentation slide decks.
Lync 2010 client	Locate and communicate with others using voice and video calls; conduct online meetings; share desktop, applications, whiteboards, and so on.

continues

TABLE 2-1: Office 365 Applications *(continued)*

Application	Use
SharePoint Workspace 2010	Access synchronized SharePoint libraries and lists locally on your PC, even when disconnected from SharePoint. Make changes offline and they will automatically be updated to SharePoint.
Access 2010	Create database applications intended to run on a single PC. Not intended for development of multiuser database applications.
OneNote 2010	Make meeting and lecture notes and store them in an organized notebook.
InfoPath 2010	Primarily used to create custom forms for use with SharePoint.
Publisher 2010	Create newsletters, brochures, postcards, greeting cards, and so on.

What Are the Disadvantages of Microsoft Office 365?

Although Office 365 is a tremendous benefit to businesses, it is not without disadvantages. To make sure that Office 365 is right for your situation, we're providing the following list of disadvantages that you might consider before building your business around it.

- **An administrator is needed:** You will need someone who is qualified to administer the various Office 365 services.

- **You're at Microsoft's mercy:** With Microsoft Office 365, and its predecessor, Business Productivity Online Services, your business enjoys the benefits of tools previously available only to large corporations that could afford the considerable expense associated with obtaining and maintaining large data centers: Exchange, Unified Communications (provided by Lync and Lync Online in Office 365), and SharePoint. Those sophisticated server applications are hosted in data centers located around the world that are owned and operated by Microsoft, but that's a double-edged sword. The other side of the story is that you no longer have physical control over your data. You are depending on Microsoft to provide security for your mission-critical data, which may require additional expensive procedures by your external auditors.

- **You still need a database host:** Although your business will not require servers to host SharePoint, Exchange, or Lync Server, you must continue to host, or to hire an outside company to host, databases that support specialized multiuser line-of-business applications.

- **Your business may become heavily dependent on Office 365:** If you begin with, say, ten employees, and keep adding staff, what happens when you need to add the twenty-sixth person to Office 365? You must switch from the small business version to the enterprise version, and you'll find yourself with significantly higher costs per employee. Plus, the upgrade from the Small Business Edition to the Enterprise edition could be complex and involve considerable administrative expensive because, for one thing, you will no longer administer a SharePoint site, you will administer a SharePoint server, which requires more experience to administer.

> **Note** Despite the disadvantages, the authors firmly believe that Office 365 could be the most important business product since the copy machine! You'll discover this when you read the next section "What Can You Do with Microsoft Office 365?"

What Can You Do with Microsoft Office 365?

What you can do with the individual components of Office 365, Exchange Online, Lync Online, SharePoint Online, and Office Professional Plus is considerable. You got a brief overview of these capabilities earlier in this chapter. However, the components of Office 365 were designed and built to work together in valuable and, actually, amazing ways. The deep integration of components is where the magic happens and the value for users arises. Later chapters of this book illustrate some of the more powerful capabilities of Office 365.

Using the Lync Client with Lync Online to Collaborate

Chapter 3 shows you how to use the Lync client to determine whether a member of the organization is available to be contacted, and how to use their contact information to initiate an online video call. You also find out how to collaborate on an

Office document in real time, including how to transfer control of the application among participants.

Sharing Documents with the Default SharePoint Document Library

SharePoint Online creates a default document library called Shared Documents that you can use for document sharing. Chapter 4 shows you how to store and retrieve documents from the Shared Documents library, connect to people who've made changes, set alerts to notify you when documents change, customize library features, keep a history of document changes, and limit changes to one person at a time. The chapter also covers how SharePoint automatically manages simultaneous edits to documents.

Creating and Managing Subsites in SharePoint

Having a central place to store and share business documents is extremely useful. However, you most likely do not want every document to be available to everyone. Although you can set library and document-level permissions to control access to sensitive content, the most effective way is to use subsites, which is the subject of Chapter 5. Specifically, you discover how collections of SharePoint sites are structured, how to create subsites, how to customize the look and feel of a team site, how groups are used to provide different user permissions, and how to set permissions that are unique for a subsite.

Coordinating Work with Task Lists in SharePoint

One of the challenges of most businesses is keeping track of who is to do what, and when. Your business can be better organized if you use SharePoint to keep track of tasks. You can use the built-in task list to store task descriptions, assign tasks to people, establish start and due dates, and to record task dependencies. After you have created a task list, you can publish it in a variety of formats. Chapter 6 shows you how to add tasks to a Team Site task list, create task dependencies, modify the task list view, add tasks in bulk using the datasheet format, create and use a calendar view of the task list, add the calendar view to the Quick Launch menu and to the Home page, create a Gantt chart of the items in the task list, and create a personal view of tasks.

Taking Advantage of the Deep Integration of Office 365 Components

Most business workers spend their work day using Outlook to send and receive hundreds of emails, schedule meetings, manage their contact list, and keep track of tasks. Because of the deep integration of Outlook 2010 and SharePoint Online, these users can have Outlook retrieve task, calendar, and other data from SharePoint. In this way, Outlook 2010 users can stay in Outlook and do not have to go to SharePoint to manage this important data. Chapter 7 shows you how to use presence information in Outlook to determine ways to contact someone, establish a video call with him or her, connect to a SharePoint calendar in Outlook 2010, and overlay a SharePoint calendar with other calendars to see a consolidated schedule. You also see how to update SharePoint calendars using Outlook 2010, and add SharePoint task lists to Outlook 2010.

Using SharePoint Lists to Track Things

Earlier this chapter, you saw how a business can stay better organized by using SharePoint to keep track of tasks. But SharePoint has all sorts of lists, and you can even create your own custom lists. Chapter 8 shows you how to use other kinds of lists to keep track of, well, just about anything. Specifically, you'll learn how to create a SharePoint list from a built-in list type, delete a SharePoint list, create a custom list, add columns to lists using site columns, create choice list columns, link a list to another list using lookup columns, add totals to a list view, and create a view showing list group structure.

Using SharePoint Workflows to Ensure Nobody Misses a Step

Do you ever want to make sure that all the concerned parties approve something? That everyone has seen, read, and agreed with a presentation, document, or Excel analysis before you take it outside the team, or to the public? SharePoint has a built-in set of workflows that will automatically notify team members that their review is wanted as well as remind them if they don't do it within the allotted time. You'll learn about these built-in workflows in Chapter 9. Of course, you can create your own workflows using SharePoint Designer. Although the process of creating such workflows is beyond the scope of this book, Chapter 9 contains a brief description of a couple examples.

Using Outlook and Lync to Schedule and Conduct an Online Brainstorming Session

Businesses often have employees who work in different locations. Everyone knows that getting people together for face-to-face meetings takes advance notice, careful planning, and significant expenditures of scarce and shrinking travel budgets. Because of the integration among the components of Office 365, using Outlook 2010 to schedule an online meeting, and to initiate or join the meeting when the time for the meeting has come, is a simple matter. After the meeting is underway, participants can share a whiteboard to brainstorm, come to consensus regarding a plan, identify next steps, and assign action items. Chapter 10 shows you how.

Using SharePoint Discussion Blogs, Wikis, and Surveys to Share Knowledge

SharePoint includes rich features that enable members to share knowledge and opinions. Team members can create blogs for others to read and comment on. Teams can share, monitor, and edit team knowledge using wikis, and they can obtain more formal team feedback via surveys. Chapter 11 shows you how easily you can do each of these items.

Using Outlook and Lync to Schedule and Conduct a PowerPoint Presentation for Customers and Partners in Widespread Locations

Participation in Lync Online meetings is not limited to users within your organization. You can use Outlook to send invitations to people inside your organization as well as to customers and partners. You can use *Meeting Options* to control who is automatically admitted to the meeting, and who has to wait in the "lobby" until admitted by a presenter. Meeting Options also allows you to control who can act as a presenter during the meeting. Lync includes a special provision for making a PowerPoint presentation, which includes special tools such as *laser pointers* and various ways to make annotations in the presentation. When the meeting concludes, you can save the annotated presentation. Chapter 12 discusses these capabilities.

What Does Microsoft Office 365 Cost?

For years, large enterprises have been using the communication and collaboration capabilities of Exchange Server, SharePoint, and Lync Server (formerly known as Office Communications Server) in conjunction with Microsoft's flagship Office suite. However, paying the rather substantial licensing costs of these products has been just the beginning of the financial outlay. To use the server products effectively, businesses have had to make substantial investments in data centers with special power, air conditioning, Internet connections, and facilities to house the servers (computers) to run the sophisticated server programs, not to mention the cost of all those servers. To ensure that the services are always available, backup copies of the data they hold are made on a regular basis, helpdesk services are available, and a seemingly endless list of other responsibilities are met. Large businesses have had to maintain a staff of highly trained information technology professionals. As a result of these significant hosting costs, the benefits of Exchange Server, SharePoint, and Lync Server have not been generally available to small and medium-sized businesses. Microsoft Office 365 changes that!

By providing online versions of Exchange, SharePoint, and Lync, Microsoft assumes the cost and responsibility of hosting these services in their continuously replicated, geo-redundant data centers, which Microsoft claims are third-party certified to international standards. In addition, Microsoft promises 99.9 percent availability and 24/7 IT Administrator support via phone, web, or email, depending on the plan you use. With IT Administrator support, the Office 365 administrator in your organization can call Microsoft's technical support any time for assistance. Web support is provided by means of an online forum monitored by the Office 365 user community. Email support provides you with the ability to submit questions to Microsoft support via email.

Microsoft offers two levels of Office 365 plans for businesses: Office 365 for professionals and small businesses, and Office 365 Plan E family for midsize businesses and enterprises. At the time of this writing, Microsoft has stated that the cost for Office 365 for professionals and small businesses (which Microsoft defines as having fewer than 25 employees) will be $6 per month per user after the initial 30-day free trial period.

> **Note**
> Think about that! A small business or professional that provides Office 365 for all 25 of its employees will pay a total of $150 a month to have most of the same capabilities that were previously only available to large enterprises with the financial wherewithal to host Exchange Server, Lync Server, and SharePoint Server! That includes 24/7 support via moderated online forums, Microsoft's financially backed promise of 99.9 percent uptime, and the peace of mind that comes from knowing that the services are hosted in Microsoft-owned and -staffed data centers. The authors believe this has to be the best business bargain ever!

Office 365 for midsize businesses and enterprises offers more advanced features than Office 365 for professionals and small businesses. As of May 2011, Microsoft is advertising four Enterprise levels of Office 365, which are shown in Table 2-1.

TABLE 2-1: Office 365 Plan E Family

Key features Cost per user per month	E1 $10	E2 $16	E3 $24	E4 $27
Advanced administration capabilities, active directory integration and 24/7 IT Administrator support	X	X	X	X
Email, calendar, contacts, personal archive, and 25GB mailbox storage	X	X	X	X
Sites to share documents and information	X	X	X	X
Instant messaging, video calls, and online meetings	X	X	X	X
Premium anti-spam and antivirus filtering—Microsoft Forefront Online Protection for Exchange and Microsoft Forefront Security for SharePoint	X	X	X	X
License rights to access on-premises deployment of Exchange Server, SharePoint Server, and Lync Server	X	X	X	X
Document viewing and light editing		X	X	X
Complete and full-featured set of office productivity applications—Office Professional Plus			X	X
Publish Access databases, share Excel workbooks, build InfoPath forms, and share Visio business processes and diagrams			X	X
Advance archive capabilities, unlimited email storage, and hosted voicemail			X	X
Enterprise voice capabilities to replace or enhance a PBX				X

At those rates, even large enterprises can enjoy considerable savings by using Office 365.

> **Note** The exact extent to which your organization can realize savings by using Office 365 depends on a number of factors, which will be unique to each organization. If your organization has a dedicated IT staff, that's the place to start your cost/benefit study. If your organization has no IT staff, then you should consult with a local IT consultant who is familiar with your industry. Also, you can work with a member of the Microsoft Partner Network (`http://www.partnerpoint.com`). For current information on Microsoft Office 365 plans and related costs, refer to `http://office365.microsoft.com/`.

What You've Learned

This chapter discussed the major components of Microsoft Office 365, including Exchange Online, Lync Online, SharePoint Online, and Office Professional Plus. You've learned some of the ways that you can put these components to work in your business, and you've read about the advantages (and disadvantages) of having Microsoft host for your team in the cloud.

What's Next?

Chapter 1 discussed *why* you might want to use Office 365 for teamwork, and Chapter 2 discussed *what* are the components of Office 365. So, what follows *why* and *what*? The *how*—how can you use Office 365, especially Lync, Outlook, and SharePoint, to solve team problems. In each chapter, we'll start with a team having trouble and then show how to use Office 365 to solve their problem. We begin in Chapter 3 with the need to work on a document together (right now!) to meet a schedule deadline. Of course, that never happens in *your* business.

Sharing Documents

This Would Never Happen in <u>Your</u> Business...

Joe Schumpeter, manager of customer support, is on the phone with Katharine Hepburn, account manager in finance:

"Hey, Katharine, how ARE you? Great to talk with you! Say, Katharine, I know you're just back from vacation, and I hate to do this to you, but Jason's headed somewhere and he wants me to get the budget to him this afternoon. Can we do it?"

"Joe, that's tough. I haven't really started on it."

"I know, I know. But, he's pushing me pretty hard."

"I'll take a look at the budget later on this morning and get back to you."

"Katharine, that might be too late." [Joe knows Katharine has a tendency to get distracted.] "How about we do it together? Email me what you have so far, and we can talk through it on the phone." After some delay and a search through his junk mail folder Joe finally has the file. "Hey, Katharine, is this the right file? This doesn't look right. Why does it say Production Planning at the top?"

"Oh, rats, I sent you the wrong one. Sorry. Let me try again." [More idle conversation while Joe waits for the file to arrive.]

"Okay, I've got it. Let me see. Hey, this still doesn't look right. Now it says Equipment and Resources on the top."

"You're on the wrong worksheet. Click the 2011 Budget tab."

"Ah, I see it. I just clicked the 2013 Budget. Okay, just walk me through it. "

At this point, Joe and Katharine have been on the phone for 23 minutes. None of that time has been on the budget, and Joe is looking at the 2013 tab of the worksheet but Katharine wanted him to look at the 2011 tab—when will they notice that?

It Doesn't Have to Be That Way...

Sharing Documents via Lync

MICROSOFT LYNC, ONE OF THE KEY COMPONENTS of Office 365, was designed to provide a virtual connection between you and the people you work with. You can use Lync to talk, share your computer desktop and applications, and work together in real time from practically anywhere. By using the built-in real-time calling and sharing features of Lync, Joseph and Katharine can avoid the problems they had with their budget file last year. Later chapters explore more about how you can use Lync to solve other difficult, and potentially expensive, business problems.

This chapter provides a quick introduction to the Lync Client application and then shows you how to use Lync's calling and Application sharing features. Specifically, you'll see how to:

- Initiate and accept calls
- Start and accept sharing of an application
- Give, accept, and return control over the application
- End sharing of the application
- End the call

Getting Started with Lync Client

Figure 3-1 shows the Lync Client. With this Microsoft Windows application, you can locate contacts, see their availability status, and connect with them in a variety of ways, including instant messaging (IM), email, Internet Protocol audio calling, and audio/video (AV) calls. With IM, audio, and AV calls, you can share your desktop, share an application that's running on your computer, share a whiteboard for brainstorming, and conduct a quick poll of participants. Later chapters explore many of these features, but for now, you see how to use the Lync Client to discuss and make real-time changes to a document (in this case, a budget draft).

FIGURE 3-1: The Lync Client Application Window

Notice that Figure 3-1 shows the Lync view. To the right of the user's (Joe's) "picture" is the user name, status (Available), and current location (Seattle). Above all of this is a box where the user has indicated what he's currently working on. Although you can't see it because this book is in black and white, a green bar runs along the left edge of the user's picture, indicating that he is available. These color status indications are part of the "presence" information in Lync. The user can see at a glance who's available to contact immediately. The user's contacts are listed in the lower part of the Lync window.

If the teammate you wish to contact is not listed, you can find the contact information by doing the following:

1. Type your teammate's name in the Find a contact search box, as shown in Figure 3-2.

2. To always display the teammate's contact information in your Lync client, hover your cursor over the teammate's contact information, and click the Pin to Frequent Contacts option in the menu that appears, as shown in Figure 3-3.

FIGURE 3-2: The Lync Client: Using the Find a Contact Search

FIGURE 3-3: The Lync Client: Pinning a Teammate's Contact Info to Frequent Contacts

As you can see in Figure 3-4, your teammate's Contact information is now listed with your other frequent contacts.

FIGURE 3-4: The Lync Client: The Teammate's Contact Info Now Showing

Now, anytime you want to contact your teammate, hover your cursor over his or her contact information to reveal some details about the teammate and to show ways you can currently contact her, as shown in Figure 3-5. Notice the fly-out window to the left of your teammate's contact information. The icons along the bottom of the pop-out (from left to right) indicate:

- Email
- Instant messaging (IM)
- Voice call
- Options, which include audio/video calls

You'll learn more about audio/video calls in later chapters. However, because Joe and Katherine will use a voice call, see the following section, which shows you a shortcut method for doing that.

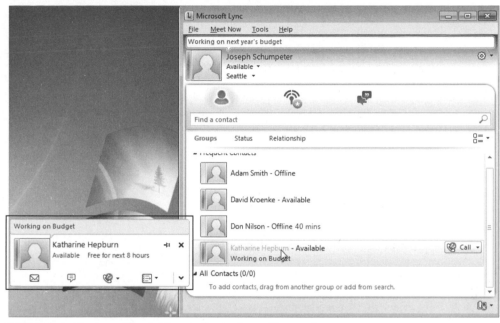

FIGURE 3-5: The Lync Client: Ways to Contact your Teammate

FIGURE 3-6: Lync Client: Click "Call"

Establishing a Voice Call

Establishing a voice call with Lync requires only two clicks of the mouse: one by the caller, and one by the person being called. In the chapter example, Figure 3-6 shows Joseph's cursor poised to click the Call button on Katharine's contact information. Figure 3-7 shows what Katharine sees after Joe clicks Call. Katharine also hears a tone to tell her that a call is coming in. All your teammate has to do is click Accept, and you and your teammate are on a Lync call.

FIGURE 3-7: Lync Session Window: Your Teammate Accepting Your Call Request

After the call is established, presence information for both you and your teammate is automatically updated to show that you are in a call and unavailable to others for the moment. This information is contained in the bar along the left side of your picture in you contact information. Figure 3-8 shows your teammate's view of the call session. Notice your new status.

FIGURE 3-8: Lync Session Window: Your Teammate's View of the Established Call

Figure 3-9 shows your Lync client with your teammate's updated status.

FIGURE 3-9: Lync Client: Your Teammate's Status Updated

Collaborating in Real Time

Now take another look at how you and your teammate could collaborate together.

Recalling the opening chapter scenario, with sharing involved, the players would interact much more efficient and effective as in the following interaction:

"Hello?"

"Hi, Katharine. I see you're busy working on the budget. I'm thinking because we're in a time crunch we could talk about it and look at it together."

"Great! I'm sharing it out to you now."

"Okay..."

To share a document with a teammate, (in this case Joe and Katharine sharing the budget workbook), do the following:

1. Expand the Share menu in the session window by clicking the small upside-down triangle.

2. Click Program, as shown in Figure 3-10.

FIGURE 3-10: Opening a Session Window:
Click Share → Program

You'll see a window that displays all the Programs that are currently open on your computer.

3. Click the draft budget, and then click Share, as shown in Figure 3-11.

FIGURE 3-11: The Share Program Window: Sharing the Budget

Figure 3-12 shows your teammate's session window where he or she can accept or decline the request.

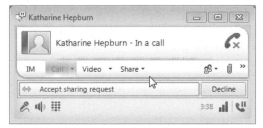

FIGURE 3-12: Session Window: Your Teammate
Accepts the Sharing Request from You

Figure 3-13 shows your teammate's session window after he accepts the sharing request.

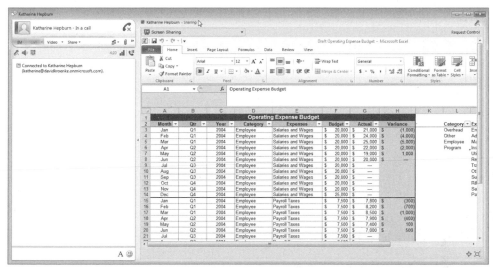

FIGURE 3-13: Your Teammate's Expanded Session Window: Joe Sees the Budget that
Katharine Is Working On

Notice that the session window has expanded significantly (in the chapter example, Joe sees the draft Excel budget workbook Katharine's working on)! What's more, your teammate does not see a static picture. He can actually see in real time cursor movements and all changes that you make as you talk about the document and decide on the needed changes.

To complete the picture to this point, the top image in Figure 3-14 shows Katharine's view of the session window immediately after Joe accepts Katharine's sharing invitation. If you want to see a preview of what your sharing, click the Preview button as shown in the top image of Figure 3-14. This causes your session window to expand and display what your sharing in a window that Lync refers to as "The Stage" shown in the bottom image of Figure 3-14.

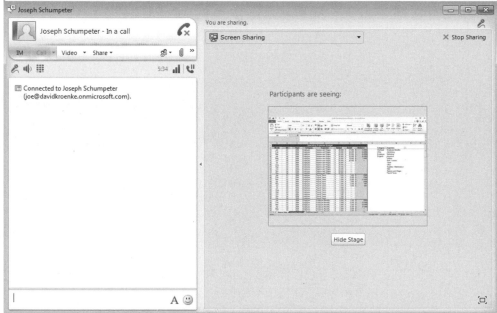

FIGURE 3-14: Your Session Window: Clicking Preview to See the "Stage," (top) Shows You What You Are Sharing (bottom)

PAUSE AND REFLECT: CONTACTING YOUR TEAMMATE AND SHARING AN APPLICATION

Let's think about what Katharine and Joe have done in the example. With very few keystrokes and mouse clicks, Joe found Katharine's contact information, initiated a call to her, and spoke with her as easily and as clearly as if he had dialed her phone number. After chatting for a while, with four clicks of her mouse, Katharine shared the draft budget she's working on so she can make changes, and Joe can see those changes in real time. No more emailing spreadsheets back and forth with all the time, frustration and risk involved!

Sharing a document has tremendous advantages as you've seen. But with Lync, you can also transfer control of the document to another person on the video call so they can make changes directly in the document.

Figure 3-15 shows how Katherine's Excel window appears. Note the tabs at the top of the screen, which have been added to the Excel window by Lync. With these tabs, you have the option of letting your teammate control your document.

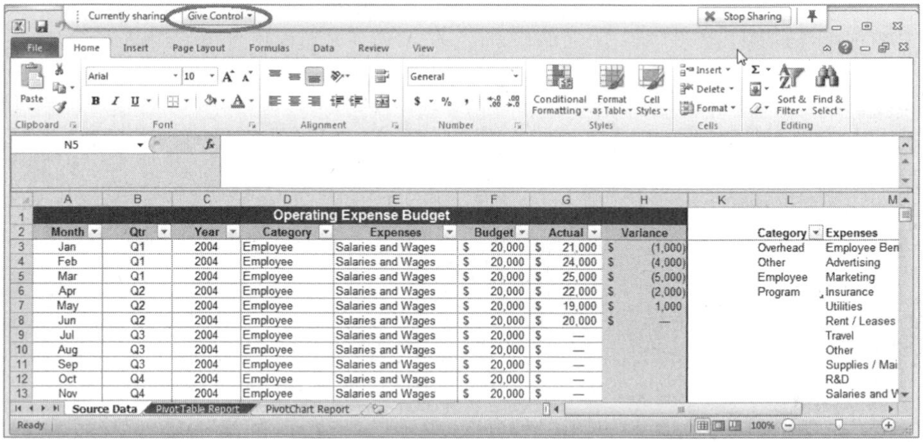

FIGURE 3-15: Excel Window: Giving Control to Your Teammate

After your teammate accepts control, he or she will see your document (in our example, when Joe accepts, Katherine's Excel window appears) as shown in Figure 3-16. Note that the text reminds you that your teammate is in control. When you finish sharing your document with your teammate and end your conversation, you can save the budget workbook, and click Stop Sharing, as shown in Figure 3-17.

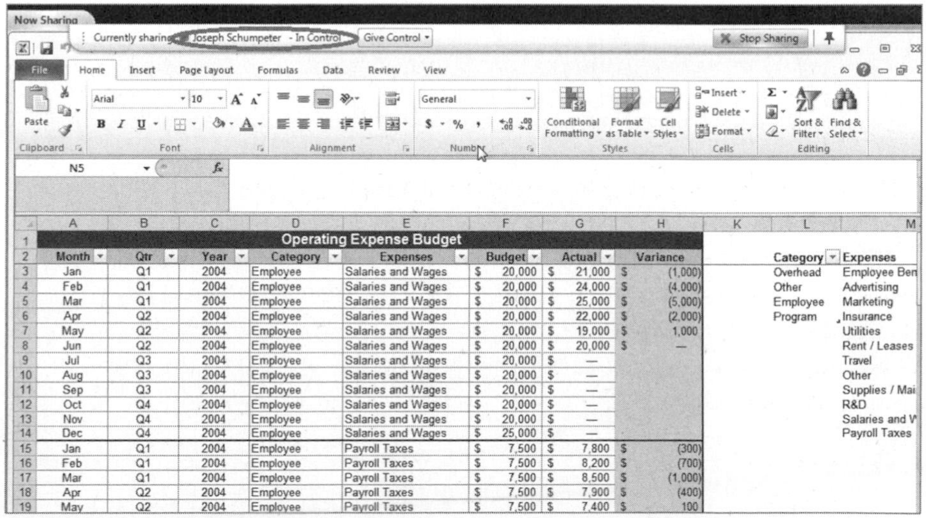

FIGURE 3-16: Excel Window: After Your Teammate Accepts Control

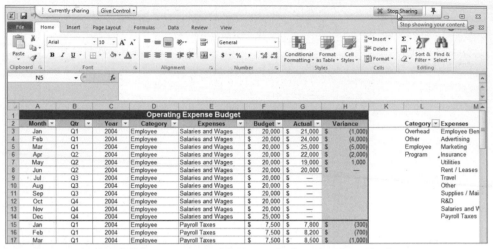

FIGURE 3-17: Excel Window: You Are Back in Control When You Stop Sharing

What You Have Learned

This chapter has provided a quick introduction to the Lync Client application, and then showed how Joe and Katharine used Lync's calling and application sharing features to:

- Initiate and accept voice calls
- Start and accept sharing of an application
- Give, accept, and return control over the application
- End sharing of the application
- End the call

What's Next?

You've just learned how to use Lync, one of the major components of Office 365, to call one of your contacts, view a computer application in common, and share control. This kind of communication is sometimes called *synchronous communication* because both callers are present at the same time. Sometimes it's not possible for people to meet at the same time, but they still may want to share a document.

For such a situation, called *asynchronous communication*, you can use SharePoint, another key component of Office 365. Chapter 4 shows you how to use a SharePoint document library for that purpose.

This Would Never Happen in Your Business...

Conversation between Tom Bridges, project manager, and Laura Listrom, team lead:

"Laura, where are they?"

"Where are what?"

"The budget numbers. I need them for Friday's meeting."

"Last I knew, Allison had them."

"Well, get them for me!"

"I'll try. She had them on her thumb drive, which she took to LA."

"Oh, great. See if you can get her to email them, okay?"

"Which spreadsheet do you want?"

"I don't know. The most recent one."

"What's the filename?"

"How do I know? Get all of them."

"All 12? They're big—that's 12 different emails."

"I don't care. And why can't I get onto the SkyDrive anymore?"

"What do you mean?"

"I need the written proposal. Jennifer said it's on the SkyDrive, but I can't get into it. She changed the password or something."

"I'll get it for you."

"How can things be such a mess in such a small company?"

"I don't know. . ."

"Remember Joan? Our admin? She knew where everything was."

"Well, hire her back!"

"Can't afford to."

"She reminded me of Joan on Mad Men."

"Yeah, she did. Hey, didn't we change this pitch? The intro I mean. Didn't we have a bunch of data about Johnson Partners at the beginning?"

"I think so."

"Well it's not there anymore."

"Which version do you have?"

"How do I know? The one Jennifer gave me."

"Sounds like she gave you the wrong one."

"I don't know, it's named Final Version, but it can't be the final one. . .where did I put that Johnson data. . ."

"No wait, she changed it—at least I think she did. I'll ask her when I can find her..."

It Doesn't Have to Be That Way...

Sharing Documents via SharePoint

MICROSOFT SHAREPOINT, one of the key components of Office 365, was designed for sharing things—documents, tasks, pictures, events, calendars—just about any kind of office document. As its name implies, SharePoint is a point where people put things to share. As such, SharePoint has built-in features, right out of the box, that prevent problems and frustrations like the ones that Tom and Laura have. Of course, there's a lot more to SharePoint than document sharing, as you'll see as you read this book.

This chapter shows you how to use Shared Documents, the default library that SharePoint creates for document sharing. You'll see how to:

- Store and retrieve documents from that library
- Connect to people who've made changes
- Set alerts to be notified when documents change
- Customize library features
- Keep a history of document changes
- Limit document edits to a single user at a time

Getting Started with Shared Documents

Figure 4-1 shows the generic SharePoint Team Site. This is the most common SharePoint site and the one you'll see many times. Chapter 5 shows you how to customize it to make it more your own, but for now, let's focus on document sharing.

The Team Site, like most SharePoint sites, includes a vertical menu on the left, which is called the *Quick Launch*. This menu is a list of links that point to resources in the SharePoint site. By default, it has Libraries (Site Pages, Shared Documents), Lists (Calendar, Tasks), and Discussions (Team Discussion). As you'll learn, the Quick Launch is easily customized to the needs of your team, but more on that in Chapter 5, as well.

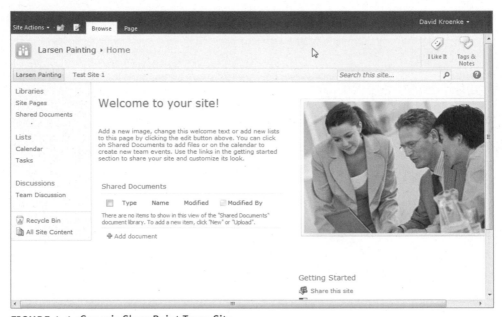

FIGURE 4-1: Generic SharePoint Team Site

A couple of things to remember as you're getting started:

- **Shared Documents library:** The default SharePoint document library, called Shared Documents, is used to store documents. Notice the name Shared Documents appears twice on this page, once in the Quick Launch and again in the lower center portion. If you click Shared Documents in the Quick Launch, SharePoint will produce a page exclusively devoted to that library. You would work on this page if you have a lot of work to do in that library. However, for convenience, SharePoint also shows an abbreviated view of Shared Documents in this first page, in the lower center part. You can work on documents in either place.

- **Adding documents to the Shared Documents library:** Because this example site is new, the Shared Documents library is empty. You can add a document by clicking Add document at the bottom of the center part of the page. If you do so, a dialog like that in Figure 4-2 appears.

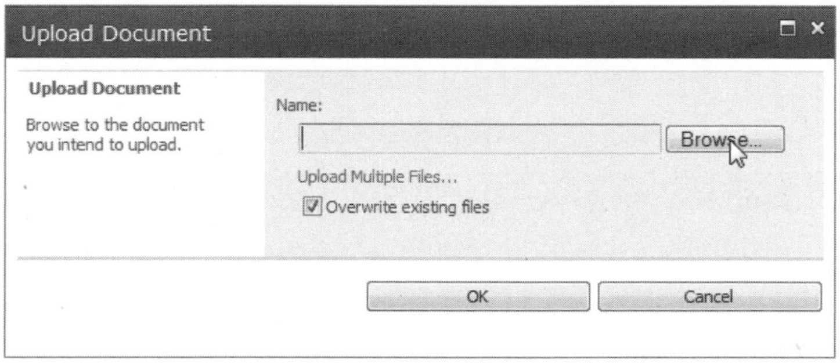

FIGURE 4-2: Uploading a Document

Next, you click Browse, find the document you want on your computer, and click OK. SharePoint adds the document to the Shared Documents library as shown in Figure 4-3.

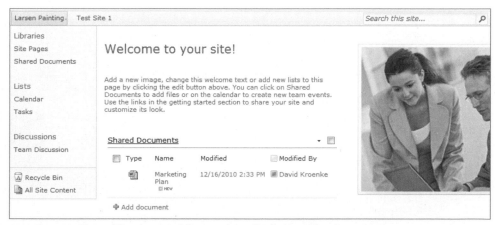

FIGURE 4-3: Shared Documents Library with a Marketing Plan Document

> **Note**
>
> Before continuing, pause for a moment. The Marketing Plan document is now available to everyone on your team. You don't need to do anything else. It's there; you and your team can get it, 24/7. No one needs to put it on a thumb drive, a SkyDrive, a disk drive, or anywhere else. Nobody can lose it at the airport. It's there, on a Microsoft server, some place in the cloud. You benefit from the work of computer scientists at Microsoft ensuring that it gets backed up, that it's protected, and that, if, God forbid, a terrible earthquake occurs where you or they are, that some other site will take over within minutes and give you your document when you want it—and all for a few dollars a month per head.

Taking Action on Shared Documents

Now, what can you and your team members do with a document in a library? If you hover your mouse just to the right of the words *Marketing Plan,* a small, drop-down arrow will appear. Click that arrow and the menu shown in Figure 4-4 appears.

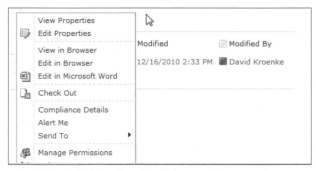

FIGURE 4-4: Actions You Can Take on a Document

As you can tell, you can do quite a number of things. *Properties* of a document are data items that describe the document. Some of the properties include Type, Name, Modified (the date and time the document was last modified), Modified By (the person who made the most recent change), and so forth. From the menu in Figure 4-4, you can View or Edit the document's properties. (By the way, such descriptive data is sometimes called *metadata*, which means data about data; here, properties are data about the document, which contains the actual data.)

Under the View and Edit properties are three choices for processing the document. You can view it in the browser, edit it in the browser, or edit it in Word. If you click Edit in Microsoft Word, SharePoint causes the document to open in Word on your computer. You can edit it and when you close the document, it is saved back to the server.

In the background, Office 365 is doing some marvelous work on your behalf. When you click Save, for example, you don't have to wait for the save to take place. Office 365 is saving it while you continue to work. Furthermore, if your computer is disconnected from the Internet while you have a document open, Office 365 saves all your changes on your local computer and integrates them into the document when you next re-connect.

If someone else is editing the document at the same time as you are, your changes are merged with theirs when the document is placed back onto the site.

> The actions that you can take in SharePoint depend on what permissions you have. In this chapter, the assumption is that you have at least Contribute permission. If you do not have permission to do something, SharePoint either doesn't show you the action at all, or shows it to you, but grays it out (disables it).
>
> What happens when two or more people edit a document at the same time depends on several factors. By default, if all are editing a Word, Excel, PowerPoint, or OneNote document, using the current version of Office, their changes are automatically merged. But if one person is editing using a browser-based Web App, changes are managed differently. Plus, if the document is checked out (see the section "Changing Library Settings" later in this chapter), only the person who checked it out can edit it. But no matter what, SharePoint notices that simultaneous editing is underway and does something to control it.

Using Presence

Because this is a single color book, you can't tell that the little square next to the name David Kroenke in Figure 4-5 is green. If you click it, the Lync application window pops up and you can email, send a text message, call, or schedule a meeting with that person.

FIGURE 4-5: Using Presence in Shared Documents

If Tom and Laura had been using SharePoint, and if Jennifer had changed this document, Tom could have used this feature to contact Jennifer in some way: send her email, a text message, call her, set up a video call, or schedule a meeting, as you'll see in Chapter 7.

Working with the Shared Documents Library

So far, you've been working with the view of Shared Documents that appears on the opening page of the Team Site. You can do more if you click Shared Documents in the Quick Launch menu (left vertical menu). When you do so, SharePoint displays the page shown in Figure 4-6.

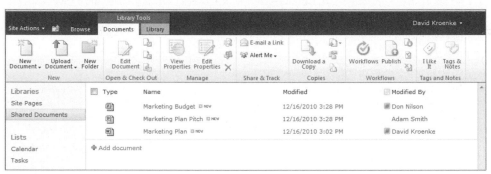

FIGURE 4-6: The Shared Documents Library View

Notice that this library now contains three documents and a different member of the team has modified each one. Also, notice that one is an Excel document, one is a PowerPoint document, and one is a Word document. Any number of different types of documents can be placed into a library. Finally, notice that both Don and David are signed into to Lync and can be reached. Adam Smith is not signed in.

Examine the ribbon at the top of this screen. The user clicked the Documents tab in the Library Tools section of the ribbon. In response, SharePoint displays the set of tools along the top of the library. However, at this point, the only tools that are enabled (can be clicked) are New Document, Upload Document, New Folder, and Alert Me. You'll see why the other tools are disabled in a minute. A little about each of these enabled tools:

- **New Document:** You can click this option to create a new Word document, as shown in Figure 4-7. Why only Word? Each document library has a default document type, and for Shared Documents, Word is the default. When you create libraries of your own, you can set the default document to whatever type of Office document you want.

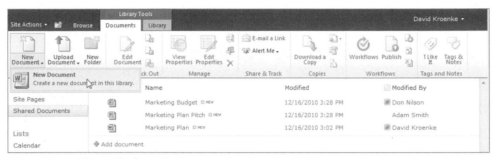

FIGURE 4-7: Library Tools → Documents

As shown in Figure 4-6, although the default for *new* documents is Word, you can upload *existing* documents of any type to the library—even (are you ready?) Acrobat PDFs!

- **Upload Document:** Use this option just like Add Document—to add a single document as shown in Figure 4-2, as well as to add multiple documents at once.
- **New Folder:** This option creates a new folder within the library, just as you do with Windows or the Mac.
- **Alert Me:** You can direct SharePoint to send you (or your teammates) emails when documents are added, changed, deleted, or under other conditions. Alerts are discussed in the next section.

All the other tools are disabled because those other tools work on a particular document, and no document is selected in Figure 4-7. For example, SharePoint can't respond to View Properties until a user indicates which document the properties should be shown for.

Figure 4-8 shows the appearance of the Ribbon after a user clicks the Marketing Plan Pitch document. Now Edit Document is enabled, along with other tools for viewing and editing properties; E-mail a Link; Download a Copy; and so on. Chapter 9 discusses the other tools, such as Publish. The options under the Tags & Notes section are beyond the scope of this book.

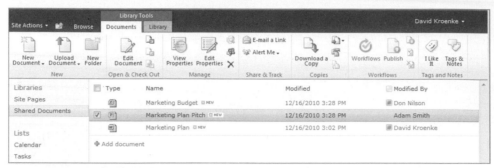

FIGURE 4-8: Library Tools → Documents, with the Marketing Plan Pitch Document Selected

Setting Alerts on Documents and Libraries

Alert Me works on whichever document (or documents) a user selects. In Figure 4-9, the user has selected the PowerPoint document Marketing Plan Pitch. With that selection, when the user clicks Alert Me, SharePoint sets an alert on that document. If a user selects several documents, then an alert is set on all of them.

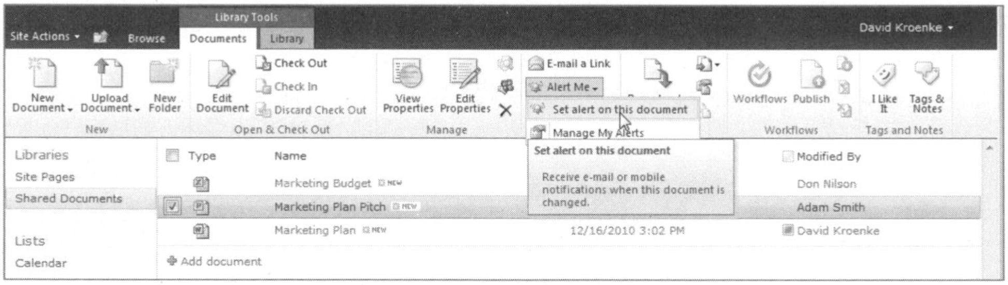

FIGURE 4-9: Setting an Alert on a Single Document

When a user clicks the Set Alert On This Document option, SharePoint displays the form shown in Figure 4-10. Here, the user, David Kroenke, is setting the alert, and he selects the Someone Else Changes a Document option, which means that any time someone other than David Kroenke changes a document, SharePoint will send an email to the users indicated. In this case, the users are David Kroenke, Adam Smith, and Joseph Schumpeter.

Suppose, for example, that after this alert has been created, Adam Smith makes a change to the document, such as the document's name. When that occurs, SharePoint sends an email (shown in Figure 4-11) describing the nature of the change to the three users specified in the alert settings. It is not possible to change the message that is sent in the email.

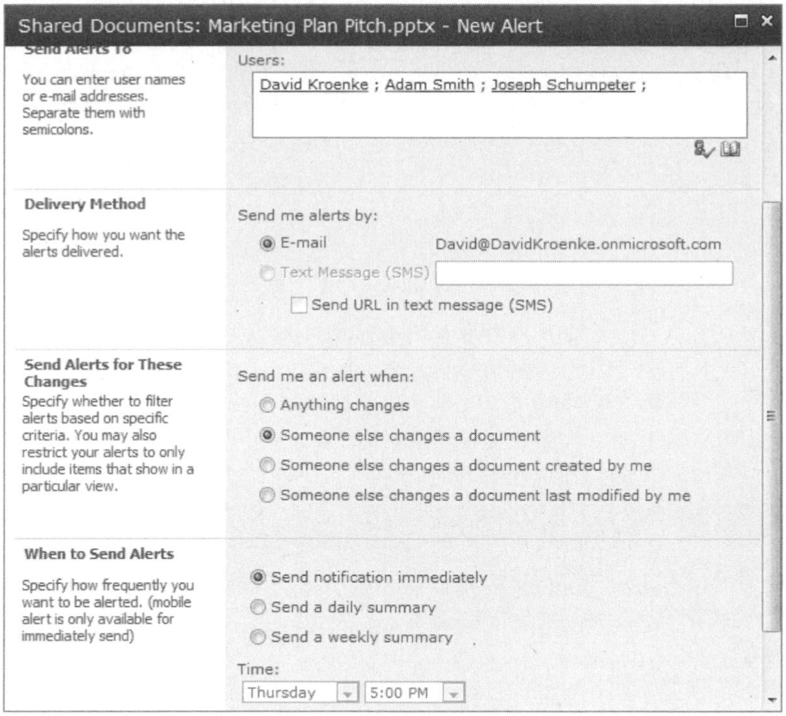

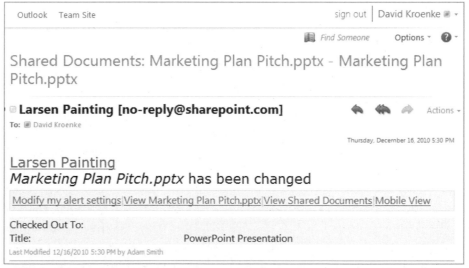

FIGURE 4-10: Specifying the Alert Conditions

FIGURE 4-11: Alert Notification Email

Alerts can also be set on the library itself, as explained in the next section.

> Alerts are very useful, but like salt and hot sauce, use them sparingly. If you set too many alerts on too many documents, you'll jam your and your team-mate's mailboxes with emails about changes. Most people respond to such overload by ignoring it, which eliminates the benefit of the alert. So, know about alerts, but use them with caution!

Changing Views and Library Settings

SharePoint provides an extensive set of tools to manage a document library. To see them, click Library Tools and then the Library tab, as shown in Figure 4-12.

FIGURE 4-12: Document Library Tools

A *view* is a presentation of a library or list. Views give incredible power and flex-ibility to SharePoint, as you'll learn later in the book. You've already seen two views of the Shared Documents library. Shared Documents in the center bottom of the page in Figure 4-1 is one view; Figure 4-12 shows a second view.

The various view options are as follow:

- **Standard View:** As shown by the shaded box in Figure 4-12, this library is cur-rently in Standard View; this is the default view that SharePoint uses unless otherwise instructed.

- **Datasheet View:** This view shows the list in the format of a table. Datasheet View is useful for many kinds of lists, especially when you're adding a lot of list items at once. It's not very useful for this example, so skip over it for now. You'll use it extensively when you create task lists in Chapter 8.

- **Create View:** There is no practical limit on the number of views. As you'll learn in Chapter 8 you can create one view that shows just items of interest to you and another that shows all items, and so forth. You can create a new view of the Shared Documents library by clicking Create View in the toolbar. Doing so puts you ahead of the discussion at hand, however, so skip it for now.

- **Modify View:** If you click this view, SharePoint presents the page shown in Figure 4-13.

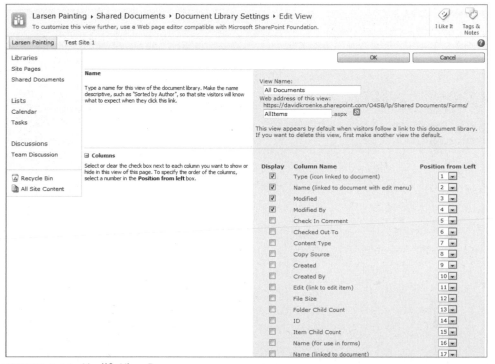

FIGURE 4-13: Modify View Page

As you can see, Shared Documents, like all document libraries, has a large number of properties that you can display in your view. One useful one is Created By, which is the name of the person who created the document. If you select the check box next to Created By and if you select a Position from Left number, say, 3, and click OK, SharePoint displays the list as shown in Figure 4-14. At present, the values of Created By and Modified By are the same; but they will not be as team members begin to review and change each other's documents.

For now, don't worry about the meaning and use of the properties listed in Figure 4-13. You'll learn about those that are of concern to most business professionals as you proceed in this book. The others are quite advanced and you probably won't need them.

FIGURE 4-14: Shared Documents View after Modification

SharePoint provides a host of tools for working on libraries, as you can see in the ribbon in Figure 4-14. We'll discuss use of the Datasheet View in Chapter 6. The Manage View section of the ribbon has tools for modifying the current view, creating a new column in document metadata, and for changing the current view. You would use this last option if you've created several views and you want to change from one to another.

In the Share and Track section, you can set an Alert on the entire library. Such alerts are similar to alerts on a document described in the last section, but if you set an alert here, it applies to any document in the library. Email a Link is straightforward and you can experiment on your own with RSS Feed.

With one exception, the rest of the tools are beyond the scope of this book. The exception is Library Settings. You will find that you use this tool more than any other. When you click it, SharePoint presents the page shown in Figure 4-15.

As you can see, SharePoint provides many tools and options for managing document libraries (and lists as well). Explaining all of them would require a 500 page book, and take us far from the basic tasks most business users need to do. So, in this book, we will show you how to use just a few of them, those that will be most useful to you.

Click Title, description and navigation to change the title of your list. That's a simple task to do, and you can do that on your own. A useful task that is a bit more complicated is to alter the versioning settings, and you will learn how to do that next.

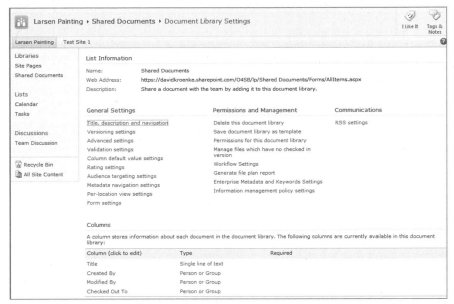

FIGURE 4-15: Document Library Settings Page

Changing Versioning and Checkout Settings

Every time you edit a document and close your editing session, you are creating a new version of that document. Prior to SharePoint, if you wanted to track versions on a file server, you'd do so by fussing with document names. Maybe you'd add the date or your initials to the end of a document. When that happens, you end up with names like MarketingPlan_Mar29_dk_dn_lt. You get the picture. Other than the ugly document names, this approach has two problems:

- You never know which version is the current version. There might be one with today's date on it somewhere, but you don't know if it exists, and if so, where it is.

- You don't know where earlier versions are located. If you want to look at the document as of last April, where would you find it?

> **Note** When you change the title in the Library Settings page, you are changing the title of the list itself, and that title change propagates into all views of the list. To see this in action, change the title of Shared Documents to something else, say, Marketing Documents. Now, go to the home page of your site and look at the title of this folder in the Quick Launch as well as the heading of the library on the main page. This kind of propagation gives you incredible bang for the buck! Just also keep in mind that it will happen.

You can set up SharePoint to track document versions for you. When you do, you and your team members always save the document under the same name; SharePoint tracks the versions. When you open a document, SharePoint always opens the most current version, automatically. If you want to go back, you can restore to an earlier version, and then open it. Versioning thus solves both of the problems of non-versioned file servers.

SharePoint provides three versioning options: none, major versions, and minor versions. A major version is created every time you edit a document and then close that document. Minor versions are created and managed differently, and involves the SharePoint publishing features and tools. Unless you're publishing the *Wall Street Journal*, you won't need them, and if you are publishing it, then someone else will have set it up.

In addition to versioning, you can also require users to checkout documents before they can edit them. Only one user can check out a document at a time, so requiring checkout means that just one person has control over a document's change.

You will learn how to setup checkout here, but it most cases, you don't need it. The 2010 versions of Word, Excel, PowerPoint, and OneNote that come with Office 365 all provide truly superb management of concurrent user changes. So unless your business requires just one person to change it at a time, don't use checkout. But if, for example, you work in a law firm, and if your firm has the policy that only one lawyer can change a contract at a time, then you should use checkout.

To change versioning and checkout settings, do the following:

1. In the Document Library Settings page, click Versioning settings. The page shown in Figure 4-16 appears.

2. In the Document Version History section, click the radio button next to Create major versions.

3. At the bottom of the page, click the Yes radio button under Require Check Out.

4. Click OK.

You've just done two things that substantially change the way documents in this library are processed:

▪ Every time you close a document, SharePoint creates a new version.

▪ No one on your team will be able to edit a document unless he or she first checks it out.

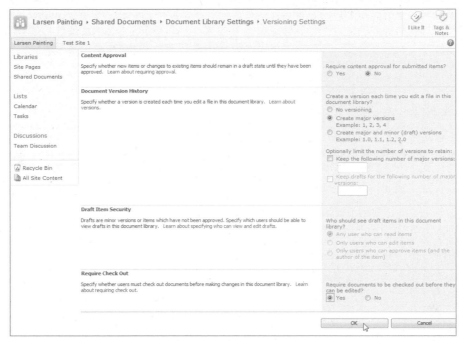

FIGURE 4-16: Changing Versioning Settings

Figure 4-17 shows the version history of the draft of this chapter at this point in time. Notice, by the way, that the presence indicator is adjacent to the name of the person who made the change. Any team member can contact that person using Lync options (refer to Chapter 3 for details).

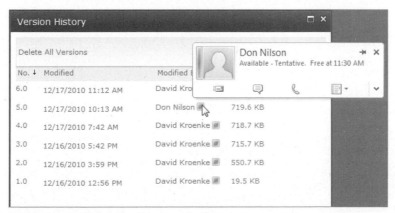

FIGURE 4-17: Using the Presence Indicator

To checkout a document,

1. Click the down arrow to the right of the document's name.

2. Click Check Out, the seventh option shown in the menu (or in the ribbon) in Figure 4-18, You now have total control over the document's content.

3. Once you are finished, close the document and check it back in. At that time, you can also type in comments about what you've done with the document.

FIGURE 4-18: Checking Out a Document

> Requiring checkout adds an extra layer of administrative tasks on team members. It can slow down teamwork and make working on documents a hassle. So, only require checkout when it is absolutely necessary. As stated, Word, Excel, PowerPoint, and OneNote control concurrent changes on your behalf quite well.

When a document is checked out, other team members know because a small green arrow appears next to the document's type icon. Hovering over that arrow causes SharePoint to display the name of the person who has the document checked out, as shown in Figure 4-19.

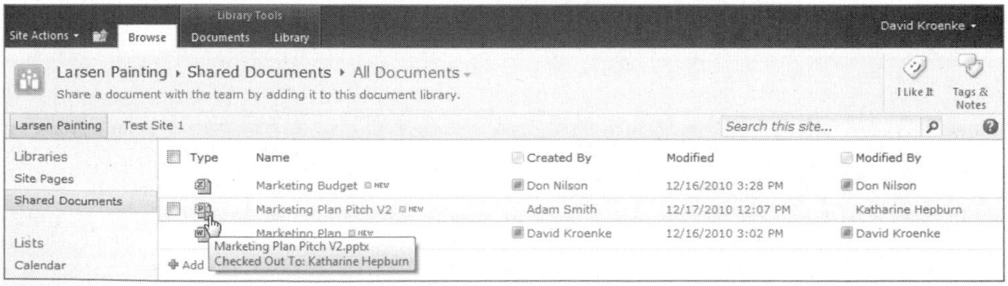

FIGURE 4-19: A Checked-Out Document

What You've Learned

This chapter has given you a basic understanding of using SharePoint document libraries. We only used the Shared Documents folder, but all the skills you've learned here will apply to other document libraries as well.

With the knowledge of this chapter, you can retrieve and store documents in a library. You also know how to use the Office 365 presence indicator to connect with document authors and editors.

Additionally, you've learned how to set alerts on documents and libraries so that you are notified when changes to the document library occur. You also saw how to change views and the basic library settings. Finally, you've learned how to instruct SharePoint to track major versions of your documents and how to use check out/check in.

What's Next?

Document sharing provides a huge productivity boost for teamwork. However, it also has some problems. What if you don't necessarily share your work-in-progress with everyone one your team? Say you want to restrict document access to few team members while the documents are in development.

One way to do that is to create a subsite with restricted permissions, and use that subsite to store work-in-progress. You will learn how to do exactly that in the next chapter!

Of Course, This Would Never Happen in <u>Your</u> Business...

Conversation between Adam Smith, project manager, and Katharine Hepburn, financial analyst:

"No, Adam, no! Don't tell me she took that PowerPoint with her!" Katharine sounds desperate.

"Yup, printed five copies and put it on her PC. She was pretty excited."

"Why did you let her?"

"I didn't know it wasn't ready. Besides, she is Laura Larsen, as in the owner of Larsen Painting..." Adam feels defensive—and worried.

"This is a disaster. Those numbers were just guesses. Those costs are way too low. I just wanted to get the format right."

"Not good. I think she's presenting it to the Glacier Peak team this morning."

"Get her on the phone—tell her not to show those numbers!" Katharine shouts.

"I can try..." Adam picks up his cell phone.

"How did she get it?"

"Off the SharePoint site."

"Can't I share ANYTHING with you guys? I wanted feedback on the format. Oh, please don't let her pitch those costs!"

"She's not answering her cell phone. Maybe I can text her. . ."

"Look, we have to have a way to share documents that are under construction. As in, documents that are NOT READY to show clients."

"Too late for that. Wait, I just got her text. She's in a rental, on her way to the meeting. What do you want me to tell her?"

"Well..."

It Doesn't Have to Be That Way...

Sharing (Only) What You Want

AS YOU LEARNED IN CHAPTER 3, SharePoint provides an easy and powerful way for sharing documents. However, such sharing comes with risks. Anyone with read permission can open documents and download them for distribution anywhere. Also, as illustrated in the opening scene, sometimes team members want to share documents with just part of the team. Sharing drafts is a good example. Another example is when some team members have access to documents that, for privacy reasons, should not be available to all team members.

You can accomplish such partial sharing in several ways in SharePoint. The easiest and most effective way is to use subsites, the subject of this chapter. Specifically, you'll learn:

- How collections of SharePoint sites are structured
- How to create subsites
- How to customize the look and feel of a team site
- How groups are used to provide different user permissions
- How to set permissions that are unique for a subsite

How Are SharePoint Sites Structured?

A *SharePoint site* is a collection of libraries, lists, calendars, tasks, and other resources. You learned about document libraries in Chapter 4 and you'll learn about numerous other SharePoint features in the rest of this book.

SharePoint sites can have one or more children sites, called *subsites*. Further, each subsite can have one more subsites itself, which would *be sub-subsites* to the first site. Figure 5-1 shows a generic collection of sites.

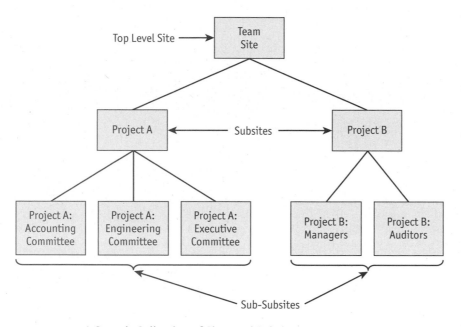

FIGURE 5-1: A Generic Collection of Sites and Subsites

By the way, Figure 5-1 shows a collection of sites. It is not labeled a *site collection,* however, because the term *site collection* has a very specific meaning to SharePoint administrators. So, if you find yourself talking with a SharePoint technical person, avoid using that term. Thankfully, you need not know anything about the "real" meaning of site collection to productively use SharePoint!

The two fundamental reasons for creating subsites are to:

- Reduce complexity
- Provide privacy

The following sections consider each reason.

Reducing Complexity with Subsites

SharePoint sites can grow large. When they do, you might find it difficult to find things. In addition, too many people may have access to more content than they want or need. To make navigating and managing site content easy, organizations create subsites that have content for particular purposes or for particular periods of time. Figure 5-2 shows a collection of sites Larsen Painting might use. This collection has two sites devoted to two of its largest projects as well as two other sites that have records of smaller jobs for the years 2011 and 2012. A summary of the content of each of these sites is as shown.

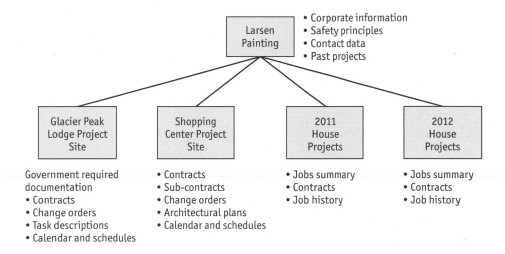

FIGURE 5-2: Example Site and Subsites for Larsen Painting

Although SharePoint allows a site to have a nearly unlimited number of subsites, as a general rule no site should have more than seven to nine subsites. After that, the subsites become unmanageable. If you need more sites, you create another level of sub-subsites. Figure 5-3 shows a collection with three levels created by a large restaurant franchiser. The top-level site is used by North American operations, the next two sites concern franchises in Canada and the U.S., and the sites below them are used by operations in different geographic regions. More levels can be created; SharePoint allows for a nearly unlimited number of levels.

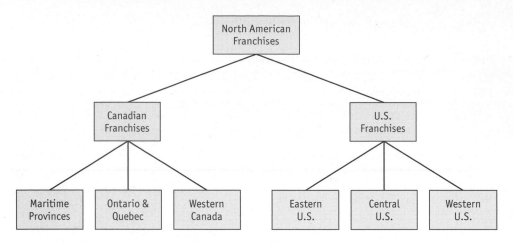

. . . Possible subsite under the regional sites . . .

FIGURE 5-3: Example Collection of Sites Used by an International Restaurant Franchiser

Creating Privacy with Subsites

By default, a subsite has the same users, groups, and permissions as its parent, and whatever you and others can do to the parent site you can do to the child site. You'll learn more about groups, users, and permissions later in this chapter, but for now, know that you can alter this default characteristic to give specific permissions to specific people or groups.

Larsen Painting, for example, could set up a subsite just for proposals and restrict permission to read or edit the contents of that site to a special group of employees. Had Katharine done that at the start of this chapter, Ms. Larsen would not have been able to access the draft PowerPoint presentation.

You find out how to restrict permissions later in this chapter. For now, however, consider the process of creating and tailoring a subsite.

How Can You Create a Subsite?

To begin, create a subsite called Test Site 1. Creating a test site enables you to isolate your learning and testing activities in one place. If you create a disaster (which is unlikely), you can always delete the test site and start over.

To create a new subsite, follow these steps:

1. Navigate to the parent site, like the one for Larsen painting shown in Figure 5-4, and click the Site Actions menu (upper-left corner).

FIGURE 5-4: Default Team Site (Top Level)

2. Select New Site from the menu. SharePoint displays a page with a floating pages image on the right side.

3. The floating pages represent the various types of subsites you can create. Click the floating pages image until the page for Team Site moves to the front on the left side of the page, as shown in Figure 5-5. Usually one click will do that.

4. On the Team Site page, type **Test Site 1** (or whatever name you choose for your site) and click Create.

SharePoint grinds away for a few moments and then takes you to the first page of your new site, which is that generic team site that you've seen before.

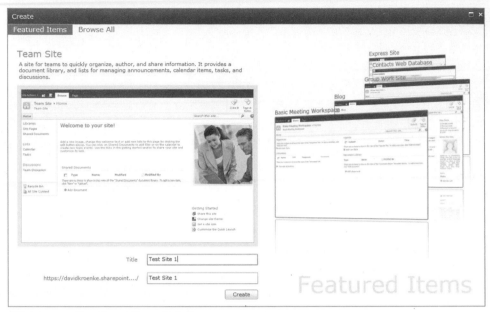

FIGURE 5-5: Creating a Team Subsite

Customizing the Appearance of a Site or Subsite

You don't have to work with SharePoint very long to become quite bored with the appearance of the default site. Of course, you want your site to look like the one for your company, and for your project, with pictures of your people, facilities, or products. Fortunately, changing the site to make it more interesting and more specific to you and your teammates is quite easy.

Changing Title and Description

To begin, change the site's title and description by following these steps:

1. Click the Site Actions menu and click Edit Page as shown in Figure 5-6. In response, SharePoint opens the current page in edit mode.

2. Mouse over the title "Welcome to your site!" and change it to something you like. In Figure 5-7, it's changed to **Larsen Painting Test Site!**

FIGURE 5-6: Edit Page Action

3. Do the same thing with the site description. Move your mouse over the paragraph that begins "Add a new image, change this..." and change that text to whatever you want. Figure 5-7 shows the text changed to **We've created this site as a place to test out what we want.**

4. Click Save & Close as shown by the cursor arrow in Figure 5-7 and SharePoint makes your changes to the site.

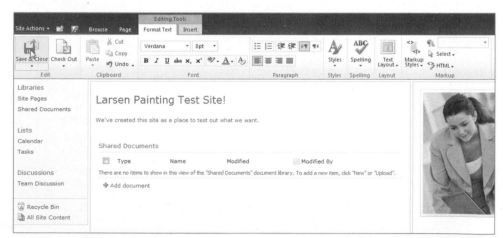

FIGURE 5-7: Saving Text Changes

Changing the Site Image

The three people in the default Team Site picture must be the three most-viewed people on the Internet! Let's hope they earn a tenth of a penny every time their faces pop up. However pleasant they appear, a picture of your own team, your own people, your own logo, is far more interesting to you and your teammates.

To change the picture, follow these steps:

1. Click Site Actions → Edit Page as you did in the last section.

2. Click the top of the picture. SharePoint displays the Picture Tools, as shown in Figure 5-8.

3. Click Picture Tools and then click Change Picture in the upper-left corner.

4. To select a picture from your computer, click From Computer, as shown in Figure 5-9. SharePoint opens a dialog box where you can select the image you want just like you would select any other file. The example in Figure 5-10 shows the selection of an image named Larsen Logo.

FIGURE 5-8: Changing the Default Picture

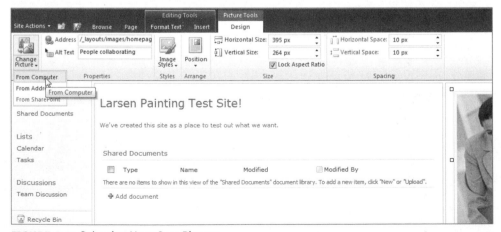

FIGURE 5-9: Selecting Your Own Picture

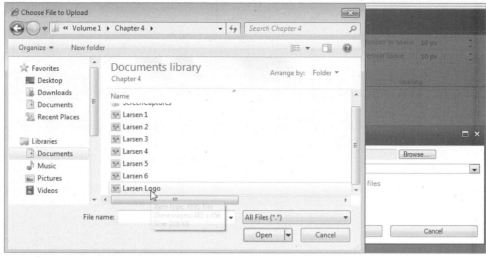

FIGURE 5-10: Uploading a Picture

5. Click Open and then click OK. SharePoint places the image onto your site.

6. The picture is likely to be the wrong size. In Figure 5-11, the picture is way too big. To reduce its size, click the handles on the corner of the image and drag it to make it a size that looks right to you. The user in this example is dragging the upper-right corner of the image in Figure 5-11.

7. With these changes, click Save & Close as shown in Figure 5-12. SharePoint saves your page with the changes you've made. Here, the page will have the title, description, and images just as shown in Figure 5-12.

FIGURE 5-11: Resizing the Picture

FIGURE 5-12: Larsen Site with Its Own Logo

Changing the Quick Launch

In Chapter 2, you learned about Quick Launch, the left-side menu that contains links to Libraries, Lists, Discussions, and site content. Quick launch, as its name implies, is an easy and fast way to access the most important or most frequently needed site content. The default Quick Launch is fine for starting, but over time, you'll want to change it to better meet the needs of your team. It is easy to change.

1. In the lower-right corner of the screen in Figure 5-12, click the Customize the Quick Launch link. In response, SharePoint displays the page shown in Figure 5-13.

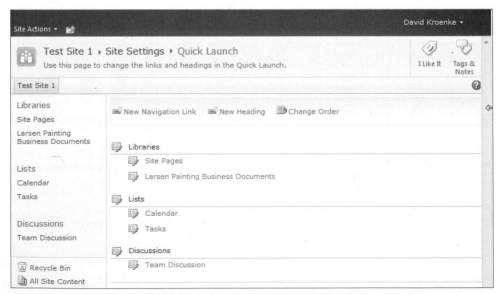

FIGURE 5-13: Editing the Quick Launch

2. As shown, from this page, you can add new navigation links, add new headings, and change the order of the items in the Quick Launch. Start with changing the order. Click Change Order and SharePoint displays a reorder page like that in Figure 5-14.

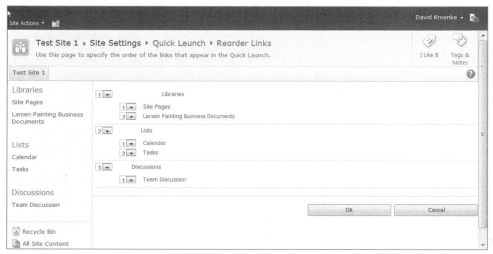

FIGURE 5-14: Changing the Order of Quick Launch Menu Items

3. To reorder the headings, for example, to make lists first and libraries second, click the down arrow next to Libraries, and change its value—in this example to 2 (or change the number in front of Lists to 1). To make Larsen Painting Business Documents appear before Site Pages, change the number in front of Larsen Painting Business Documents to a 1. (Alternatively, change the number in front of Site Pages to 2.)

4. Click OK, and your site will appear like that shown in Figure 5-15.

   Notice in Figure 5-15 that Lists is now first in the Quick Launch and Larsen Painting and Business Documents is first in Libraries.

> **Note** The menu item *Site Pages* is a link to a library that is important in SharePoint, but is beyond the scope of this discussion and beyond the scope of the needs of most non-technical people. Most likely you have no need for a link to it in Quick Launch; its link is just taking up critical space, so you should delete it. Keep in mind, however, that you're deleting the *link* to Site Pages; not the Site Page library. In fact, if you were to delete the Site Pages library, you would have a disaster on your hands! As long as you stay within the confines of the pages you see by clicking Customize the Quick Launch, you'll be fine. You won't have a chance to delete the library itself.

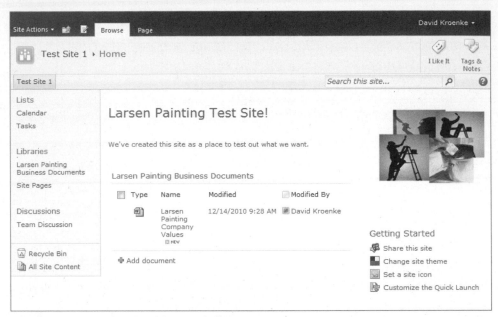

FIGURE 5-15: Results of Quick Launch Change

5. To delete this link to Site Pages, click Customize the Quick Launch and in the page that appears, click the edit icon next to Site Pages (looks like small document with a pencil). SharePoint displays the page in Figure 5-16.

6. Click Delete, confirm that action, and SharePoint will delete the *link* to the Site Pages in the Quick Launch.

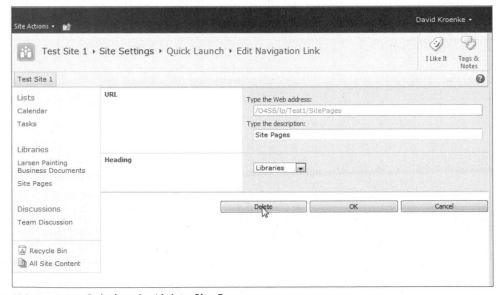

FIGURE 5-16: Deleting the Link to Site Pages

Note You may be wondering how to remove or move a subsite. Deleting one is easy. Just click Site Actions → Site Settings and, in the second column, under the heading Site Actions, click Delete this site.

Moving a site to a different parent site is more difficult. You must save it as a site template with content, then re-create the site from that template. Then, you delete the original site. These steps are beyond the scope of this book. Search the Web for the topic **saving a site as a template** for more information.

Changing the Site Theme

A *site theme* is a graphic design that includes typefaces, sizes, and colors, as well as screen background colors. SharePoint includes many different site themes that you can apply to your sites. When you apply a theme, the structure of your site does not change. Instead, the overall look of your site is altered.

You don't necessarily need to change the site's theme. If you like what you see so far, you can skip all of this. However, you might want to experiment just to see the dramatic visual changes you can make with a few simple clicks.

To apply a different theme to your site, follow these steps:

1. Click Change site theme in the lower-right corner of your site's Home page (the page shown in Figure 5-15). SharePoint displays the screen shown in Figure 5-17. The themes available are shown with names like Azure, Berry, and Bittersweet in the list box on the right.

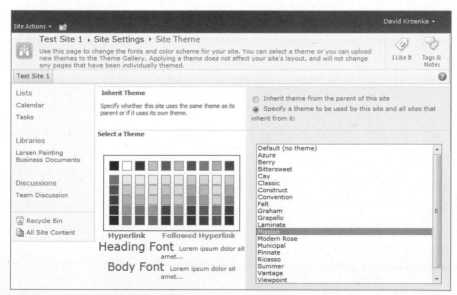

FIGURE 5-17: Changing the Site Theme

2. Click around in this list to see the colors that are selected for that theme. Figure 5-17 shows the colors available for the Mission theme.

3. When you find a color you like, you can do one of three things:

   ▪ **Preview:** This button lets you try out your theme before applying it.

   ▪ **Apply:** Click Apply (it appears at the bottom of the screen in Figure 5-17, but it was cut off from this screen capture) to apply the theme.

   ▪ **Current versus subsites:** You also have the choice of applying this theme only to the current site, or applying it to the current site and all subsites of this site.

4. Click Apply. SharePoint makes the changes. The application of the Mission theme to Test Site 1 is shown in Figure 5-18. As you can see, while changing the site, the content has quite a dramatic effect on the appearance of the site, the content is unchanged.

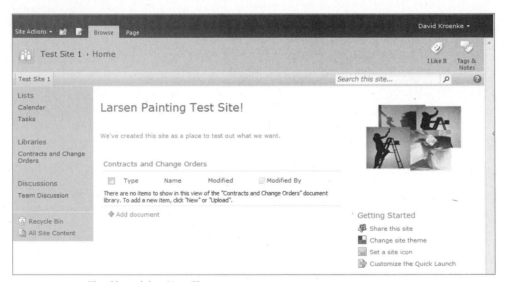

FIGURE 5-18: The Site with a New Theme

Customizing Subsite Permissions

SharePoint has an elaborate set of permissions that you can use to limit activity in very specific and detailed ways. If you want, you can limit the clicking of a particular button to left-handed, green-eyed people. But, unless you're using SharePoint to publish the daily edition of the *Wall Street Journal*, you probably do not need to use, or even know about, SharePoint's elaborate permissions and groups.

However, you probably will want to create subsites that have simple, but unique permissions. In fact, Larsen Painting, the company you read about at the start of this chapter, could have avoided its near-catastrophe if it has customized the permissions of a subsite for use by team members who are creating draft documents. All the assets of such a subsite could have been shared with the working team, and at the proper time, moved to another site that could have been accessible by everyone.

This section shows how to do create such a subsite. It carefully threads the way through the robust and complex SharePoint security system. When you do these tasks yourself, just copy what you see here; don't get off the tracks. It's a jungle in there!

Basic SharePoint Security Groups

Most business professionals and teams can get by with the three basic groups and permissions listed in Table 4-1. In fact, when SharePoint creates the top-level site in a collection, it creates the groups in this table. People in the top-level site owners group can add and remove people to and from any of these groups.

TABLE 4-1: SharePoint Security Groups and Their Permissions

Group	Permissions
Visitors	Read: Can view and download site content.
Members	Contribute: Can add, edit, read, and delete site content.
Owners	Full control: Contribute plus change the structure and appearance of site. Can create subsites and change site groups and permissions.

Subsites Inherit Permissions by Default

To generate the screenshots for this book, the authors created a top-level site named **Office 365 in Business.** As part of that site, SharePoint created the following three groups:

- Office 365 in Business Visitors
- Office 365 in Business Members
- Office 365 in Business Owners

These groups have the permissions shown for visitors, members, and owners in Table 4-1. Initially, the groups had only one person; the person who created the top-level site. That person, however, added more users to each group. Any person who was added to the Owners group could then add other people to the groups as well. People in the Owners group can also remove users from all the groups.

Larsen Painting is a subsite of the site Office 365 in Business. When SharePoint created Larsen Painting, by default it assigned Larsen Painting the same groups the parent site, Office 365 in Business. When this was done, the subsite Larsen Painting was said to "inherit permissions from its parent."

You can verify whether or not a site is inheriting from its parent. To do so for the chapter example, select Site Actions → Site Settings, and click Site Permissions as shown in Figure 5-19.

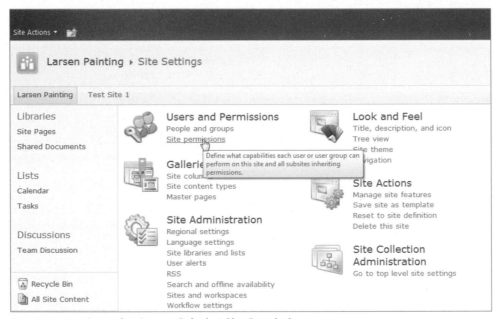

FIGURE 5-19: Accessing Larsen Painting Site Permissions

In response, SharePoint shows the three groups in Figure 5-20. Notice the phrase "This Web site *inherits permissions* from its parent" in the box between the Ribbon and the Library lists.

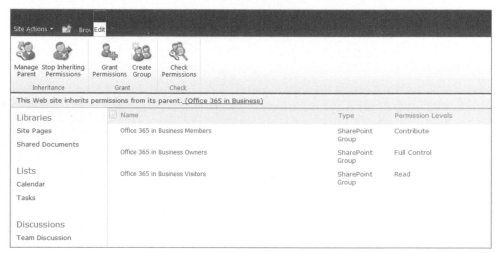

FIGURE 5-20: Larsen Painting Inherits Permissions from Its Parent Site, Office 365 in Business

Such inheritance by default makes sense; most of the time, you want a subsite to have the same users, groups, and permissions as the parent site. However, sometimes, you want a site to have its own private set of permissions, called *unique permissions*. In the chapter example, Larsen Painting needs a site with unique permissions for people to develop bids and proposals without exposing those items to the entire company.

Test Site 1 is a subsite of Larsen Painting, and when you created it earlier in this chapter, SharePoint automatically inherited its permissions from the Larsen Painting site. But, as you just saw, Larsen Painting inherits from the top-level site Office 365 in Business. So Test Site 1 has the same permissions as Office 365 in Business.

Changing the Default Permissions

If you decide you want to change the default permissions, you can set up unique permissions for Test Site 1, follow these steps:

1. Navigate to Test Site 1.

2. Click Site Actions → Site Settings.

3. Under the heading Users and Permissions, click Site Permissions. SharePoint displays a page like that shown in Figure 5-21.

4. To stop inheriting permissions, click Stop Inheriting Permissions in the upper-left corner as shown in Figure 5-21 When you do that, SharePoint gives Test Site 1 unique permissions.

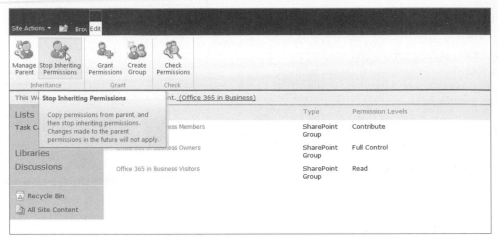

FIGURE 5-21: Breaking Permission Inheritance

The result is shown in Figure 5-22. Note the phrase, "This web site has unique permissions."

You need to be careful here, however. All you have done to this point is to break the requirement that the subsite and site (Test Site 1 and Larsen Painting) always have the same permissions. Notice in Figure 5-22 that SharePoint left the three original groups in place on this site. Because you've broken permissions, you can remove these groups from Test Site 1. You can also create new groups and give them permissions on this site without SharePoint's automatically adding them to other inheriting sites.

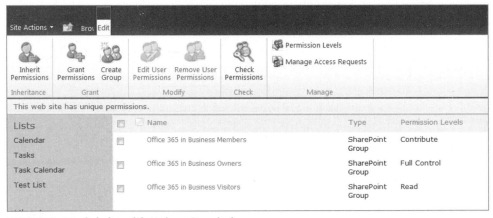

FIGURE 5-22: Subsite with Unique Permissions

Most of the time, permission inheritance is a good idea. If you have a collection of sites with, say, 75 subsites and sub-subsites, breaking inheritance will create an administrative nightmare. So, only use unique permissions when you must.

Creating a New Group and Deleting Old Groups

The groups that were left on this site (those listed in Figure 5-22) are still used by other sites. If you change, add, or remove someone to or from one of these groups, you are changing that group both here and in every place that group is used. So, if you want truly unique permissions, the safest course of action is to create new groups, just for this site, and remove the existing shared groups from this site. You will learn how to do that next.

To create a new group, follow these steps:

1. Click Create Group in the Grant section of the ribbon previously shown in Figure 5-22. SharePoint displays a large form.

2. At the top of the form, enter a name for the group, something like **Test Site 1 Viewers**. Then lower in the form, select the permissions you want this group to have. For this example, the user selected Read, as shown in Figure 5-23.

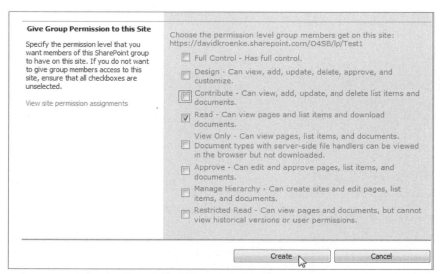

FIGURE 5-23: Setting Permissions for a New Group

3. Click Create. In response, SharePoint opens a form that you can use to add members to this group as shown in Figure 5-24. Here Adam Smith and Katherine Hepburn have been added to the new group.

4. Click OK and the new group are created with these two people.

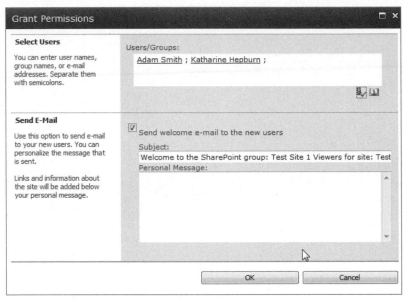

FIGURE 5-24: Adding Members to the New Group

Figure 5-25 shows the new group with three people. David Kroenke is automatically a member of the group because he created it.

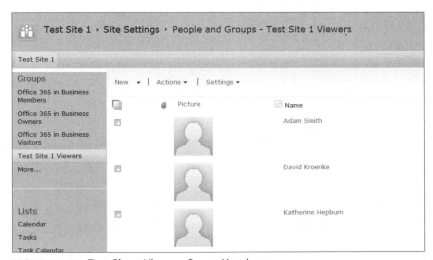

FIGURE 5-25: Test Site 1 Viewers Group Members

> **Note** Later on, if you want to add or remove users from the new group, click Site Actions → Site Settings → People and Groups. On the left, select the group you want to modify. With that group highlighted, click New and select people to add to the group you've highlighted. To remove users from a group, highlight the group as just described, select the box next to the person or people you want to removed, and click Actions → Remove Users from Group.

5. Follow steps 1-4 to create groups with Contribute permissions and groups with Full Control permissions. If you do so, the results appear as shown in Figure 5-26. Notice that the three new groups have been created, but the three original groups are still there. To finish this customization, you need to remove the original groups from Test Site 1.

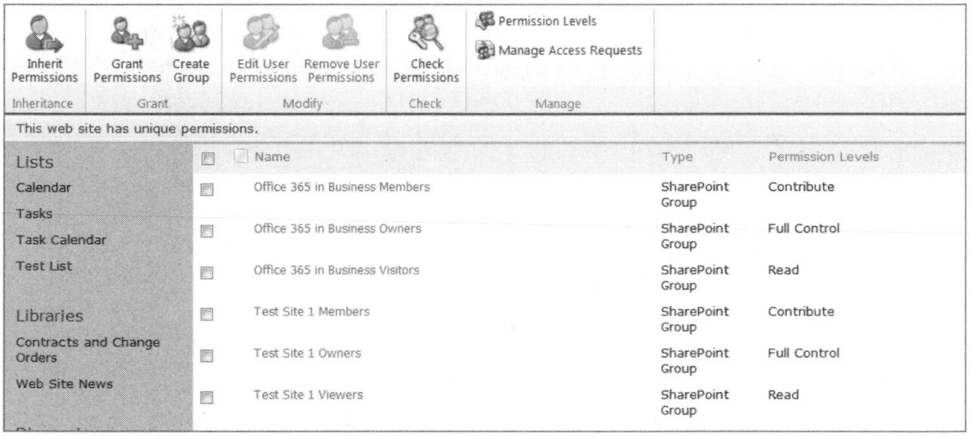

FIGURE 5-26: Test Site 1 with Three New Groups

6. To remove the three Office 365 in Business groups, select the box next to each of their names and then click Remove User Permissions as shown in Figure 5-27.

Figure 5-28 shows the result. Test Site 1 now has permissions that are different from its parent site. In particular, only Adam Smith and Katharine Hepburn can view the site's contents.

Groups in Test Site 1 are managed independently of its parent site. User and Group changes made to the parent do not affect Test Site 1, and changes made to Test Site 1 do not affect the parent.

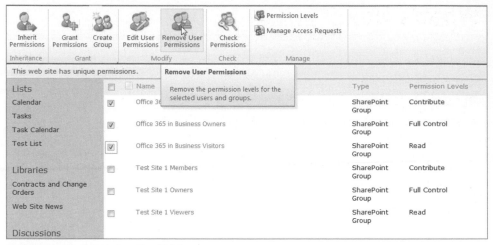

FIGURE 5-27: Removing the Old Groups

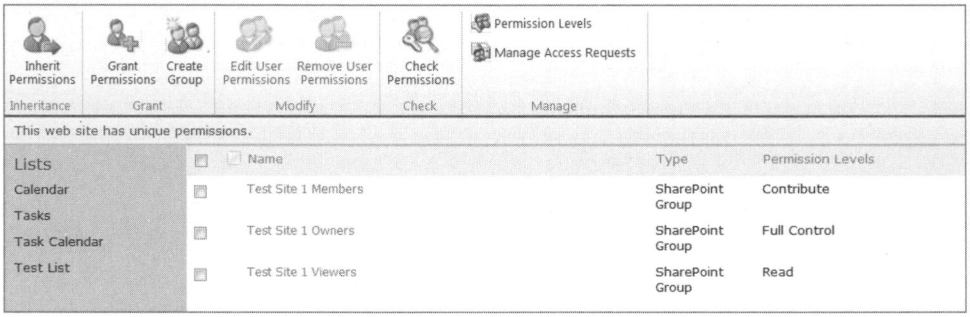

FIGURE 5-28: Test Site 1 with New Permissions

What You've Learned

In this chapter, you've learned the structure of SharePoint sites and the relationship of sites and subsites. You've seen how to reduce complexity with subsites as well as how to create privacy with them.

With the knowledge from this chapter you now know how to create a subsite, customize the appearance of any site, and customize subsite permissions.

You have the knowledge to prevent the problem at Larsen Painting that started this chapter. You know how to create a subsite for proposal development and how to customize the permissions of that subsite so that only people authorized to see proposals-in-process could access it. If Larsen Painting had such a site, Laura Larsen would not have had access to the draft PowerPoint, let alone download it before it was ready.

What's Next?

Alas, the problems are not over for Larsen painting. In the next chapter, you will learn how the "left hand didn't know what the right hand was doing" on the crucial Glacier Peak job. As a consequence, many labor hours were wasted. It didn't have to be that way; they could have used SharePoint task lists to keep track of who is supposed to do what, next.

Coordinating Work

Of Course, This Would Never Happen in <u>Your</u> Business...

Adam Smith, job supervisor, drives up to the Glacier Peak Lodge to check progress on the painting of the first floor. He's outraged to find the crew sitting around a big fire in the lodge fireplace, chatting.

"Why are you guys just sitting there? Don't you have some walls to paint?"

"Yeah, Adam, we do. But to paint walls, you actually have to have paint!" this comment from Steve, a part-time employee hired for the Glacier Peak job.

"Joe was supposed to pick up the paint. I'm surprised he's not here." Adam looks around in frustration.

"I don't think he was planning on it when he went home yesterday." Steve, embarrassed by his earlier comment, is trying to be helpful.

"Really? I told him to get it last week."

Jennifer, another painter on the job jumps into the conversation. "I talked to him this morning on his cell phone. They didn't have it when he was there last week. And today, there was some problem on the door trim color. The only way to get it today was to drive to Seattle."

"To Seattle?" Adam's face is turning bright red.

"Yeah, he had to drive down to the big city because the Alderwood store didn't have the right base tint. The designer specified something special, I guess."

"I told him to figure that out last week. Okay, no paint. So finish the prep—like that trim on the balcony. Get out your scrapers and get going. You do have scrapers, right?"

"Yup, Adam, we've got scrapers. No problem there," Steve says, repressing a chuckle as he looks at Jennifer and the rest of the group.

"So get going!" Adam barks.

"How are we going to get up there?"

"What do you mean? Use a ladder."

"Good plan. Except the ladders are on Joe's truck... so I thought I'd sit by this nice fire until he comes back," Steve says as he arranges a pillow on the stone hearth.

It Doesn't Have to Be That Way...

Coordinating Work with Tasks Lists

LARSEN PAINTING IS A SUCCESSFUL BUSINESS that has been painting houses and commercial properties for 25 years. It's a well-run company, but when it wins big jobs like the Glacier Peak Lodge, coordinating people, tasks, equipment, and resources, such as paint, becomes challenging. Larsen Painting needs an easier way for its managers and employees to create and access a list of tasks.

SharePoint was designed, in large part, to manage lists. It has features and functions for keeping track of many different kinds of lists. One of the most popular and useful SharePoint lists are lists of tasks. When we created the Test Site 1 team site in Chapter 5, SharePoint automatically created a Tasks list.

Larsen Painting could use SharePoint Tasks lists to keep track of who is going to do what and by when. It is unlikely that painters or laborers will use SharePoint, but managers, supervisors, and office personnel who are concerned with scheduling personnel, assigning equipment, allocating resources, establishing task start and due dates, and meeting budgets could all benefit by using SharePoint Tasks lists.

This chapter shows you how to:

- Add tasks to a Team Site task list
- Create task dependencies
- Modify the task list view
- Add tasks in bulk using the datasheet format
- Create and use a calendar view of the task list

- Add the calendar view to the Quick Launch menu and to the Home page
- Create a Gantt chart of the items in the task list
- Create a personal view of tasks

Entering Tasks into the Task List

Test Site 1, the site you created in Chapter 5, is based on the Team Site template which includes, by default, a list called Tasks. As shown in Figure 6-1, if you click Tasks in the List Category of the Quick Launch, SharePoint displays a page showing the task list, which initially is empty.

FIGURE 6-1: Task List in Team Site

A company like Larsen Painting can use the Tasks list to schedule work on projects, and for more than that, as you will see. To do so, they first need to enter tasks into that list. They can do so one-at-a-time or in bulk. You should consider each method to determine how it fits in with your game plan. The following sections give you a step by step walk through of each method.

Adding Tasks One at a Time

To add a task to the list shown in Figure 6-1, follow these steps:

1. Click Add new item. SharePoint displays the default form for entering items, as shown in Figure 6-2.

2. Type in a value for Title and add one of the people in your group (here Adam Smith) for the Assigned To property.

3. Specify values for Description, Start Date, and Due Date, and then click Save.

Note We won't use the other fields in this form in Figure 6-2 for now. Predecessors are discussed in the next section "Modifying the Current View" and Status is discussed in Chapter 9.

FIGURE 6-2: Entering a New Task

ADVICE By default, SharePoint only allows one person to be entered into the Assigned To property. You can allow for more than one person in Assigned To by going to the List Tools section of the ribbon, clicking List, and then off to the right, clicking List Settings. Under the Columns heading, click Assigned To, and click Yes under the phrase Allow multiple selections.

4. Enter additional tasks by repeating steps 1–3.

5. Click Add new item, and SharePoint displays the form shown in Figure 6-3. When SharePoint displays that form, it places all existing tasks in the Predecessors

list. If any of the existing tasks must be completed before the current task is started, select those existing tasks and click Add. SharePoint will add them to the list in the box to the right of the Add and Remove buttons.

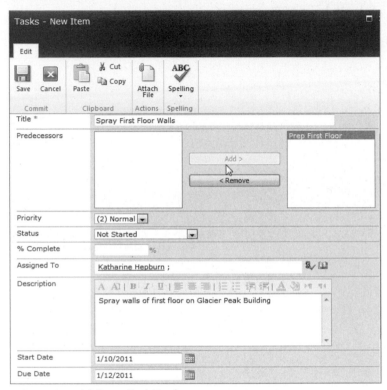

FIGURE 6-3: Adding a Task Predecessor

In this example, the Prep First Floor task must be completed before the Spray First Floor Walls task can be started. Because this is so, in Figure 6-3, the user clicked Prep First Floor and added it to the list of predecessors.

FIGURE 6-4: Default View of Tasks

Modifying the Current View

The Tasks list with two tasks is shown in Figure 6-4. Notice that the second task has the value Prep First Floor in the Predecessors property. You'll see how SharePoint uses predecessor data later in this chapter. Tasks can have more than one predecessor tasks.

Larsen Painting does not use a task priority system. Consequently, the Priority values shown in Figure 6-4 are needlessly taking up space. Thankfully, removing unwanted columns is easy.

To do so, follow these steps:

1. Click List Tools → List in the ribbon and then click the edit icon to the left of the words Current View. (If your screen is maximized, SharePoint may show the phrase Modify View instead of the edit icon.) In response, SharePoint displays the page shown in Figure 6-5.

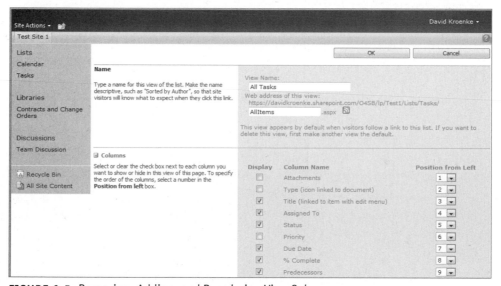

FIGURE 6-5: Removing, Adding, and Reordering View Columns

2. Specify which columns you want in the view by selecting or deselecting the column's Display Checkbox.

3. Specify the order of the column in the view by changing the values of Position from Left. This is similar to specifying the order of the items in the Quick Launch that you saw in Chapter 5.

4. Click OK.

Note   You can customize the columns that you've just created. To do so, see Chapter 8.

Here, the user deselected Attachments, Type, and Priority to remove them from the view. He also selected Start Date, which is cut off in the screenshot in Figure 6-5. When the user clicks OK, SharePoint displays the new view format shown in Figure 6-6.

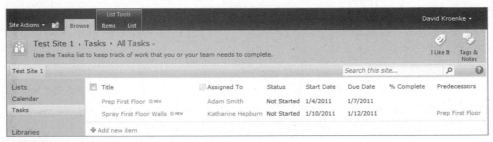

FIGURE 6-6: The New Tasks View

ADVICE   SharePoint lists and libraries have many different views. As you'll soon see, creating even more views is easy. When you remove a column from a view, you are *not* removing the column from the list itself. The column is still in the list, and it still has values, and it may appear in other views. It just won't appear in the view that you're modifying.

If you want to remove a column from the list itself, navigate to List Tools → List and click List Settings. Under the Columns heading, find the name of the column you want to remove and click its name. In the page that appears, click Delete.

Warning! When you remove a column from a list, it is removed from all views of that list, even views that you never use and views that you don't even know exist. Deleting a column can create problems for other users, so be careful.

You can also customize columns by changing their names and other characteristics. See Chapter 8.

Adding Multiple Tasks Using the Datasheet

If you have many tasks to add, clicking Add new item and filling out the form for each one is time consuming and inconvenient. To save time, you can do the following:

1. Click List Tools → List in the ribbon.

2. Near the left-hand side of the ribbon, click Datasheet View, as shown in Figure 6-7.

FIGURE 6-7: Switching to Datasheet View

3. In the view that appears, you can now add tasks just as if you were entering data into spreadsheet. Fill in the values for each task in a row of its own, as shown in Figure 6-8.

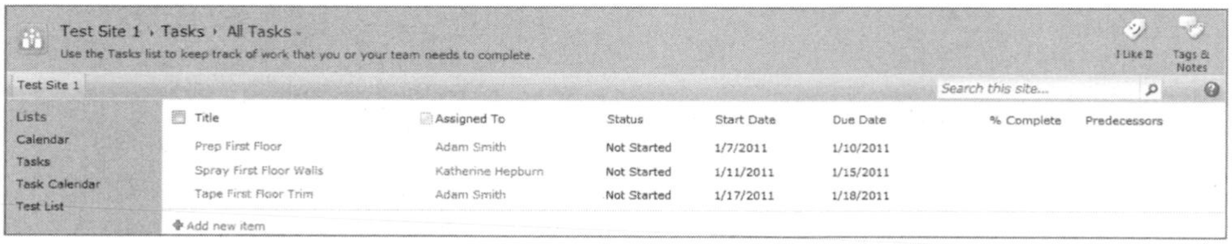

FIGURE 6-8: Add Task Data in Datasheet View

4. In Figure 6-8, the user has not specified values for Predecessors for the new tasks. The reason for this is that until you save new tasks in SharePoint, they are not available to use as predecessors. To make them available, you need to save the data by clicking Standard View. This forces SharePoint to add the new task data to its database.

5. Click Datasheet View again and all the just-entered tasks will appear as possible predecessors, as shown in Figure 6-9.

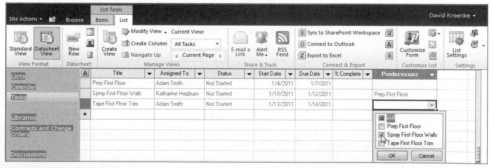

FIGURE 6-9: Setting Predecessors after Saving Newly Entered Task Data

> **Note**
>
> The tasks shown in Figure 6-9 are not detailed enough to prevent the management problem that Adam had at the start of this chapter. He needs to add tasks for checking paint colors, picking up paint, supplying ladders to the site, and so forth. Because this book is about Office 365 and not about running a painting company, it omits these details.
>
> Although this book does not describe the use of Office 365 in the painting industry, you can find information about using Office 365 for CPA firms, for law firms, and for other industries at `www.365forBusiness.com`.

Working with List Views

SharePoint provides five different list view types:

- Standard View
- Datasheet View
- Calendar View
- Gantt View
- Access View

You have already seen the first two: Standard View (Figure 6-8) and Datasheet View (Figure 6-9). The remaining part of this chapter discusses the Calendar and Gantt views. Access Views causes SharePoint to open Microsoft Access and allows you to create Access forms and reports on this list. Working with such views requires knowledge of Microsoft Access and is beyond the scope of this book.

> **Note**
>
> To learn more about Microsoft Access and database processing, see *Database Concepts, 5th Edition*, by David Kroenke and David Auer, Pearson, 2010.

In addition to these built-in view types, you can also customize your own view using SharePoint Designer. This option enables you to be very creative in the way you portray list data; you can make lists appear unlike anything in SharePoint if you want. You need knowledge of SharePoint Designer to do so, however, and we will not address this option in this book.

Using the Calendar View

The calendar view is just what you'd expect: SharePoint places the items in your list on a calendar according to a date value that you've assigned in the list. Most often tasks are placed on a calendar according to their Start and Due Dates. But, if you have other dates in your list that are more appropriate, you could use them for placing tasks on your calendar instead.

Larsen Painting could organize its tasks on a calendar and give printed copies of the calendar to supervisors and employees on painting crews. Doing so might have enabled Joe to remember to pick up the paint. Viewing tasks on calendars also helps to identify schedule conflicts and over-allocation of employees and resources.

> **Note** For more on information on actually managing your Outlook calendar and viewing tasks via Outlook, see Chapter 7. For more on allocating resources, see Chapter 8.

Viewing Tasks on a Calendar

To create a calendar view of the tasks entered in the previous section, follow these steps:

1. Click List Tools → List in the ribbon and then click Create View, as shown in Figure 6-10. In response, SharePoint displays the possible view formats, as shown in Figure 6-11.

FIGURE 6-10: Creating a New Task List View

2. Click Calendar View.

3. In the form that appears, shown in Figure 6-12, type in the name of your calendar view.

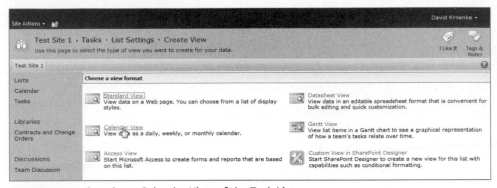

FIGURE 6-11: Creating a Calendar View of the Task List

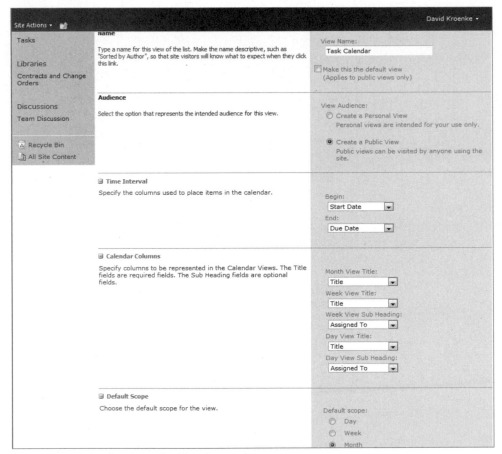

FIGURE 6-12: Setting Calendar View Properties

4. In the Time Interval section of this form, click the down arrow under Begin, and select Start Date. Similarly, click the down arrow under End, and select Due Date.

5. In the Calendar Columns section, select Title for Month View Title, Title for Week View Title, and Title for Day View Title. All these selections are required. If you want, you can also specify subheadings for Week View and Day View. This example shows Assigned To selected for subheadings.

6. You can also specify the default scope as being day, week, or month. In Figure 6-12, the user accepted the default selection of Month.

7. Click OK. Figure 6-13 shows the result.

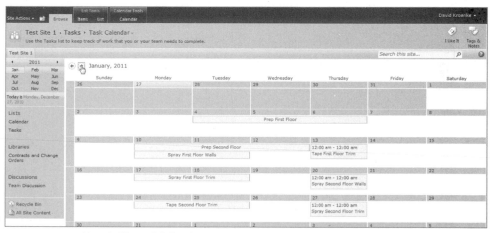

FIGURE 6-13: Month View of Calendar

> If you enter dates for tasks and you do not specify a time for them, SharePoint assumes the tasks fill a 24-hour period.

8. You can change the scope of the calendar by clicking Calendar Tools → Calendar in the ribbon. Then click Day, Week, or Month. In Figure 6-14, the user clicked Week, and SharePoint responds by showing the weekly calendar shown in Figure 6-15.

The user can navigate from week to week by clicking the forward and back arrows to the left of the week's dates.

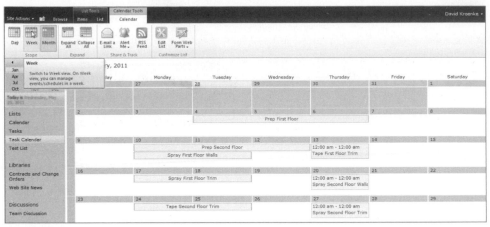

FIGURE 6-14: Changing Calendar Scope to Week

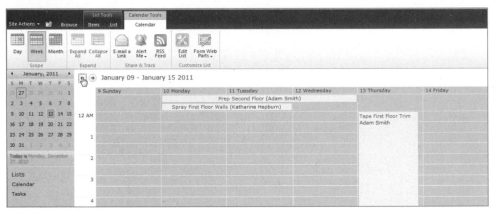

FIGURE 6-15: Week Calendar View

Adding the Calendar View to the Quick Launch

Because the calendar view is a useful way of learning what tasks are to happen, and when, many teams want to make such views readily accessible to team members. One way to do that is to add it to the Quick Launch so that team members can easily access the calendar with one click.

To insert a link to a calendar view (or any view for that matter), you must know the URL of the view. The URL is the long string of often weird-looking text that appears in your browser's address window when you view the calendar. It starts with the characters `https://` and ends with the characters `Calendar.aspx`.

To add the Calendar to the Quick Launch, follow these steps:

1. Copy the URL string of characters onto your Clipboard. To do so, in your browser, click in the address box to the right of `.aspx`. The entire URL is highlighted. Then press Ctrl + C. This places the value of your URL on the Clipboard.

2. Navigate to the site's Home Page by clicking Browse in the ribbon and then clicking Test Site 1.

3. In the lower-right corner of the Home Page, click Customize the Quick Launch (you did this in Chapter 5).

4. In the page that appears, click New Navigation Link. The page in Figure 6-16 appears.

5. Click the box under Type the Web address and delete the letters that are there.

6. With the cursor in this box, press Ctrl + V. Your calendar site's URL is pasted into that box. Figure 6-16 shows the last portion of the URL for the calendar on the site used to create these examples.

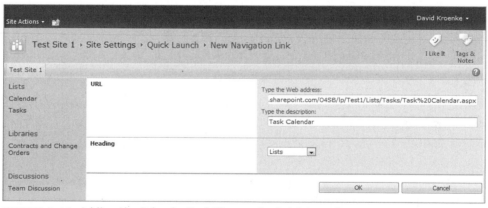

FIGURE 6-16: Adding the Calendar Task View to the Quick Launch

7. Enter a label for the new menu item in the box under Type the description. In Figure 6-16, the user entered **Task Calendar**.

8. You want this new link to appear in the Lists category, so in the box opposite Heading, click the down arrow and select Lists. Figure 6-17 shows the result.

The Task Calendar menu item appears under Lists, and when the user clicks it, SharePoint displays the calendar.

The calendar gives you a graphical view of task relationships that are difficult to see when the tasks are in the form of a list. For example, in Figure 6-17, you can see that Prep Second Floor and Spray First Floor Walls are occurring at the same time. Is this OK? Because you're not a painter, you wouldn't know, but Larsen supervisors will. Also, there is just one day delay between Spray First Floor Walls and Tape First Floor. Is that long enough for the paint to dry? Again, Larsen employees will know. You can also infer from this calendar the dates on which spraying equipment is unused. This data helps Larsen managers to allocate equipment to other jobs, if appropriate.

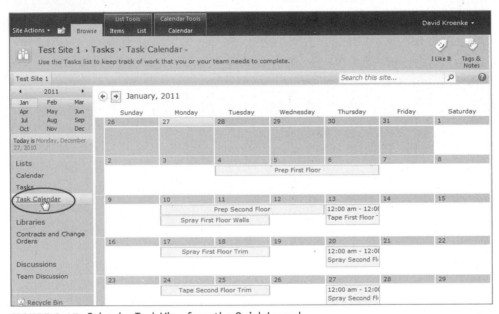

FIGURE 6-17: Calendar Task View from the Quick Launch

Adding the Calendar View to the Home Page

Placing the calendar view in Quick Launch makes it accessible to team members. Another, even more impactful way of showing the tasks calendar is to place it on the Home Page. When you do this, anyone who opens the site will see the calendar without doing anything.

To place a calendar view on the Home Page, you first must add the task list to the Home Page and then change the view of that list to the calendar view.

To edit the Home Page, follow these steps:

1. Navigate to the Home Page and click Site Actions.

2. Click Edit Page, which places the Home Page in edit mode, as shown in Figure 6-18.

3. Place your cursor where you want to add the calendar, and in the ribbon click Editing Tools → Insert.

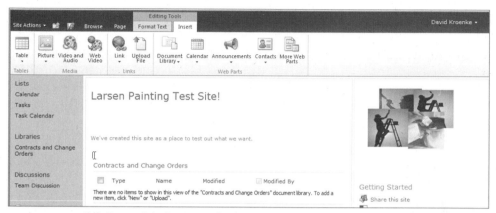

FIGURE 6-18: Edit Page with the Cursor in the Location for Task List

4. Click More Web Parts.

5. In the page that appears (shown in Figure 6-19), click Lists and Libraries on the left, click the Tasks icon, and then click Add. SharePoint places the default Tasks list view into the Home Page.

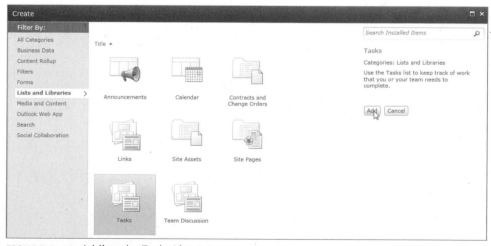

FIGURE 6-19: Adding the Tasks List

6. Click Save & Close to save your work so far.

7. Now, to change the default Tasks view into the Task Calendar view, on the Home Page, click the Tasks list and then click the down arrow in its upper-right corner. Select Edit Web Part, as shown in Figure 6-20.

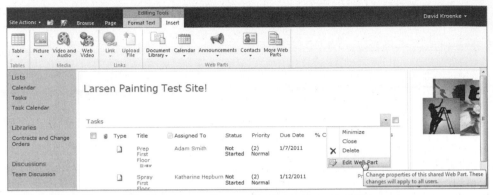

FIGURE 6-20: Choose Edit Web Part to Change the Home Page Task View

8. SharePoint displays a small work area on the right side of your screen. If you don't see it, you may have to scroll over to the right until you can see the work area labeled List Views. In the List Views area, change the value of Selected View to Task Calendar.

9. Click OK in response to the warning message that appears, as shown in Figure 6-21. (We don't care about this warning right now because we haven't made any changes to the list we just placed on the home page.)

10. Click OK in the List Views area and your Home Page will appear as shown in Figure 6-22. Voilà! You have added the Task Calendar view to your Home Page!

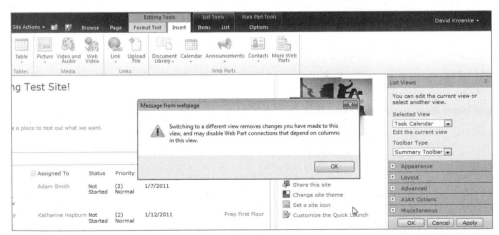

FIGURE 6-21: Warning Message—click OK (for This Example)

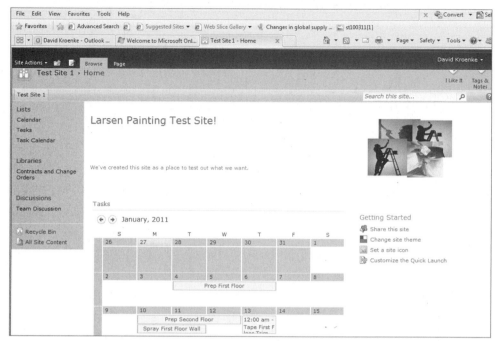

FIGURE 6-22: Home Page with Calendar View of Task List

Now the users of this site cannot avoid the calendar. It's right in front of them, whenever they visit their SharePoint site. If Joe, at Larsen Painting, is a SharePoint user, he'll have a hard time explaining to management why he didn't know about a task that was on the Home Page of their site!

Creating a Gantt Chart of the Task List

A Gantt chart is a graphical display that places tasks on a timeline and shows dependencies among those tasks. Gantt charts are easy to create in SharePoint as you will see. Earlier in this chapter you saw how to enter task dependencies by specifying task predecessors. A Gantt chart is just a graphical way to show those dependencies.

The principal value of Gantt charts is to display what needs to be done before what. At Larsen Painting, you can't buy the paint until the designer has chosen a paint color. Similarly, you can't paint the walls until you have the paint, and so forth.

One of the major uses of Gantt charts is to assess the consequences of schedule changes. A common question is, "If we're late on Task 1, what other tasks will also be delayed?" Or, another common query is just the opposite. "If we finish Task 1 early, does that help us with the scheduling of other tasks?"

The Gantt charts that SharePoint produces are relatively simple. If you know about project management, know about critical path analysis, resource scheduling, and so forth, you may find SharePoint's version of Gantt charts too simple. If so, you can export your Gantt chart into Microsoft Project, where you have many more features for processing task dependencies and managing schedules.

> The interface between SharePoint and Microsoft Project is, ahem, less than perfect. You can readily import Gantt charts and tasks into Project, no problem. However, if you use features of Project that are not supported by SharePoint, when you bring your task list back into SharePoint, you may lose some of your work.
>
> Processing tasks with both SharePoint and Project is useful, but just be careful. Experiment before you put a lot of work into a project schedule using Project and then try to importing it into SharePoint.

1. Navigate to the tasks list; if you're on the Home Page, just click Tasks under Lists in the Quick Launch. In the ribbon, click List Tools → List and then click Create View. SharePoint displays the page shown in Figure 6-23; this is the same page you used to create the Calendar view (Figure 6-11).

2. This time, rather than clicking Calendar View, click Gantt View.

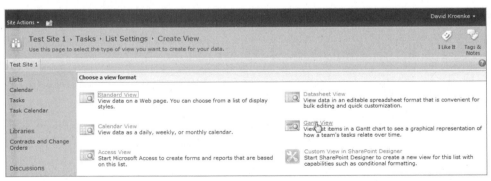

FIGURE 6-23: Creating a Gantt View

3. Name your view just as you named the calendar view and scroll down to the section in the form labeled Gantt Columns.

4. As shown in Figure 6-24, specify Title for Title, Start Date for Start Date, and Due Date for Due Date.

5. Select Predecessors for Predecessors.

> **Note** The selections in steps 3–5 are necessary because, in more advanced applications, you might want to use columns other than these obvious choices.

FIGURE 6-24: Setting the Gantt Chart Columns

6. Click OK, and SharePoint displays the Gantt chart shown in Figure 6-25.

7. To make the Gantt chart the default view, click List Tools → List in the ribbon and then click the Modify View icon (to the left of Current View). Then select the Make this the default view checkbox, as shown in Figure 6-26.

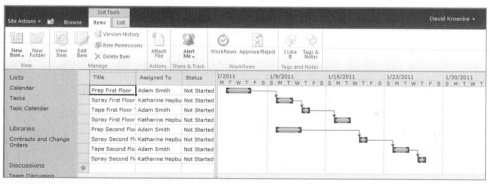

FIGURE 6-25: Gantt Chart View of Task List with Predecessor Arrows

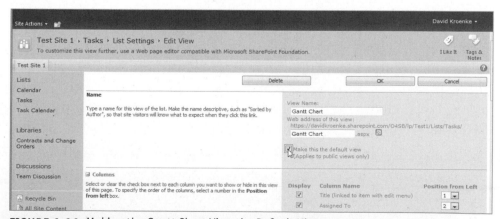

FIGURE 6-26: Making the Gantt Chart View the Default View

Now, what does this Gantt chart tell you? It shows that the first floor tasks are a chain. It also shows that there are some gaps in time between the tasks. For example, the task, "Tape First Floor" is done on a Thursday, and the task that depends on it, "Spray First Floor" doesn't begin until the next Monday.

Is that delay important? We don't know, but Larsen Painting will. Maybe it's bad because the tape will stick on the walls. Or, maybe given the delay, Larsen needs to use special tape that won't stick. Or, maybe there is an event over the weekend and the tape will be removed without Larsen's knowledge.

As stated earlier, tasks can have more than one predecessor. If so, then a task would have two or more arrows flowing into it. Those predecessor tasks might appear in the list view on separate pages and it could be difficult to know that both exist. They will jump out quickly on the Gantt chart.

Before leaving this topic, notice that the vertical bar between the task list items and the graphical chart is a slider bar. By clicking and dragging it to the left or right, you can change the amount of real estate devoted to the list items or to the graphic. See Figure 6-27. When you want to view or change task data, move the bar to the right. When you want to see more time on the calendar, move the bar to the left.

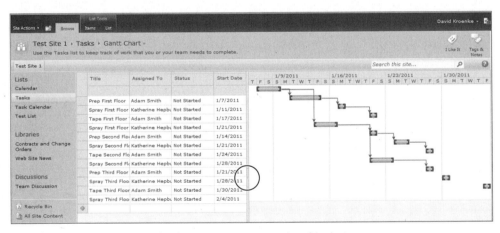

Slider bar moves to expose more or less of the chart

FIGURE 6-27: Using the Gantt Chart Slider Bar

Making a Personalized Task List

As you might imagine, the tasks list can become quite large. When this occurs, some people like to have a view of the task list that shows only their own tasks. This makes it easier for them to understand just what they are responsible for.

SharePoint makes it easy to do this. You need only create a new view and specify that SharePoint should filter the items in the list to remove all but those that belong to you. In the task list, the field Assigned To has the name of the person who is responsible for the task. So, you need to tell SharePoint to select only those tasks that have your name as a value of Assigned To.

SharePoint knows your name. At least it knows the name you gave it when you signed in. So you don't have to insert your real name as the filter value. Instead, you use a special keyword [Me]. SharePoint will substitute your name for that value when it creates the list.

The beauty of this feature is that [Me] can change. When Joe is signed in, the value of [Me] is Joe. When Adam is signed in, the value of [Me] is Adam. Thus, the personalized list will work for all users on the team.

To create such a personalized view, follow these steps:

1. Navigate to the tasks list and click List Tools → List in the ribbon.

2. Click Create View and select Standard View.

3. Enter some appropriate name in View Name.

4. Scroll down to the Filter section of this form and click "Show items only when the following is true." Then, as shown in Figure 6-28, select the following:

   ▪ Under "Show the items when column," select Assigned To.

   ▪ Select "is equal to" in the box under Show the items

   ▪ Type the characters **[Me]** in the last box, making sure to include the square brackets [ ] around the word Me.

5. Click OK.

In step 4, you are using that special keyword [Me]. Because it takes the value of whoever is signed in when the view displays, it always shows tasks for the current user.

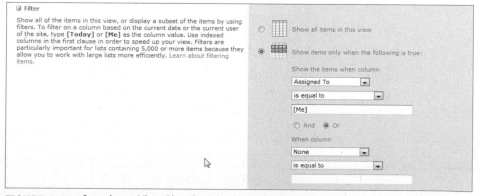

FIGURE 6-28: Creating a View Showing the Signed-in User's Tasks

Figure 6-29 shows the tasks that display when Adam Smith is signed in. Notice his name in the upper-right corner of the page. And note that only tasks assigned to him are shown.

FIGURE 6-29: Personal Task View When Adam Smith Is Signed In

ADVICE Some teams place two views of the Tasks list on the Home Page. One view shows all tasks (as, say, a Gantt chart) and another shows tasks just for the current viewer. You can place two views on the Home Page by adding the Tasks list twice to the Home Page. You then edit the web part to select different views as discussed in the section "Adding the Calendar View to the Home Page."

What You've Learned

In this chapter, you've seen how to use SharePoint Tasks lists to schedule work. You know how to enter task data either one task at a time or in bulk. You know how to modify views of tasks to eliminate files you don't want and to reorder the appearance of task data in a list.

You also learned how to create a calendar view of tasks more readily available by placing a link to it in Quick Launch and how to put the calendar itself on the Home Page. You learned how to create Gantt charts and how to interpret task dependencies from them. Finally, you saw how to create a list view that contains just the tasks assigned to you.

What's Next?

Now that you know how to create task lists and calendars in SharePoint, you might want to display them using Outlook. We take up that topic in Chapter 7.

Of Course, This Would Never Happen in <u>Your</u> Business...

Joe Schumpeter, Manager of Customer Support is on the phone with Katharine Hepburn, account manager in finance:

"Joe, I got your email. Thought I'd follow-up on the phone."

"Glad you called, Katharine! I'm really confused. Why has all the scaffolding been moved to the 3rd floor?"

"Don't you remember, we decided Tuesday to do the 3rd floor before the 2nd. The client wants the 3rd floor finished first."

"When did we decide that?"

"Oh, that's right, you missed that meeting."

"WHAT meeting?"

"The one on Tuesday. Did you look at the project calendar?"

"No, it's in SharePoint and, well, I haven't looked at it much."

"So, you use Outlook. Put it there!"

"How?"

"It's easy, I'll show you. But, hey, if you haven't put the calendar in Outlook, you probably don't have the task lists there either."

"Are you kidding? I don't know anything about this."

"OK, let's set up a video call, share your desktop, and I'll do it for you while you watch."

"You can do that?"

"Yes! Just watch!"

It Doesn't Have to Be That Way...

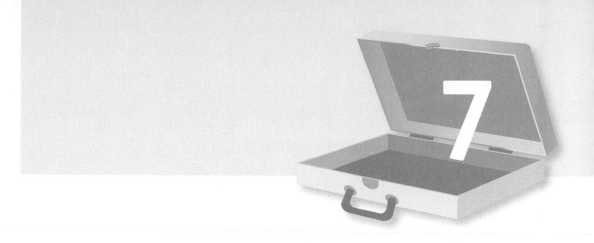

Managing Calendars and Tasks in Outlook

JOE MISSED A TEAM MEETING, an important one. Even worse, he didn't do several tasks that were assigned to him because he didn't know he had them. He would have known about them if he had checked SharePoint, but he didn't. Who knows why? He's not lazy: maybe he's just too busy to learn another way of doing things.

Joe's management can force him to learn SharePoint, and he will comply when he can. But, another alternative is available for Joe and his manager. Joe is an active user of Outlook, and because of the deep integration of Outlook and SharePoint in Office 365, he can have SharePoint send the task data he needs to Outlook, where he can view and edit it. In this way, he can stay with Outlook, a program that he knows and likes, and learn SharePoint later when he's not so busy managing painting jobs.

Even better, connecting SharePoint to Outlook is easy to do. Plus, because Lync, Outlook, and SharePoint are also deeply integrated in Office 365, Katharine, one of Larsen's employees, can use Lync video and desktop sharing to show Joe how to have SharePoint send calendar, task and other data to Outlook. She can show him how to create a combined overlay view of multiple calendars as well.

By connecting SharePoint to Outlook, Joe can consolidate calendars to avoid scheduling conflicts, save time by managing SharePoint calendars from the familiar environment of Outlook, and stay up to date by viewing SharePoint lists and documents stored in SharePoint, also from within Outlook.

> **Note**
>
> This chapter is different than the chapters on SharePoint, which are more procedural in nature. This chapter, as well as Chapters 7, 10, and 12 use a narrative approach because they involve communication, and the authors believe the best way to learn these topics is to see examples.

Specifically, in this chapter, you'll learn how to:

- Use presence information in Outlook to determine ways to contact someone, and establish a video call with them

- Connect to a SharePoint calendar in Outlook and overlay a SharePoint calendar with other calendars to see a combined schedule

- Update SharePoint calendars using Outlook

- Add SharePoint task lists and document libraries to Outlook

Using Lync Presence Information in Outlook to Initiate a Video Call

Most people who use live video images enjoy the experience because it allows users to communicate without the possibility of the misunderstandings encountered in emails and IM. You see your colleague's facial expressions and body language, and you can hear each other's voice.

In this section, you see how to initiate a video call using the Lync presence information in Outlook. *Presence information* is a status indicator that conveys the ability and willingness of a potential communication partner to communicate. In Outlook you can use presence information to tell at a glance whether the person who has emailed you is currently available to be contacted. That information is shown in a small square immediately to the left of the contact's name. The color of the square indicates whether the person is available (green), away (yellow), or busy (red). A grey square indicates that presence information for the contact is not available. By placing your cursor over the contact's name you can see more details about ways you can communicate with him or her.

The icons under Joe's image in Figure 7-1, from left to right, are presented in Table 7-1.

TABLE 7-1: Communication Icons

Icon	Name	Description
	Email	Clicking this sends an email to the user.
	IM	Clicking this sends an instant message to the user.
	Phone	Clicking this initiates a Lync or phone call to the user.
	Options	This expands to reveal additional choices for communicating with the user (options are shown in Figure 7-1).

In this example, after receiving an email from Joe, Katherine checks Joe's contact information as shown in Figure 7-1. Katherine could choose initially to initiate an Instant Message (IM) with Joe, then convert that conversation to a video call, but she feels it would be best, in this case, to initiate a video call with Joe. To do that, Katharine clicks Start Video Call in the drop-down list as shown.

To initiate an Instant Message session (IM) and Lync conversation with a teammate, follow these steps:

1. Click the IM icon, as shown in Figure 7-1. A new Lync IM session window opens, as shown in Figure 7-2.

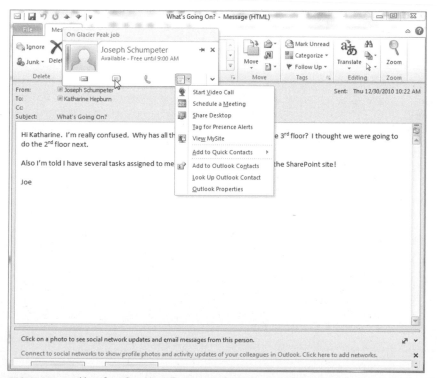

FIGURE 7-1: You Can See Your Teammate's Contact Information

FIGURE 7-2: You See a New Lync IM Window

2. Click Video → Start a Video Call, as shown in Figure 7-3. You've now initiated a Lync call. In the example, Joe's Lync phone rings on Joe's desktop.

FIGURE 7-3: Starting a Video Call with Your Teammate

3. Your teammate can answer your call by clicking Accept, as shown in Figure 7-4.

FIGURE 7-4: Your Teammate Accepts the Video Call

A few seconds after your teammate accepts the video call, a video of you will appear on your teammate's desktop, as shown in Figure 7-5.

FIGURE 7-5: Your Teammate Can Now See You

4. Your teammate must now click Video → Start My Video at the top of the session window so that you can see your teammate (see Figure 7-6).

FIGURE 7-6: Your Teammate Starts His Video

After a few seconds, your teammate's live video image appears in your screen, as shown in Figure 7-7.

FIGURE 7-7: You Can Now See Your Teammate

Notice that on your screen, your teammate's video image is large and detailed, whereas the embedded image of you is small. The smaller picture in picture image is there to make sure that your image isn't cut off or crooked. If it is, you can adjust your position until you look right in the smaller picture.

Sharing the Desktop and Granting Control to a Teammate

When you need help with something on your computer, it's extremely useful to be able to show a teammate what your desktop looks like. In this way, your teammate can direct you to take some action on your computer in an effort to help solve whatever issue you are having. But with Lync in Office 365, you can go one step further and actually grant control of your desktop to your partner so he or she can actually perform the necessary steps on your computer as you watch!

In this chapter's example, Katharine can show Joe how he can view and update calendar and task information in Outlook. She can do this by having Joe share his desktop with her then taking control of his desktop.

To share a desktop with your teammate, follow these steps:

1. Click Share → Desktop near the top of the session window. If you have multiple monitors hooked up to your computer, click Main Monitor, as shown in
   Figure 7-8.

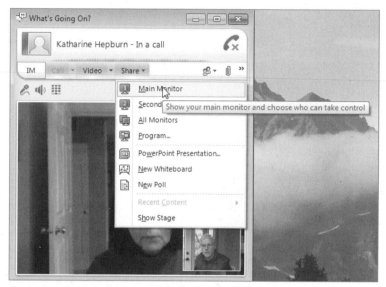

FIGURE 7-8: Your Teammate Shares His Desktop

FIGURE 7-9: A Warning Message Appears when
You Share Your Desktop

2. Your teammate user must click OK. The other user's screen will appear as shown
   in Figure 7-10. Doing this will make your teammate's screen appear as shown in
   Figure 7-11.

Note that your teammate won't automatically see what he's sharing. In order
to do that, he must click Preview, as shown in Figure 7-10.

FIGURE 7-10: Your teammate Clicks Preview to See What He's Sharing

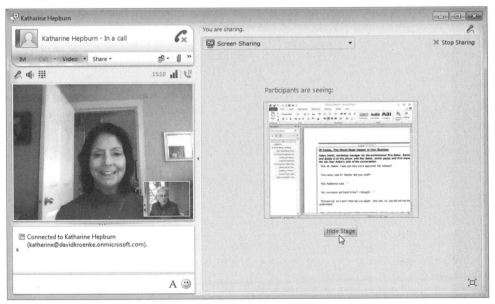

FIGURE 7-11: Your Teammate Sees a Preview of What He's Sharing

The first user will receive a sharing request and must accept it, as shown in Figure 7-12.

FIGURE 7-12: You Accept the Sharing Request

After a few seconds, the other user's computer desktop appears on the first user's screen as shown in Figure 7-13.

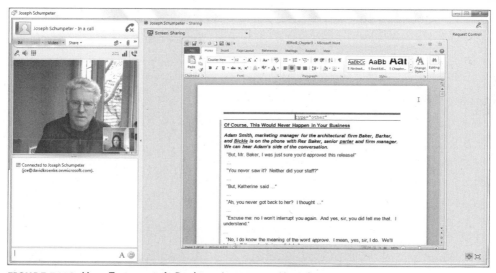

FIGURE 7-13: Your Teammate's Desktop Appears on Your Screen

Controlling Another Computer's Desktop

While you're sharing your computer with another user, you can request control over another user's computer. This enables you to show your teammate how to do specific tasks using his or her monitor to illustrate the tasks. In the case of Joe and Katharine, Katharine shows Joe how to connect SharePoint calendars and tasks to Outlook so that he can keep up to date and make his own changes right from Outlook, and not have to go to SharePoint for that. The possibilities for sharing are endless; besides showing how to link Outlook and SharePoint, you can show colleagues how to access a specific part of the server, how to fix or alter a computer setting or how to access and use any program.

To share your computer with another user, follow these steps:

1. Share your desktop as outlined in the previous section "Sharing the Desktop."

2. Click the Request Control link, as shown in Figure 7-14. Your teammate will see a request for control. In this example, Joe sees a request from Katharine.

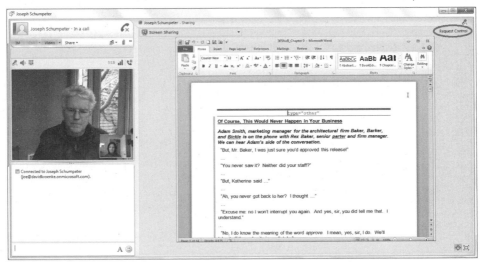

FIGURE 7-14: Requesting Control of Your Teammate's Desktop

3. Your teammate must click Accept when he or she sees your request (see Figure 7-15).

4. Now, not only can you view your teammate's desktop, but you can also move your cursor around the desktop as if you were sitting in his or her office, as shown in Figure 7-16.

FIGURE 7-15: Your Teammate Grants Control of His Desktop to You

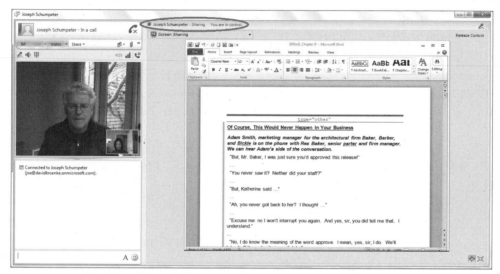

FIGURE 7-16: You Have Control of Your Teammate's Desktop

5. If your teammate wants control back, he or she can expand the Give Control drop-down menu and then click Take Back Control as shown in Figure 7-17.

FIGURE 7-17: Your Teammate Can Take Back Control at Any Time

PAUSE AND REFLECT: THE POWER OF PRESENTING REMOTELY

Think about the power of this for a moment. With this capability IT professionals can assist with PC issues remotely, or your organization can conduct remote white-boarding sessions as illustrated in Chapter 10. You can also do remote PowerPoint sales presentations as illustrated in Chapter 12. No doubt you can easily think of other valuable ways to use this capability!

Connecting to a SharePoint Calendar in Outlook

In the opening scenario to this chapter, Joe missed an important team meeting. He would have known about the meeting if he had checked SharePoint, but he didn't. With Office 365 he can get calendar information automatically downloaded to Outlook.

In the chapter example, after Katharine has control of Joe's computer desktop, she can show Joe how to access SharePoint and set it up so that SharePoint calendar information is automatically downloaded to Outlook.

To connect the SharePoint Calendar to Outlook, follow these steps:

1. Click Calendar in Outlook. The Outlook calendar appears, as shown in Figure 7-18.

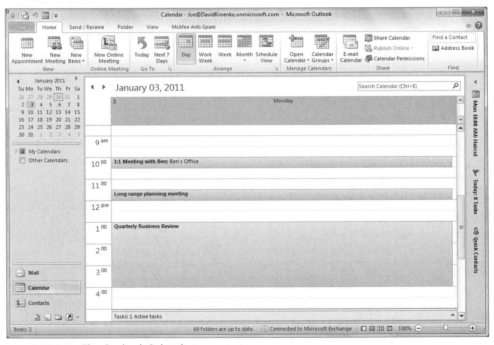

FIGURE 7-18: The Outlook Calendar

2. Select the Day view in the Arrange section of the Outlook ribbon. In this example, Katherine selects Monday, January 3 from Joe's calendar.

3. Using your browser, navigate to the desired SharePoint site. In this example, Katharine navigates to the Larsen Painting Test Site 1, as shown in Figure 7-19.

A calendar view of the SharePoint task list appears in the home page, but it may not be the one you want to appear in Outlook.

4. Click Calendar (circled in Figure 7-19). This opens up the team calendar in SharePoint, as shown in Figure 7-20.

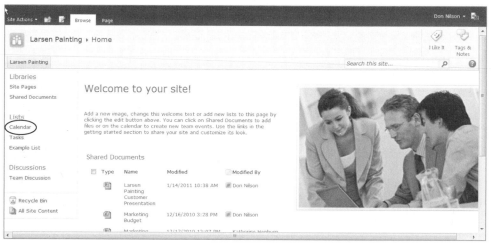

FIGURE 7-19: The Home Page

5. Click the Calendar tab in the Calendar Tools tab of the ribbon, shown in Figure 7-20. The calendar tools appear, as shown in Figure 7-21. You'll see a whole set of tools for managing your calendar.

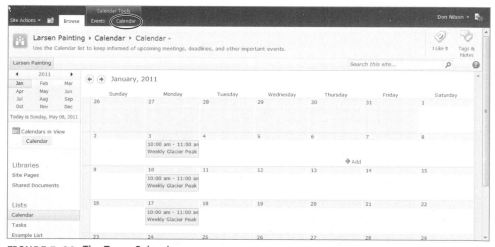

FIGURE 7-20: The Team Calendar

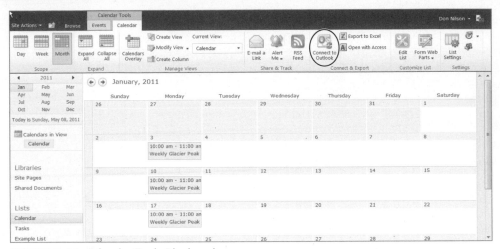

FIGURE 7-21: Calendar Tools Displayed

6. To connect the SharePoint calendar to Outlook, simply click Connect to Outlook, as shown in Figure 7-21.

7. A series of warning dialog boxes appear, as shown in Figures 7-22, 7-23, and 7-24. Click to allow the SharePoint website to open a program on your computer and to connect SharePoint to Outlook.

After you accept all the warnings, the SharePoint team calendar appears side by side with the user's Outlook calendar, as shown in Figure 7-25.

The side-by-side view is one view for these calendars; the SharePoint calendar is added to the Outlook navigation pane under a new heading: Other Calendars.

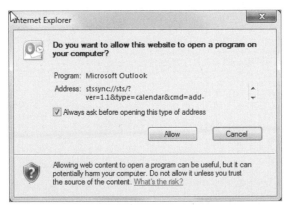

FIGURE 7-22: Internet Explorer's Allow Website to Open a Program Dialog Box

FIGURE 7-23: Internet Explorer's Allow a Website to Open Web Content Dialog Box

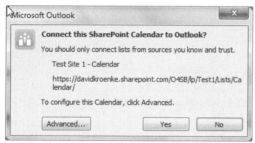

FIGURE 7-24: Outlook's Confirm Connect to SharePoint Calendar Dialog Box

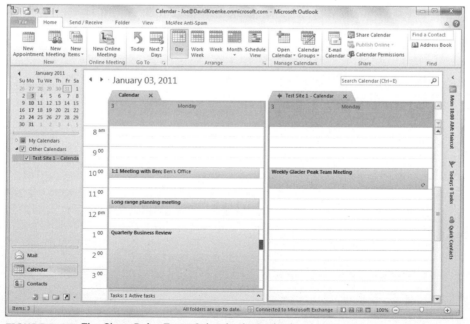

FIGURE 7-25: The SharePoint Team Calendar in Outlook

Viewing Schedule Conflicts

You can have Outlook overlay multiple calendars so you can see a composite view. To do this, click the arrow at the top of the SharePoint calendar where the cursor is pointing in Figure 7-26. This gives you a consolidated view of the two calendars in Outlook, as shown in Figure 7-27. You can see where conflicts exist between your Outlook and SharePoint calendars. In the chapter example, Joe needs to reschedule his one-on-one meeting with Ben on Monday so he won't miss the team meeting.

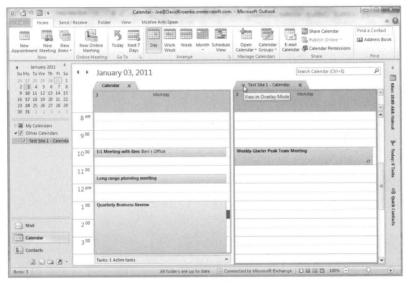

FIGURE 7-26: Cursor Pointing to Overlay Mode Arrow

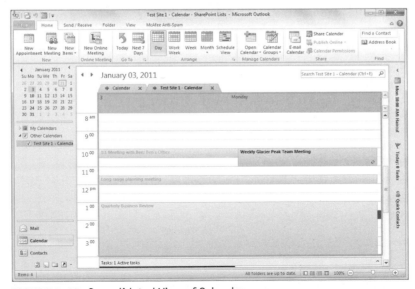

FIGURE 7-27: Consolidated View of Calendars

Adding Items on SharePoint via Outlook

If you need to add something to the SharePoint calendar and you're in Outlook, you don't need to go through SharePoint for that. The procedure is just like scheduling an appointment in any Outlook calendar.

Follow these steps:

1. Click the arrow in the SharePoint site Calendar tab (in this example, Test Site 1) to show the calendars side by side again, as shown in Figure 7-28.

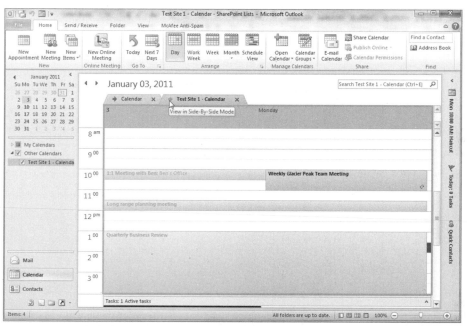

FIGURE 7-28: Click the Arrow to View Calendars Side by Side

2. Click the Month view so you can see more than just one day in the calendars (see Figure 7-29).

3. Double-click the box for the date you want to add to the SharePoint calendar. A new appointment appears.

4. Fill in the Subject, Location, Start Time, End Time, and a description, and then click Save and Close, as shown in Figure 7-30.

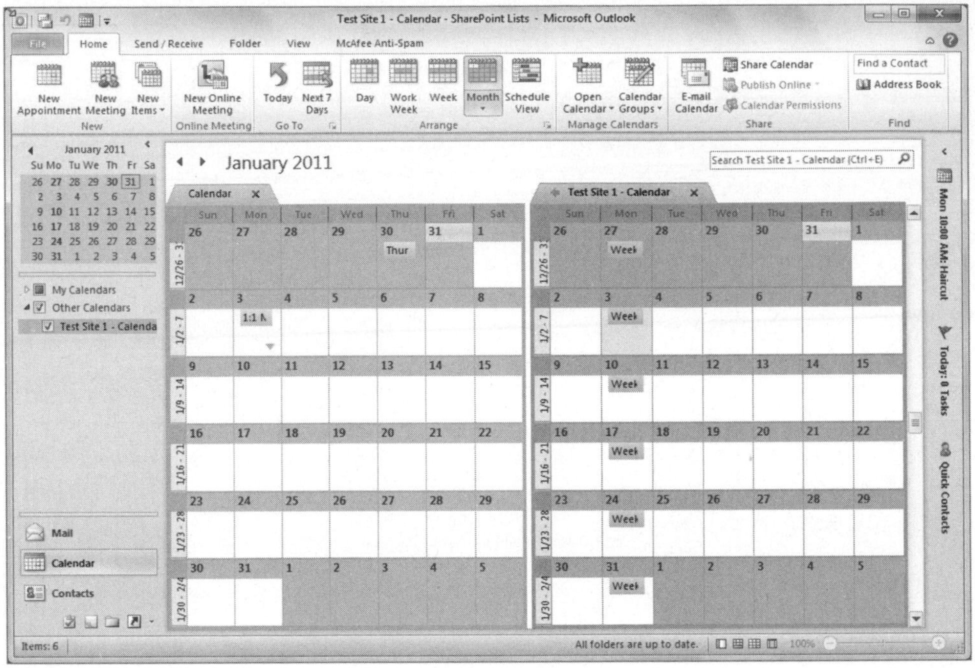

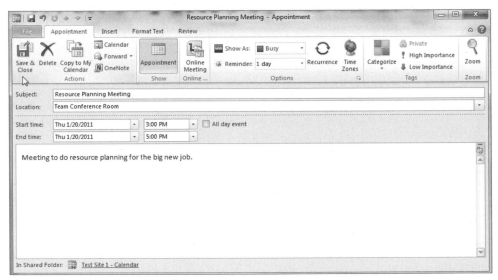

FIGURE 7-29: Calendars Shown Side by Side in Month View

FIGURE 7-30: Completed New Appointment

The new appointment appears in the SharePoint calendar (in this example, (Test Site 1) in Outlook, as shown in Figure 7-31.

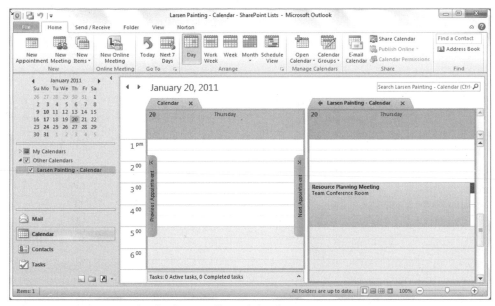

FIGURE 7-31: New Meeting in the Test Site 1 Calendar

The appointment will automatically appear on the calendar on the SharePoint site (see Figure 7-32).

FIGURE 7-32: The New Meeting Is Automatically Added to the SharePoint Calendar

> **Note** You might see a slight delay after you add the new meeting to the Outlook calendar before it shows up in the SharePoint calendar. That's because Outlook performs a Send-Receive All process periodically. If you get impatient and want to see things synced up right away, you have the option of clicking the Send/Receive tab of the Outlook ribbon, and then clicking Update Folder (see Figure 7-33).

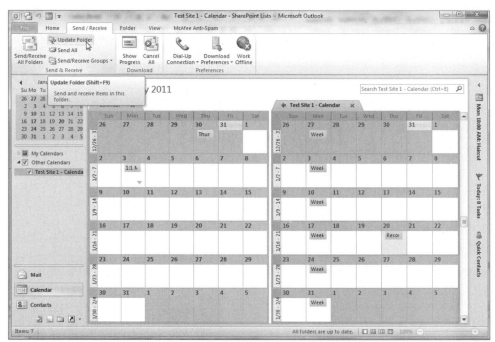

FIGURE 7-33: Click Update Folder to Sync with SharePoint

Connecting to SharePoint Task Lists and Document Libraries

When your team uses SharePoint task lists to keep projects on track, you may miss task assignments if you forget to periodically go to the team SharePoint site. With the integration of SharePoint and Outlook in Office 365, it is a simple matter to enable Outlook to automatically download tasks from SharePoint. You can even create new tasks in Outlook and they will automatically be uploaded to SharePoint.

The process of getting your SharePoint task and document lists to appear in your Outlook is basically the same as connecting SharePoint and Outlook's calendars. To do so, follow these steps:

1. In SharePoint, navigate to the list you want. The example navigates to the Glacier Peak task list.

2. Click List in the List Tools tab.

3. Click Connect to Outlook as shown in Figure 7-34.

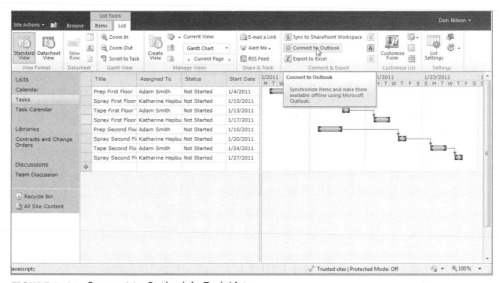

FIGURE 7-34: Connect to Outlook in Task List

After you have the tasks in Outlook you can update them and add new ones right from Outlook and they automatically are added to the SharePoint site.

> Unfortunately, when adding a new task from Outlook, you cannot specify a precedent task. You must do that in SharePoint.

4. To view a list of documents from a SharePoint document library, navigate to the library you want to connect to, click Library in the Library Tools tab, and then click Connect to Outlook just as you did earlier for connecting your task list to Outlook (see Figure 7-35).

FIGURE 7-35: Connect a SharePoint Document Library to Outlook

> **ADVICE**   A word of advice about accessing the document libraries in Outlook. This
> feature is great for keeping up with what's in the library, and even reading
> the documents without having to go to SharePoint. However, you probably don't
> want to edit documents from Outlook. It takes the document offline, and unless
> you lock the document, you'll have a problem if somebody makes changes to the
> same document. When you add the document back to the SharePoint library,
> you'll overwrite any changes made by the other user. Going to SharePoint, where
> SharePoint will keep track of simultaneous changes and make sure they all get
> into the document properly, is best.

What You've Learned

In this chapter you have seen how to:

- Use presence information in Outlook to determine ways to contact someone, and establish a video call with them

- Connect to a SharePoint calendar in Outlook and overlay a SharePoint calendar with other calendars to see a combined schedule

- Update SharePoint calendars using Outlook

- Add SharePoint task lists and document libraries to Outlook

What's Next?

In Chapter 8, you will earn how to use SharePoint lists to keep track of just about anything. You'll see how Majestic River Ventures can use lists to track trip leaders, trips, equipment, and equipment reservations. You'll also learn how to link data in one list with data in a second list.

Specifically, you'll learn how to:

- Create a SharePoint list from a built-in list type
- Delete a SharePoint list
- Create a custom list
- Add columns to lists using site columns
- Create choice list columns
- Link a list to another list using lookup columns
- Add totals to a list view
- Create a view showing list group structure

Of Course, This Would Never Happen in <u>Your</u> Business...

Majestic River Ventures offers guided river rafting and dory trips on major rivers in the western United States and Alaska. The following is a conversation between Ringo Nash, the lead trip guide, and Aaron Butterworth, a customer at the start of a recent trip down the Snake River:

"Look, Mr. Butterworth, I'm sorry."

"All I want is the private tent I paid for."

"I know you do and I know that you paid for it, but the problem is..."

"Don't tell me your problems; tell me how you're going to get me a private tent."

"Mr. Butterworth, we're here at the river, about to start our trip. Our permit gives us a two-hour window to start. I can't get back to Boise to find a tent for you and still get off on time."

"So, where's the tent I was promised."

"Honestly, it's in repair. We didn't..."

"Why did you rent me a tent that is in repair?"

"Well, someone made a mistake and I'll get to the bottom of that, but I can't do it now. I can promise you we'll refund your payment, for sure."

"I don't want a refund. It's not the money. It's that I don't want to sleep with that teenage kid over there."

"Okay, I understand. Hey, these nights are warm and beautiful. Why don't you sleep outside?"

"Tell me something Bingo or Ringo or whatever your name is—why do they call it the <u>Snake</u> River?"

It Doesn't Have to Be That Way...

Keeping Track of Things with SharePoint

MAJESTIC RIVER VENTURES IS A SMALL COMPANY that offers river rafting and kayak trips on western U.S. and Alaskan rivers. As a seasonal business, their staff varies widely. In the winter, they employ five people, but that count mushrooms to more than 25 part-time employees and contractors during the height of the season.

With such dramatic staff change, inevitably some personnel will not follow standard processes and procedures. Whoever took Butterworth's reservation assumed that all of MRV's tents were available and didn't know to check for outages due to repair. MRV needs an easy way to keep track of tents and their status and other equipment as well.

In Chapter 6, you learned how to use SharePoint to keep track of tasks. In this chapter you'll learn how to use other kinds of lists to keep track of, well, just about anything. Here you'll see how MRV can use lists to track trip leaders, trips, equipment, and equipment reservations. You'll also learn how to link data in one list with data in a second list.

Specifically, in this chapter you'll learn how to:

- Create a SharePoint list from a built-in list type
- Delete a SharePoint list
- Create a custom list
- Add columns to lists using site columns

- Create choice list columns

- Link a list to another list using lookup columns

- Add totals to a list view

- Create a view showing list grouping structure

> **!** You can readily use SharePoint to keep track of many types of things. Lists are easy to set up and easy to process. However, if you go too far, creating, say, dozens of lists with many relationships and hundreds of rows, you'll soon fall into problems that are better solved using database processing technology. Thus, for large or complicated tracking problems, use tools like Microsoft Access, SQL Server, Oracle, or MySQL because these products were purpose-built for keeping track of things in an industrial-strength way.
>
> However, the proper use of such tools is beyond the scope of this book and beyond the technical skills and knowledge of most business professionals. Thus, as you'll see in this chapter, when a tracking problem becomes too hard to do well in SharePoint, simplify the problem. If you can't do that, then hire a professional to help you or license an application that was designed for your particular tracking problem. You can find more details about this issue later in this chapter in the section, "Are Lists Too Much of a Good Thing?"

Creating Lists

In addition to the tasks lists that you learned about in Chapter 6, SharePoint includes many other types of list, including lists for announcements, contacts, issue tracking, web links, and others.

When you have a tracking problem, examine the list of built-in list types. To do so, go to Create and click Filter by: List. SharePoint will display the types of built-in lists that your site supports. It's possible that one of them is close to what you need. This section will consider using the built-in Contacts list, but will ultimately reject using that list. Rejecting it may or may not be a good idea, as you'll see.

Creating a List from a Built-in List Type

Suppose that MRV wants to keep track of its Trip Leaders; these people are part-time employees and contractors that vary from season to season. MRV wants a list that will contain their contact data. Because SharePoint includes a built-in list named Contacts, consider using it.

To do so, follow these steps:

1. Click Lists in the Quick Launch. Then, as shown in Figure 8-1, click Create.

FIGURE 8-1: Creating a New List

2. In the page that appears, click List in the Filter By column. As stated, SharePoint responds with the selection of lists that are available to your site. For tracking contact data about MRV trip leaders, the list type named Contacts sounds appropriate, so, as shown in Figure 8-2, click Contacts, name the list, and click Create.

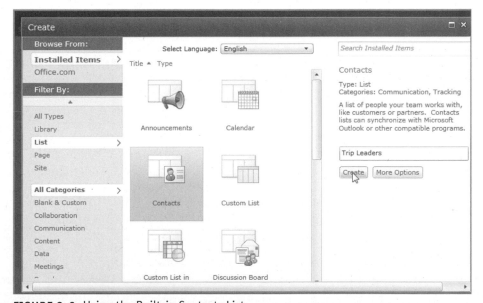

FIGURE 8-2: Using the Built-in Contacts List

SharePoint will create a new Trip Leaders list based on the Contacts format.

3. To see what's in that new list, click the name of your new list, in this case, Trip Leaders, in the Quick Launch and then click List Tools → List in the ribbon. Click List Settings and scroll down to the section labeled Columns. Your list will have the columns shown in Figure 8-3.

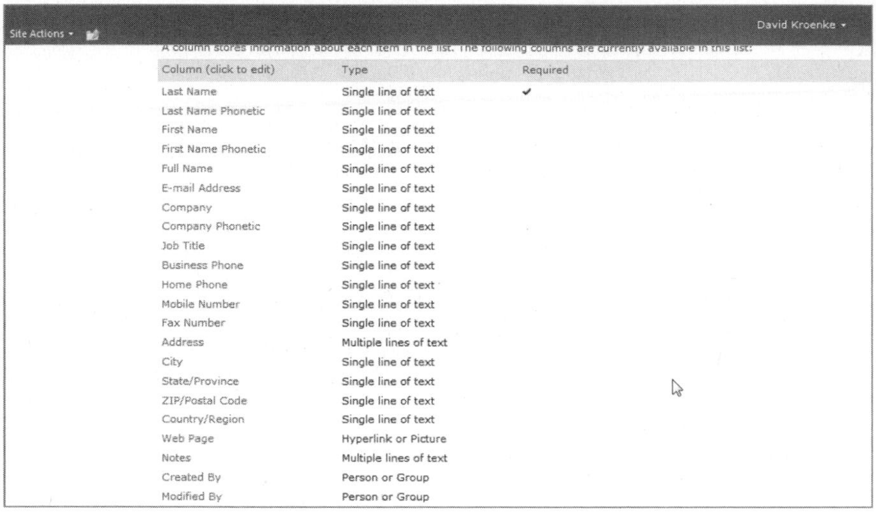

Column (click to edit)	Type	Required
Last Name	Single line of text	✓
Last Name Phonetic	Single line of text	
First Name	Single line of text	
First Name Phonetic	Single line of text	
Full Name	Single line of text	
E-mail Address	Single line of text	
Company	Single line of text	
Company Phonetic	Single line of text	
Job Title	Single line of text	
Business Phone	Single line of text	
Home Phone	Single line of text	
Mobile Number	Single line of text	
Fax Number	Single line of text	
Address	Multiple lines of text	
City	Single line of text	
State/Province	Single line of text	
ZIP/Postal Code	Single line of text	
Country/Region	Single line of text	
Web Page	Hyperlink or Picture	
Notes	Multiple lines of text	
Created By	Person or Group	
Modified By	Person or Group	

FIGURE 8-3: Fields in the Built-in Contacts List

The default Contacts List contains many columns; many more, in fact, than MRV needs. MRV can either ignore these columns, or create views that omit most of these columns, or delete the unwanted columns from the list. However, for reasons that are beyond the scope of this book, SharePoint will not allow some columns to be deleted.

Because MRV's needs are modest, it decides not to use this list, instead deleting it and using a custom list constructed in-house.

Note

Do not assume from this example that the built-in lists in SharePoint are not useful. The opposite is the case. The built-in list formats are, understandably, rich and complex. The decision not to use the built-in Contacts list is not necessarily the right decision. MRV might find later that those who constructed the SharePoint default Contacts list knew what they were doing and that MRV needed most of the columns that were in this list.

In general, when creating a list for a common task, start by looking at the built-in SharePoint lists types. Create a list based on one or more of them, as just shown; if you don't like a list, deleting it is easy.

Deleting a SharePoint List

To delete a list, follow these steps:

1. Scroll back up the page shown in Figure 8-3, or, in the ribbon, click List Tools → List → List Settings.

2. Click Delete this list, as shown in Figure 8-4. SharePoint presents a warning message that asks you to confirm that you mean it.

3. Click OK.

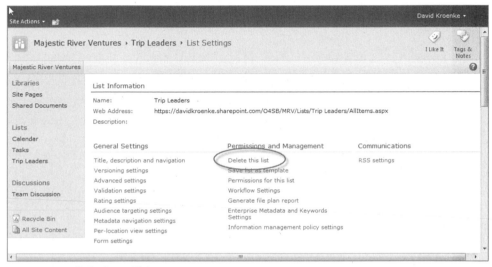

FIGURE 8-4: Deleting a List

Creating a Custom List

A custom list can be, well, anything you want it to be. When you create a custom list, SharePoint creates a list with just three columns: Title, Created By, and Modified By. After it's created, you can add more columns to fit your particular needs. Quite a number of column types can be created. Some of the more useful column types are:

- Single line of text
- Multiple lines of text
- Number
- Currency
- Date

- Date and Time

- Yes / No

- Person or Group

- Hyperlink

You can also create columns containing multiple values to choose from as well as columns that obtain data from other SharePoint lists. You will learn how to do that later in this chapter.

With this wide selection of data types, SharePoint allows you to create lists that will track almost anything.

To create a custom list, follow these steps:

1. Just like in the last section, click Lists in the Quick Launch and click Create.

2. This time, click Custom List, name the list **Trip Leaders** (you can reuse that name as long as you've deleted the prior Trip Leaders list), and click Create (see Figure 8-5). As stated, SharePoint creates a custom list with three columns: Title, Created By, and Modified By. It also creates default views with just Title in them.

Note You can rename the Title, Created By, and Modified By columns, but SharePoint will not allow you to delete them.

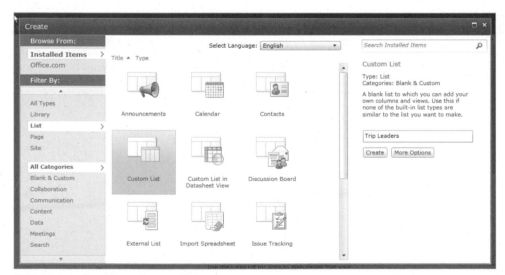

FIGURE 8-5: Creating a Custom List

3. Title is not useful for MRV's Trip Leaders, so you can rename that column for something else, like First Name. To do that, click List Settings, scroll down to the Columns section, and click on Title.

4. In the page that appears, change Title to First Name and click OK.

Customizing Lists with Columns

Now that you have created the basic custom list, you can customize it for your circumstances. Here you will learn how MRV customized their list to track Trip Leaders.

This section discusses adding a column to a list, adding a lookup column or a choice column as well as how to link a list to a lookup column.

Adding Columns to Lists

To add a column to a list, follow these steps:

1. Click Trips in the Quick Launch, and then click on List Tools → List.

2. As shown in Figure 8-6, click the Create Column icon in the ribbon. If you've maximized your window, that Create Column icon will be labeled Create Column.

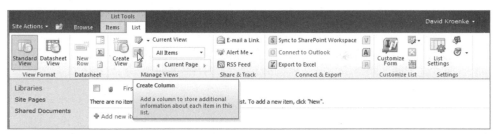

FIGURE 8-6: Creating a New Column

3. In the page that appears, enter Last Name for the Column name, and while you're at it, change the maximum length from 255 to something reasonable, perhaps 50, as shown in Figure 8-7.

4. Click OK.

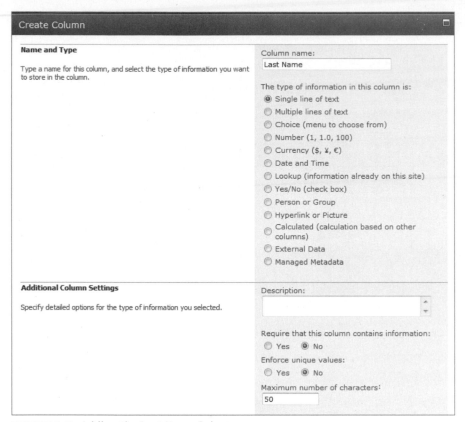

FIGURE 8-7: Adding the Last Name Column

Adding Columns Using Existing Site Columns

You can add all the columns you want to a list using the process described in the last section. However, you can shorten that process and likely create a better list if you use the built-in column types available to your site. To do so, follow these steps:

1. Go to the Trip Leaders list, click List Tools → List, and then click Create Column.

2. Scroll down in the page that appears to the bottom of the Columns section. The last two columns in the Trip Leaders list are Created By and Modified By. Two lines after that, click the phrase "Add from existing site columns," as shown in Figure 8-8. In response, SharePoint displays the page shown in Figure 8-9.

Created By	Person or Group
Modified By	Person or Group

Create column
Add from existing site columns
Column ordering
Indexed columns

FIGURE 8-8: Selecting an Existing Column

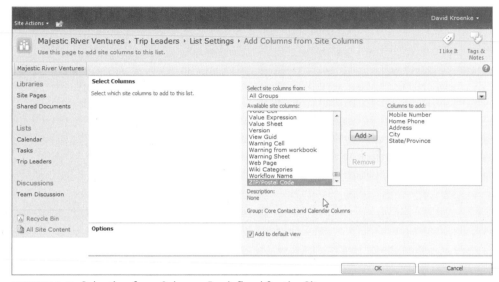

FIGURE 8-9: Selecting from Columns Predefined for the Site

3. Columns that have already been defined in your site are shown in the left list box (Available site columns). To add one of these columns to your list, highlight it and then click the Add button. In Figure 8-9, the user has already added five columns and is in the process of adding ZIP/Postal Code.

4. Click OK. SharePoint adds these columns to your list; in this case, the Trip Leaders list, as shown in Figure 8-10.

> **Note** The columns that appear in the Available site columns list box in Figure 8-9 depend on how your site collection was set up; the list in your site may look different than the one shown. Large organizations use this SharePoint feature to enforce data standards by offering predefined columns that conform to their standards. If you're working in a small business, however, you need not worry about this. Just use whatever columns fit your needs; if you don't see a column that you want, create a column as discussed in the section "Add Columns to Lists."

Columns

A column stores information about each item in the list. The following columns are currently available in this list:

Column (click to edit)	Type	Required
First Name	Single line of text	✔
Last Name	Single line of text	
Mobile Number	Single line of text	
Home Phone	Single line of text	
Address	Multiple lines of text	
City	Single line of text	
State/Province	Single line of text	
ZIP/Postal Code	Single line of text	
Created By	Person or Group	
Modified By	Person or Group	

FIGURE 8-10: Columns in the Trip Leaders List

Note

When you create a column, you have the option of stating that a value is required (in the bottom section of Figure 8-7). If you do so, then SharePoint won't allow you to create a new list item without a value for that column. In Figure 8-10, you can see the only required column is First Name. If MRV is small enough, that probably works. However, for a larger organization, Last Name should be required and maybe one of the phone columns as well.

You can create a list with no required columns; SharePoint won't object. But, in general, you should create lists with at least one required item. Otherwise, you could have list items with no values of any column.

Figure 8-11 shows the example list after the user has added five rows.

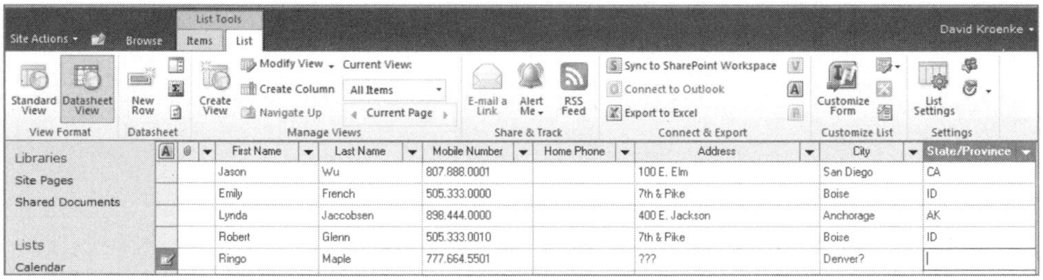

FIGURE 8-11: Entering Trip Leader Data in Datasheet View

ADVICE

You can use the techniques you learned in Chapter 5 to customize the default Home Page of the Team Site. Figure 8-12 shows this site after the user has customized the Home Page with text and a picture, removed Libraries and Discussions from the Quick Launch, and moved the Trip Leaders list to the top of the Lists category.

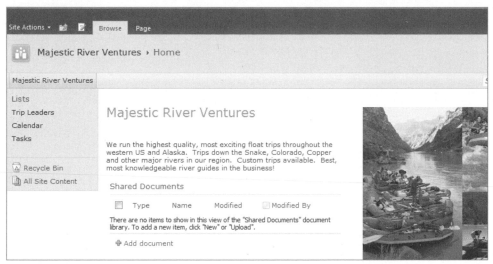

FIGURE 8-12: Majestic Site with Trip Leaders List First in the Quick Launch

Obtaining Column Values from Other Lists

MRV would like to create a list to track planned river trips, and it wants to include the trip leader's name as part of that list. Rather than duplicate trip leader data, you can cause SharePoint to obtain that data from the Trip Leader list. In this section, you'll learn how to do that.

First you need to create a new Trips list. To do so, follow these steps:

1. Create a custom list as shown in the section, "Adding Columns to Lists."

2. Add columns to the list from the Site Columns as just demonstrated in the preceding section. Figure 8-13 shows the process of adding three columns to the Trips list.

MRV wants to include the name of the Put In Site (where the rafts are put into the river), but not surprisingly, no predefined column exists for that purpose. Instead, MRV added City from the predefined list and then renamed that column Put In Site. It chose City because a "put in" is a particular geographic location like a city, and so the definition of the City column is likely to be close to what MRV needs.

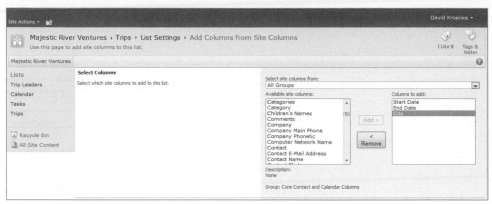

FIGURE 8-13: Selecting Site Columns for the Trips List

Creating a Choice Column

MRV's trips can either use kayaks, rafts, or both. Because this is so, it wanted the person who is creating the trip record to choose among these three types. To enable that choice, the company created a column named Trip Type and defined it to be a Choice column, as shown in Figure 8-14.

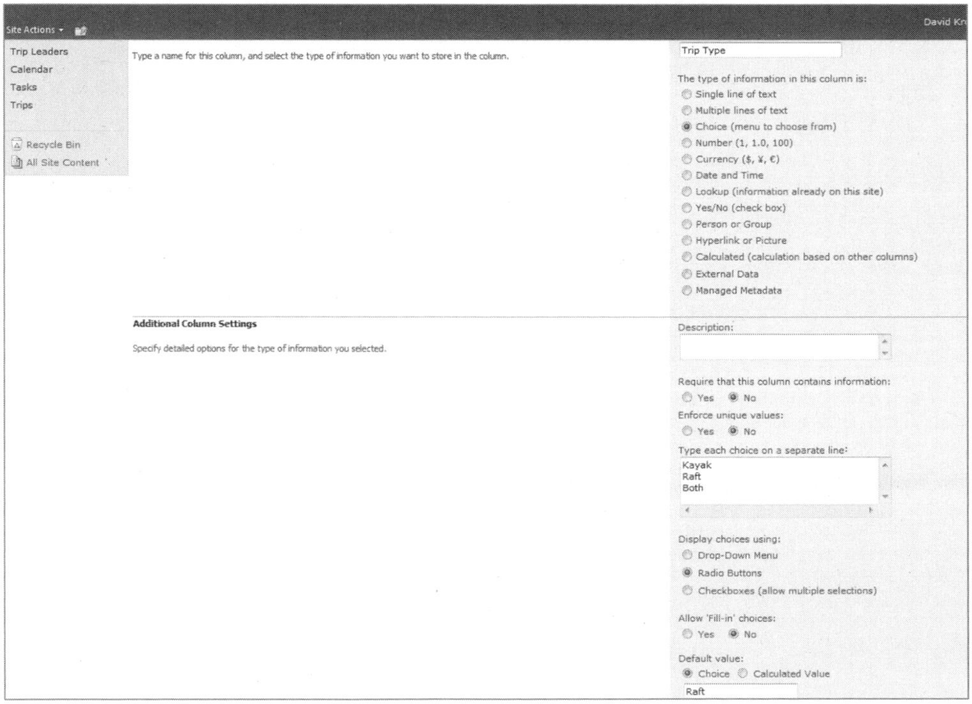

FIGURE 8-14: Creating Trip Type as a Choice Column

To define a Choice column, type each of the choices you want the users to see on a separate line in the box labeled "Type each choice on a separate line." In Figure 8-14, the list creator at MRV has typed the choices **Kayak**, **Raft**, **Both**. The list creator left the default value for display choice as a Radio Button and then typed in **Raft** as the Default value.

Creating a Lookup Column

As stated earlier, MRV wants the Trips list to include the name of the trip leader. It could add Trip Leader column as another text column to the Trips list to do this. However, two problems exist with that approach:

- It requires more keying, and the possibility exists that names will be misspelled.

- More important, if the data is duplicated in the Trips list, then when Trip Leaders change—say one leaves MRV, or changes names, or new leaders are created—then the Trips list will be outdated and inaccurate.

Consequently, a better alternative is to create a column that links the name in the Trips list to the name in the Trip Leader list. Such columns are called *lookup columns*.

To create a lookup column, follow these steps:

1. Create a new column as shown in the section "Add Columns to Lists" and name the column Trip Leader.

2. As shown in Figure 8-15, select Lookup (information already on this site) as the column type. In response, SharePoint adjusts the page and presents a new set of column settings.

3. In the Additional Column Settings, do the following:

   1. Under Get information from: Select Trip Leaders from the drop-down list. This selection tells SharePoint to obtain a value from the Trip Leaders list.

   2. Select a column (in this example, Last Name) from the In this column drop-down list. This selection tells SharePoint to take values from Last Name in Trip Leaders and use one of them as the value of Trip Leader in the Trips list.

FIGURE 8-15: Creating a Lookup Column

Figure 8-16 shows the columns in the finished Trips List.

Columns

A column stores information about each item in the list. The following columns are currently available in this list:

Column (click to edit)	Type	Required
Trip Name	Single line of text	✔
Start Date	Date and Time	
End Date	Date and Time	
Put In Location	Single line of text	
Trip Type	Choice	
Trip Leader	Lookup	
Created By	Person or Group	
Modified By	Person or Group	

FIGURE 8-16: Columns in the Finished Trips List

PAUSE AND REFLECT: WHAT'S GOING ON IN FIGURE 8-15?

Quite a bit is going on in Figure 8-15. Without inadvertently stumbling into the deep morass of database design, consider several of the other entries in the Additional Columns Settings of this figure. If you select Enforce unique values, then a particular value of Last Name will only be allowed to appear in the Trips list once. In the MRV example, this restriction means that a particular trip leader will be allowed to lead just one trip. Such a restriction isn't appropriate for MRV and hence the value for Enforce unique values was set to No in Figure 8-15.

Under the selection of Last Name, you have the option of setting Allow multiple values. If you do not check that box, a trip can only be guided by one Trip Leader. If you check Allow multiple values, then a given Trip can be guided by more than one Trip Guide. At MRV, trips have just one leader so this box was not checked.

Putting the choices for these options together, SharePoint will enforce four kinds of relationship between two lists. Using the MRV example, they are:

- 1 to 1: A Trip Leader leads at most one Trip, and a Trip has at most one Trip Leader.

- 1 to many: A Trip Leader can lead more than one Trip, but a Trip has at most one Trip Leader (this is the case specified by the selections shown in Figure 8-15).

- Many to 1: A Trip Leader can lead at most one Trip, and a Trip can have many Trip Leaders

- Many to many: A Trip Leader can lead more than one Trip, and a Trip can have many Trip Leaders.

If this is not clear, do not worry about it. It is quite a feat that SharePoint will do this, however!

One last point about Figure 8-15: Once a Trip Leader list item is associated with Trips, SharePoint can bring in additional columns from the Trip Leader list. As you can see in Figure 8-15, you can add any of the columns in Trip Leader to the Tripslist.

After you create the lookup column, SharePoint automatically makes the connection between the Trip Leaders and Trips lists. For example, in Figure 8-17, the user adds a new Trips list item. Notice how the user can select Trip Leader names from the drop-down list box in this form. If you change the leader data in the Trip Leaders list, this form automatically picks up the changed values the next time you use it.

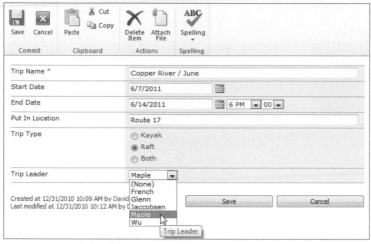

FIGURE 8-17: Selecting a Trip Leader for a Trip

Figure 8-18 shows how this column appears in the Datasheet View.

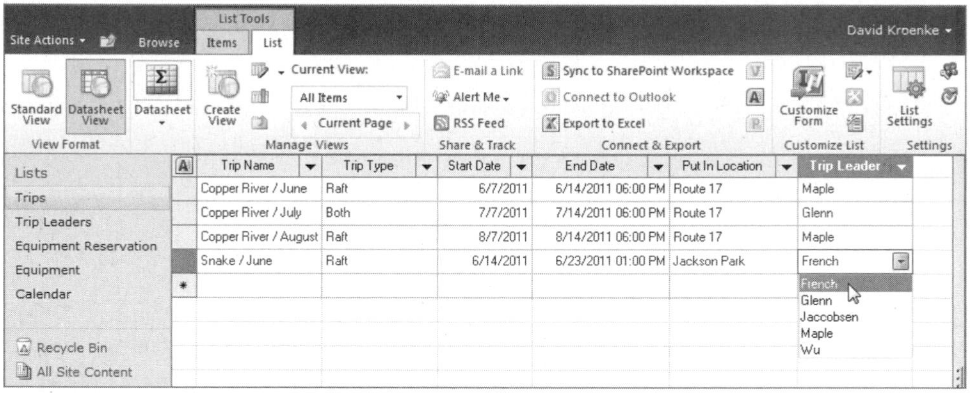

FIGURE 8-18: Entering Trip Data Using the Datasheet View

As you can see in Figure 8-19, the values of Trip Leader data appear in the list as if they were local to this list and not taken from the Trip Leaders list.

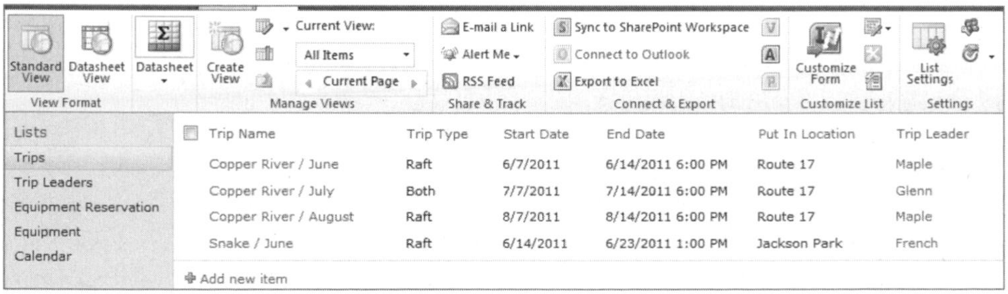

FIGURE 8-19: Trips Data in Standard View

Are Lists Too Much of a Good Thing?

Lists are easy to create and even easier to use, so expanding the use of lists and lookups to all of MRV's business is tempting. In addition to Trips and Trip Leaders, MRV could create a Customer list, a Reservations list, an Equipment list, and an Equipment Reservations list, and then connect all these lists using lookup columns.

Figure 8-20 shows a diagram of such lists and their relationships. Notice how the items in different lists are related. A single customer row relates to (potentially) many Trip Reservation rows because a customer can go on more than one trip. That one-to-many relationship is what the forked arrow and the N mean. One Customer row relates to many Trip Reservation rows. Similarly, the relationship between Trip Leaders and Trips is one-to-many because a given leader can lead more than one trip. In the same vein, a Trip Reservation can have many equipment items reserved, and a given piece of equipment can be reserved many times.

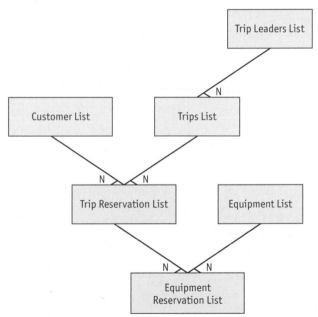

FIGURE 8-20: Possible Reservation System Using SharePoint Lists

Although creating the lists like this in SharePoint is possible, such a course is not recommended. SharePoint provides the rudiments for managing such inter-related data, but it lacks many of the features and functions that one might want. For example, MRV may want a report that combines some data from each of these lists, and creating such a report using SharePoint is difficult, if not impossible. Similarly, MRV may want to query data in lists in a variety of ways. For example, they may want to search for all the trips taken by a particular customer in a given year.

These reporting, querying, and other data management functions are difficult in SharePoint, but they are baked into the fabric of database management systems (DBMS) like Microsoft Access or Oracle, for example. So, if you have a requirement that necessitates the management of many integrated lists, you probably should not attempt to meet that requirement within SharePoint. Instead, develop the solution in Access or another DBMS. Later, if you want, you can import parts of that solution into SharePoint. However, such development is not for the non-IT business professional. Instead, hire a professional to help you. He or she has the knowledge and skill to design the database and create the application features and functions that you need.

If you don't have the budget to hire help, the other course of action, and the one taken in this chapter, is to simplify the problem. Create a bare-bones system that will solve your basic problem. In MRV's case, it needs a way to track equipment and its uses. So, the next section builds a set of two lists that does just that.

Creating a Simple Equipment-Tracking Solution

To prevent problems like the one that started this chapter, MRV needs to keep track of equipment and reservations to use equipment. To do so, it must create Equipment and Equipment Reservation lists.

To create the Equipment list, you can create a custom list and add columns as shown in the sections "Creating Lists" and "Customizing Lists with Columns" discussed previously in this chapter. Figure 8-21 shows the columns that MRV added to this list. Status has one of three values:

- Available
- In Repair
- No Longer Serviceable

Because status has only those three values, creating a Choice column, rather than a single line of text column, is tempting. However, as you'll see, MRV wants status values to appear in another list, and this is not possible for Choice columns. Hence, the company creates status as a single line of text.

Columns

A column stores information about each item in the list. The following columns are currently available in this list:

Column (click to edit)	Type	Required
Equipment Name	Single line of text	✔
Acquisition Date	Date and Time	
Acqusiiton Cost	Currency	
Description	Single line of text	
Status	Single line of text	
Created By	Person or Group	
Modified By	Person or Group	

FIGURE 8-21: Columns in the Equipment List

Note, too, that Acquisition Date is of the type Date and Time and that Acquisition Cost has been given the type of Currency.

PAUSE AND REFLECT: COMPUTING MONETARY COSTS

When lists contain numeric or currency columns, configuring SharePoint to compute sums, averages, maximums, and so on, on those numeric or currency columns is possible. To do so, follow these steps:

1. Go to the Equipment list, click List Tools → List and click the Modify View icon. In the page that appears scroll down to the Totals section.

2. If that word *Totals* is preceded by a +, that group is closed. Click the plus sign to open the group.

3. To cause SharePoint to compute the sum of Acquisition Cost, select Sum from the drop-down list to the right of its name as shown in Figure 8-22.

FIGURE 8-22: Specifying a Total in a View

continues

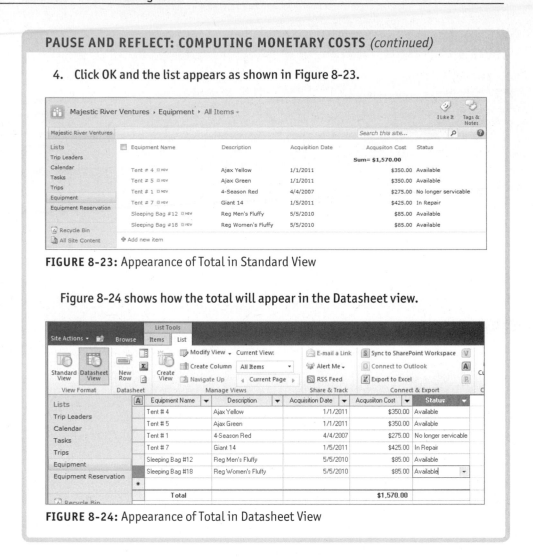

PAUSE AND REFLECT: COMPUTING MONETARY COSTS *(continued)*

4.   Click OK and the list appears as shown in Figure 8-23.

FIGURE 8-23: Appearance of Total in Standard View

Figure 8-24 shows how the total will appear in the Datasheet view.

FIGURE 8-24: Appearance of Total in Datasheet View

Building an Equipment Reservation Report

In an ideal world, MRV would have an information system that automatically prevents equipment that is in repair or is already reserved from consideration when enrolling a customer on a trip. However, that solution requires more expertise than MRV has available, as previously described, and so the company decides to create a simpler system. This simpler system allows equipment to be allocated without restriction, but it also can create a report that makes problems easy to detect so they can be corrected before the trip starts.

Figure 8-25 shows the report MRV wants for that simpler solution. It lists each MRV Trip in alphabetical order and then displays the equipment reservations for clients on that trip. If Ringo had been able to see this report before driving to the Snake River to start the trip, he would have known that Butterworth had been allocated a tent that is in repair. He also would have foreseen a problem that he as yet doesn't know about—that the tent allocated to Adam Smith was no longer serviceable. Instead, Ringo will learn that he has two unhappy campers—Mr Butterworth who is having to share a tent, and Adam as he tries to set up his tent and finds that the tent zippers are broken.

Also, examine the reservations for the June Copper River trip. Two people have been allocated the same sleeping bag! Unless Larsen and Jones are very close, they're going to be unhappy as well.

Again, this solution isn't perfect, but it will do for a company like MRV.

Client Name	Equipment	Equipment:Description	Equipment:Status	Trip	Trip:Start Date	Trip:End Date
⊟ **Trip : Copper River / July (1)**						
Wu	Sleeping Bag #12	Reg Men's Fluffy	Available	Copper River / July	7/7/2011	7/14/2011 6:00 PM
⊟ **Trip : Copper River / June (2)**						
Larsen	Sleeping Bag #18	Reg Women's Fluffy	Available	Copper River / June	6/7/2011	6/14/2011 6:00 PM
Jones	Sleeping Bag #18	Reg Women's Fluffy	Available	Copper River / June	6/7/2011	6/14/2011 6:00 PM
⊟ **Trip : Snake / June (3)**						
Butterworth	Tent # 7	Giant 14	In Repair	Snake / June	6/14/2011	6/23/2011 1:00 PM
Schumpeter	Sleeping Bag #18	Reg Women's Fluffy	Available	Snake / June	6/14/2011	6/23/2011 1:00 PM
Smith (Adam)	Tent # 1	4-Season Red	No longer servicable	Snake / June	6/14/2011	6/23/2011 1:00 PM

FIGURE 8-25: Needed Equipment Reservation List

The Equipment Reservation List

The report in Figure 8-25 is based on a new list, Equipment Reservation, which has lookups into two existing lists: Trips and Equipment. However, notice that this list not only looks up Trip name, it also looks up the Start and End Dates for each trip. Similarly, this list looks up the name of Equipment as well as obtains the Description and Status of each equipment item.

The additional lookup data is easy to include. Figure 8-26 shows the form that was used to define the Equipment column in the last section. Notice that it is of type Lookup, and it gets its information from the Equipment list. Below that, however, notice that the additional fields of Description and Status are selected—these selections tell SharePoint to add the values of Description and Status when it looks up a row of Equipment.

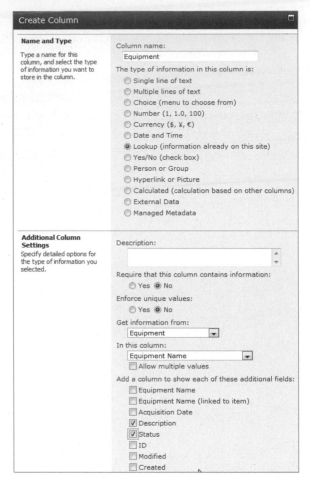

FIGURE 8-26: Columns in the Equipment Reservation View

A similar technique was used to add Trip, Start Date, and End Date to the Equipment Reservation list.

The completed list has the columns shown in Figure 8-27.

Columns		
A column stores information about each item in the list. The following columns are currently available in this list:		
Column (click to edit)	Type	Required
Client Name	Single line of text	✔
Equipment	Lookup	
Equipment:Description	Lookup	
Equipment:Status	Lookup	
Trip	Lookup	
Trip:Start Date	Lookup	
Trip:End Date	Lookup	
Created By	Person or Group	
Modified By	Person or Group	

FIGURE 8-27: Columns in the Completed Equipment Reservation List

PAUSE AND REFLECT: BEWARE OF REQUIREMENTS CREEP!

For the Equipment Reservation list, the Client Name column is a single line of text. This means that client names could be duplicated many times in the list, once for each time someone reserves equipment. If you follow the principles of this chapter, you might be tempted to make a new list called Client and store all of the client data in that list. Then, the Equipment Reservation list could take Client Name as a lookup from the new Client list.

That's workable, but if you go that far, you should probably also allocate Clients to Trips. To do that, you need to create a new list called Client Trip Reservation, and create a relationship between it and Equipment Reservation. In doing all of this, you create a list for all the items shown in Figure 8-20. But, as stated in the section "Are Lists Too Much of a Good Thing?" that much complexity is better placed in a database management system such as Access rather than SharePoint lists.

This situation illustrates a common phenomenon that arises in the development of information systems, called *requirements creep*. That term refers to the situation that occurs when one little requirement leads to another one, which leads to another one, and soon the system is large, complex, and difficult to build. This book avoids that problem and just uses Client Name as a text column into which you write client data, thus relying on manual procedures to ensure that the named client is actually on the trip of the date shown.

Creating Equipment Reservations

After you create the Equipment Reservation list, you can use it to record client equipment requests. However, when you enter data into this list, the standard New Item form is less than ideal. As you can see in Figure 8-28, you can select equipment names and trip names, but the secondary data such as equipment Description or trip Start Date do not appear.

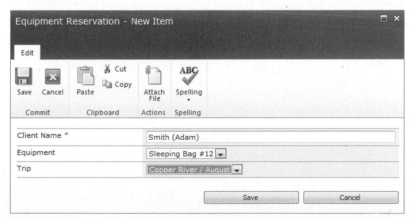

FIGURE 8-28: Creating a Reservation Request with the Standard New Item Form

Because of this limitation, many users prefer using the Datasheet view for lists with lookups. As shown in Figure 8-29, the secondary columns such as Equipment Description and Status do appear in the datasheet. However, to make them appear, you must first select the lookup values (shown in Figure 8-29) and then click a different row, such as the empty row below the new entry. When it receives that second click, SharePoint looks up the secondary values and places them into the datasheet as shown in Figure 8-30.

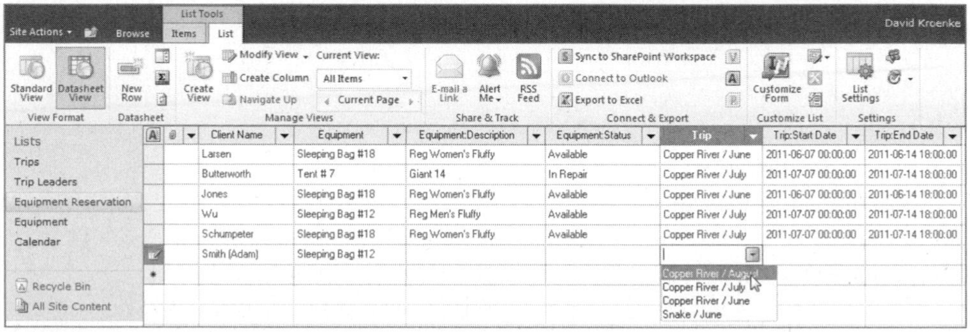

FIGURE 8-29: Entering Lookup Values (secondary columns not yet shown)

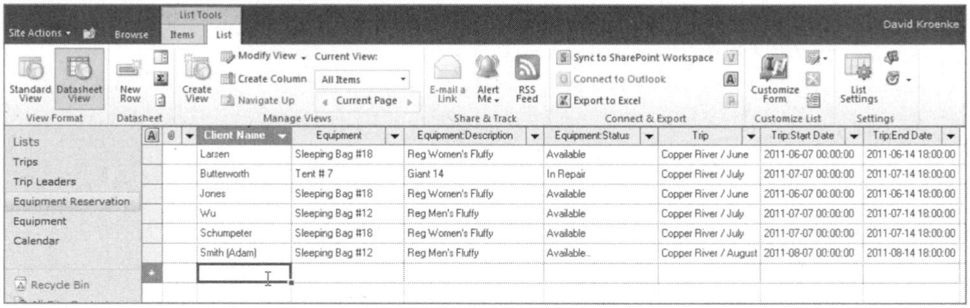

FIGURE 8-30: Clicking the Next Row Brings Forth Secondary Values

Creating the Solution with Grouping

We want to create the view in Figure 8-25, and, given the lists we've just created, it will be easy.

1. Go to the Equipment Reservations list and select List Tools → List and then click Create View.

2. Click Standard View.

3. Leave all the columns in the view and scroll down to the Group By section.

4. Select Trip for the value of "First group by the column" as shown in Figure 8-31.

5. Click OK and you will see the view shown in Figure 8-25.

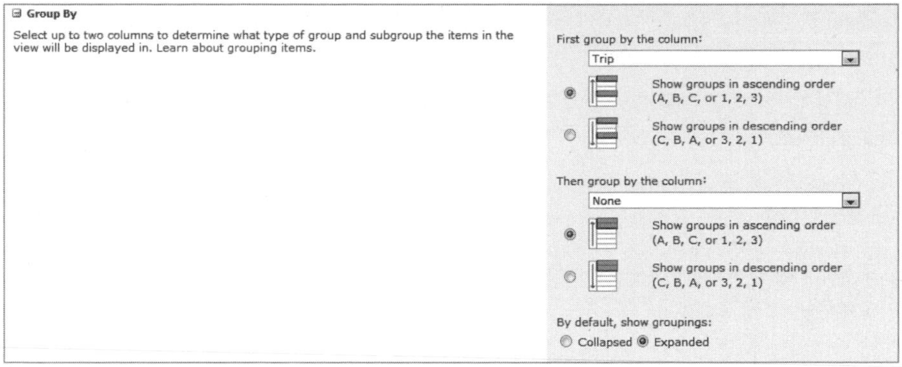

FIGURE 8-31: Grouping Equipment Reservations by Trip

MRV now has a view (report) that it can use to detect equipment outages and conflicts. Of course, this report is only useful if users are taught not only that they should use it but also how to use it. Thus, MRV must create user procedures and train users on how to use them. This solution, as in all information systems, is only as good as the users who employ it!

What You've Learned

This chapter has presented considerable information to you. You learned how to create a list from one of SharePoint's built-in lists, how to learn what's in such a list, and how to delete it.

You also learned how to create a custom list, add columns to it manually as well as via the existing site column definitions. Furthermore, you learned how one list can obtain data from another list via Lookup columns as well as how to create a choice column. This chapter also discussed the decision to solve a tracking problem in SharePoint versus solving one with database technology.

Finally, you learned how to use group-by to organize data in a view, a feature that is particularly useful for lists that contain Lookup columns.

What's Next?

The next chapter continues the discussion of the SharePoint and Exchange components of Office 365. You will learn how SharePoint controls workflow to ensure that the proper people take appropriate actions at appropriate times, in accordance with pre-defined workflow patterns. You will also see the role that Exchange plays in alerting team members of the need to take action as well as receiving emails about workflow progress.

Of Course, This Would Never Happen in _Your_ Business…

Adam Smith, marketing manager for the architectural firm Baker, Barker, and Bickle is on the phone with Rex Baker, senior partner and firm manager. We can hear just Adam's side of the conversation.

"But, Mr. Baker, I was just sure you had approved this release!"

. . .

"You never saw it? Neither did your staff?"

. . .

"But, Katherine said. . ."

. . .

"Ah, you never got back to her? I thought. . ."

. . .

"Excuse me: no I won't interrupt you again, and yes sir, you did tell me that. I understand."

. . .

"No, I do know the meaning of the word approve. I mean, yes sir, I do. We'll take it off the website immediately."

. . .

"Well, yes, that is unfortunate but Katherine's a good writer!"

. . .

"But sir, I'm sure she thought your wife's name is Nancy."

. . .

"No sir, I'm certain it was a coincidence. No one here knows about the first Mrs. Baker."

. . .

"Yes sir, yes, I understand you're telling me her name was, er, is Nancy. Mrs. Nancy Baker. Yes, she was your first wife, but not now. I know the current Mrs. Baker's name is Sarah."

. . .

"No sir, I'm not being flippant. I'm sorry this has happened!"

. . .

"It's on Facebook?"

. . .

"Your club? What can I do about the rumor at your club?"

It Doesn't Have to Be That Way…

Controlling Workflow

BAKER, BARKER, AND BICKLE (BBB) is a successful architectural firm employing nearly 100 people with major projects worldwide. BBB staffs a small marketing group of three people who manage the firm's public relations, advertising, promotional events, and produce content for the firm's public website.

As a general rule, content that is to be placed on the website is supposed to be pre-approved by three people: Smith, the manager of the marketing group, and two others in the firm's management. However, that rule is enforced by custom and manual procedure. The possibility exists, as the conversation to the left indicates, for news or other items to slip through this manual procedure without proper approval.

SharePoint provides a facility called *workflows* to automatically enforce procedures and policies for items such as approvals. In this chapter you will learn:

- How SharePoint enforces business processes via workflows
- How to create and use an approval workflow
- How to create and use a three-state workflow
- Other possibilities for using SharePoint workflows

How SharePoint Enforces Business Processes via Workflows

A SharePoint *workflow* is a sequence of tasks or steps that SharePoint assigns and controls. For example, you can define an approval workflow so that SharePoint gives a particular person, say, Adam Smith, the task of reviewing and approving a document. If Adam approves the document, then another person, say, Joseph Schumpeter, is given the same task, and so forth, through as many people as the creator of the workflow specified.

As shown in Figure 9-1, at each stage, SharePoint assigns tasks to one or more people or groups of people and inserts those tasks into a task list. Optionally, the task assignees are sent an email notifying them of the task as well. When a person completes a task, by setting the task status or other variable to a completed state, SharePoint closes the task, generates optional emails to personnel that the task has been completed and then creates tasks for the next step in the workflow.

As indicated in Figure 9-1, all of this activity is recorded in a workflow log. Users with proper permissions can request SharePoint to process that log to produce a workflow report.

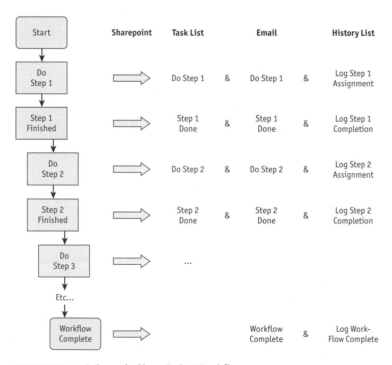

FIGURE 9-1: A Generic SharePoint Workflow

Workflows can implement complicated processes. You can specify that tasks be accomplished in sequence or in parallel. The tasks in Figure 9-1 are done in sequence; for a parallel workflow, some steps are done at the same time. For example, Step 1 could be followed by Steps 2 and 3 running concurrently.

You can have multiple stages in workflows, with the output of one stage feeding the input of another. Having logic in workflows so that the results of one step are evaluated to determine the step that should be taken next is also possible.

SharePoint includes several predefined workflow templates that you can use to create workflows. In addition, more advanced users can employ SharePoint Designer to create their own custom workflow templates. This book does not address that capability. However, creating workflow templates in SharePoint Designer does not require computer programming, and users who have an analytical mind and who are willing to learn SharePoint Designer can easily perform this task. Beyond that, serious software developers can use programming languages like C# and Visual Studio to program their own workflow activities and workflow templates. Such programming is so far beyond the scope of this book as to be in another universe. However, it can be done!

You will have the most success if you stick to the workflow templates that are predefined in SharePoint. The particular templates available depend on the SharePoint installation, but most SharePoint sites have the following four:

- Approval
- Collect Feedback
- Collect Signatures
- Three-state

This chapter illustrates the creation and use of both approval and three-state workflows. Collect feedback and collect signature workflows are similar to the approval workflows and if you understand it, you should be able to use the collect workflows without a problem. The idea of all three of these workflow types is that a list of employees is given a task to perform: Approve (Approval), provide feedback (Collect Feedback), and sign a document (Collect Signatures). Employees are sent emails and their actions are logged, as shown in Figure 9-1.

The Approval Workflow

As the name implies, approval workflows are used to obtain approval for something: a document, a proposal, a problem definition, or whatever. The item for approval can be stored in the SharePoint site, but it need not be. You can create an approval workflow, for example, to gain approval for website design, for the proposed location of a new office, or for some other proposal.

An approval workflow consists of one or more stages. At each stage, one or more people are asked to approve the item under consideration. If the people at one stage do not approve, then the next and subsequent stages of the approval workflow are not executed.

Thus, BBB might have an approval workflow that consists of a stage of a approval within the marketing department. If all the reviewers at that stage approve, then the workflow could start a second stage of approval by senior managers, and that could be followed by a third stage of approval by partners. At each stage, the approvals can be sequential, one person following another, or they can be in parallel. If the approval is not obtained at any stage, then additional stages of approval are cancelled.

To create a workflow, follow these steps:

1. Navigate to the library or list on which you want to create the workflow.

2. Click Library Tools → Library.

3. Click the workflow symbol as shown in Figure 9-2.

4. In the menu that appears, click Add a Workflow.

FIGURE 9-2: Adding a Workflow to a Library (or List)

> **Note** You can create a workflow on any library or list. If the workflow involves approval or feedback on documents, create the workflow on the library that contains them. If the workflow involves tasks, create it on the list that has the tasks you want to manage.

The actions that you take next depend on the particular workflow template you use. The following section covers creating a workflow based on the Approval template.

Creating an Approval Workflow

Approval workflows are great for obtaining approvals and creating a log to document them. BBB at the start of this chapter, needed a workflow to ensure that a document was not published on their website without appropriate review.

Suppose that the BBB marketing department has a site of its own, and that the site includes a library for creating documents for publication outside the firm that is named *Public Documents*. Assume that you want to create an approval workflow for documents in that library.

1. When you click Add a Workflow, SharePoint produces a sequence of pages for defining the parameters of that workflow. The first task is to select the template that you want to use. Figure 9-3 shows the selection of the Approval workflow.

FIGURE 9-3: Selecting the Approval Workflow

2. As shown in Figure 9-4, you next need to provide a name for the new workflow and to specify a list for SharePoint to use to store workflow tasks. You can use the default Task list of your site, or you can specify that a new task list be created just for the purposes of this workflow. Figure 9-4 shows the default Tasks list selected. The workflow history list is a list in which SharePoint stores the workflow log. As shown, SharePoint creates a new list for this purpose.

3. In the last section of this first page, you specify how the workflow will be started. Several options are possible, as shown. Figure 9-4 shows that this new workflow can be started either manually or automatically when someone adds a document to the library (not shown in the figure, but this workflow is based on the Public Documents library).

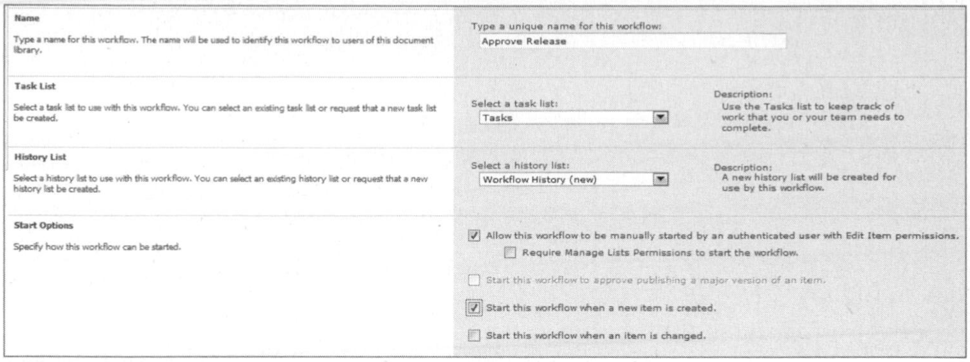

FIGURE 9-4: Specifying Approval Workflow Parameters (1)

4. Figure 9-5 shows the second page used to define an approval workflow. In the top part of this page, you specify the names of the people on your site who are to approve the documents. In this example, users Joseph, Adam, and Stanley are on the list of approvers. You can specify whether the approvals are to be obtained in sequence or in parallel. Here, the user has selected in sequence.

You also have the option of defining the following:

■ **Add a new stage:** You can select additional approval stages by clicking the Add a new stage option. This example defines just one stage. However, if BBB wanted to have one stage for the Marketing Department, one for Senior Managers and one for Partners, they would set that up here.

■ **Expand Groups:** You use this option to assign tasks to groups. This example ignores this option.

■ **Due Date for All Tasks:** You can specify a date by which the entire workflow needs to be accomplished.

■ **Duration Per Task:** You use this option to specify the number of days (or other unit of time) allowed for each approval. If the approval is not obtained by that date or time, SharePoint will send reminder emails.

■ **CC:** You can use this option to specify additional people who are to receive emails about the status and progress of this workflow.

5. In the last part of this page, you specify whether or not to reject the document if it is rejected by any approver.

6. You can specify that the workflow is to be terminated if anyone changes the document while the workflow is underway. SharePoint will enforce all of these selections.

7. Click Save (not shown in Figure 9-5, but at the bottom of that page) to create your workflow.

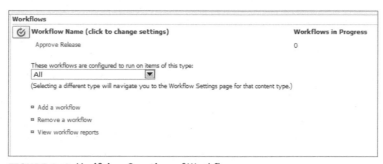

Approvers	Assign To		Order
	Joseph Schumpeter ; Adam Smith ; Stanley Larsen ;	&/📖	One at a time (serial) ▼
	◻ Add a new stage		
	Enter the names of the people to whom the workflow will assign tasks, and choose the order in which those tasks are assigned. Separate them with semicolons. You can also add stages to assign tasks to more people in different orders.		
Expand Groups	☑ For each group entered, assign a task to every member of that group.		
Request	Please approve this document for public release		
	This message will be sent to the people assigned tasks.		
Due Date for All Tasks	4/15/2011		📅
	The date by which all tasks are due.		
Duration Per Task			
	The amount of time until a task is due. Choose the units by using the Duration Units.		
Duration Units	Day(s)		▼
	Define the units of time used by the Duration Per Task.		
CC			&/📖
	Notify these people when the workflow starts and ends without assigning tasks to them.		
End on First Rejection	☑ Automatically reject the document if it is rejected by any participant.		
End on Document Change	☑ Automatically reject the document if it is changed before the workflow is completed.		

FIGURE 9-5: Specifying Approval Workflow Parameters (2)

8. To ensure your workflow has been created. Go to the library, select Library Tools → Library, and click Workflow Settings. The page shown in Figure 9-6 appears. Because the new workflow Approve Release is listed, you know that SharePoint has successfully created it. Note that the value of Workflows in Process is zero, indicating that none have been started.

Workflows

🛡 Workflow Name (click to change settings)	Workflows in Progress
Approve Release	0

These workflows are configured to run on items of this type:

All ▼

(Selecting a different type will navigate you to the Workflow Settings page for that content type.)

▫ Add a workflow
▫ Remove a workflow
▫ View workflow reports

FIGURE 9-6: Verifying Creation of Workflow

Using the Approval Workflow

After you have defined a workflow, SharePoint will execute it, creating tasks, sending emails, and writing to the log as just described. The log provides documentation of all workflow events. Logs are useful if team members need to be able to demonstrate compliance with organizational policy. They are essential in situations in which a group might need to show compliance with accounting and legal standards.

For the workflow just created, the act of uploading or creating a document in the Public Documents library will cause SharePoint to start the workflow. In Figure 9-7, the user David Kroenke has placed the Quarterly Report document into this library. The Approve Release workflow is listed in that library and its status for this document is In Process.

FIGURE 9-7: Adding a Document Causes SharePoint to Start the Workflow

The basic process for working with the approval workflow as follows:

1. Navigate to the library or list that has the workflow. Verify that the workflow is underway by checking Workflow Settings on that library or list and noting that Workflows in Progress has a value of 1, as shown in Figure 9-8. Also, when the workflow is started, SharePoint creates a review task and places it into the Tasks list as shown in Figure 9-9.

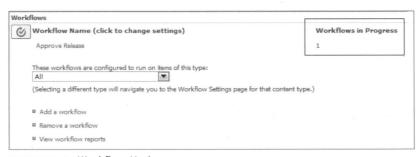

FIGURE 9-8: Workflow Underway

FIGURE 9-9: Task Created for First Reviewer

2. Click the task in the list that needs approval. In this example, if Joseph Schumpeter clicks the words Please approve Quarterly Report, SharePoint displays the dialog shown in Figure 9-10.

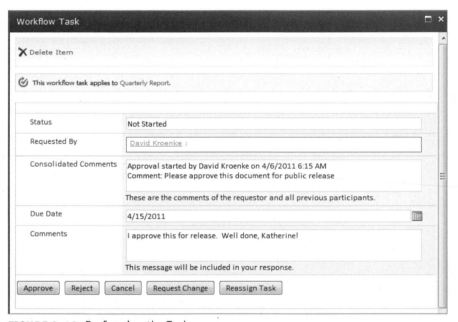

FIGURE 9-10: Performing the Task

3. If you wish to approve the item under review, type an approval message in the Comments textbox and click Approve. If not, you can click Reject or take some other action as indicated.

> **Note**
>
> As shown in Figure 9-10, Joseph has been assigned this task. He can reassign the task of approving the document to someone else if he wants to. By the way, in this example, if any user other than Joe tries to take action on this task, SharePoint will inform that person that this is not his or her task and ignore the action.

4. After you approve the document, SharePoint generates an approval task for the next person who needs to give approval, in this example Adam Smith, as shown in Figure 9-11. Had this workflow been set up as a parallel workflow, then SharePoint would have created all such tasks at one time.

		Type	Title		Assigned To	Status	Priority	Due Date	% Complete	Predecessors	Related Content	Outcome
			Please approve Quarterly Report ☐ NEW		Joseph Schumpeter	Completed	(2) Normal	4/15/2011	100 %		Quarterly Report	Approved
			Please approve Quarterly Report ☐ NEW		Adam Smith	Not Started	(2) Normal	4/15/2011			Quarterly Report	

✛ Add new item

FIGURE 9-11: Task List with Task for Second Approver

As shown in Figure 9-12, the approval state for the documents under Approve Release is still In Progress.

5. At this point, it doesn't appear that any work has been done. However, clicking the words In Progress causes SharePoint to open the dialog shown in Figure 9-13. As you can see from the example, Joseph has approved the document and it now awaits Adam's approval, followed by Stanley's.

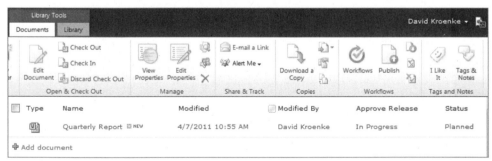

FIGURE 9-12: Click In Progress to View the Task Status Diagram

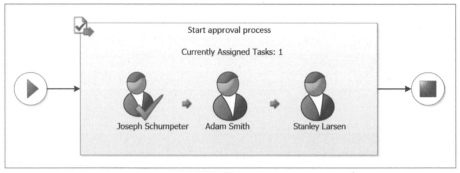

FIGURE 9-13: Task Status Diagram

6. The tasks for the second and third people on the approval chain (Adam and Stanley) will be the same as for the first (Joseph), so they are not repeated here. After all three have approved the document, however, the status of Approve Release will change to Approved as shown in Figure 9-14.

7. Clicking the word Approved opens the dialog box shown in Figure 9-15.

FIGURE 9-14: Approval Completed

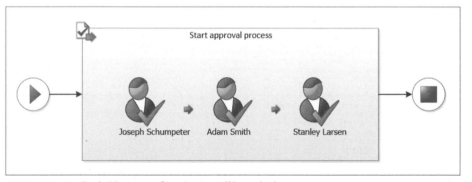

FIGURE 9-15: Task Diagram after Approval Completion

SharePoint has been sending emails to the participants in this workflow as stipulated when the workflow was created. When a workflow completes, it sends a final email like that shown in Figure 9-16.

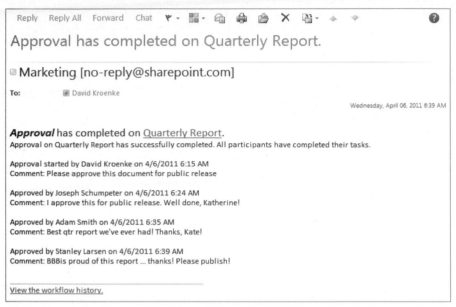

FIGURE 9-16: Email at Approval Completion

This email summarizes the approvals, the dates and times of those approvals, and comments made about the document. This email is sent to the person who placed the document into the library. It could be sent to other people or groups in the organization as well.

The Three-State Workflow

Figure 9-17 shows four built-in workflows (with the Three-state workflow selected) that are included in most SharePoint sites. The preceding section discussed the approval workflow. As stated earlier, the two collect workflow templates operate very similarly to Approval, so they are not addressed here. The three-state workflow, however, is different both in action and character from the other three workflows, so this section covers how to create and use one.

Three-state is a generalized pattern that can be applied to any work assignment. Work is assigned, someone does it, and the work is accepted (or not). The task could be resolution of problems, the painting of walls, or getting a haircut. Because of this generality, it is most useful.

Note that unlike approval and collect feedback workflows, which can work on libraries, three-state workflows work only on task lists.

FIGURE 9-17: Typical Built-in Workflows

To understand how three-state workflows operate, consider the diagram in Figure 9-18 in which actors (people) are shown on the left, actions are shown in the middle, and states are shown on the right.

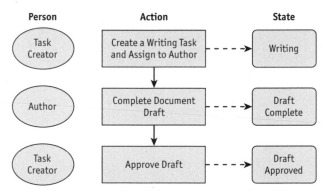

FIGURE 9-18: Example of a Three-state Workflow Action

The process is as follows:

- **Writing:** When a writing task has been created and assigned to someone, that person is (one hopes) engaged in writing that document. So the state of the workflow is Writing.

- **Draft complete:** When the document is complete, the author notifies someone that the document is finished. At that point, the workflow transitions from the Writing state to the Draft Complete state.

- **Draft Approved:** Next, someone (in Figure 9-18, the task creator) reviews the draft, and if he or she approves it, the workflow is put into its third state, Draft Approved. If the draft is not approved, the task creator would cancel this workflow and start another task, such as Rework Draft. That task would follow the same flow.

All this fuss about these transitions is for a reason. When you create a three-state workflow, you must tell SharePoint what you want done when the workflow goes from no value to Writing. You must also indicate what you want done when the state goes from Writing to Draft Complete. However, you don't need to specify anything about the state change from Draft Complete to Draft Approved. When that state is reached, the workflow is finished and SharePoint already knows what to do.

Bottom line: A three-state workflow has three states and three transitions, but you need only provide instructions to SharePoint for the first two of them. You'll see how all this fits together in a few pages.

Setting Up the Task List

To function, three-state workflows require the task list upon which they are based to include a choice column with at least three values. Figure 9-19 shows a portion of the three-state creation page. When you get to this spot, your list will need to have such a column, so you'll need to create it before starting to define your workflow.

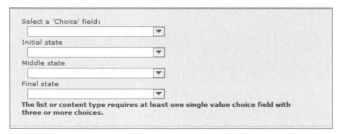

FIGURE 9-19: Three-state Requires a Choice Field in the List

For this example, create a custom list called Writing Assignments that has four columns: Document Name, Created By, Author, and Status. To create these columns list, follow these steps:

1. Create a custom list as shown in Chapter 8.

2. Change the name of the Title column to Document Name. SharePoint will automatically add Created By, so you need not add it.

3. Create an Author column and set its type of People or Group, but restrict it to just People.

4. Create the Status column as shown in Figure 9-20. Add three choices as the values of the state of your workflow (Writing, Draft Completed, Draft Approved). Select Drop-Down Menu so that Status can have only a single value. Do not allow 'Fill-in' choices.

FIGURE 9-20: Three Choice Values for the Example Workflow

The resulting list is shown in Figure 9-21. Task assigners will start the workflow by creating an item as you'll see in the section "Using a Three-State Workflow."

FIGURE 9-21: The Writing Assignments Task List

Creating a Three-State Workflow

With a list in place, you can now create the workflow:

1. Navigate to the list and click List Tools → List.

2. Click Workflow Setting → Add a workflow. In the page that appears select Three-state, and type in a name for the workflow. Figure 9-22 shows the workflow creator has typed the name Manage Draft Documents.

3. If you want a custom task list, select that option here. This example uses the standard site Tasks list. Workflow History is the name of the list that will contain the workflow log. As shown, the workflow creator accepted the default name of *Workflow History*.

> **Note** Two tasks lists are involved here. One is the custom task list for recording writing assignments that you just created. The other (here the default Tasks list) is a task list that has tasks for workflow processing of the Writing Assignments task list. You'll see how this works when you run the workflow.

4. Select only the "Allow this workflow to be manually started by an authenticated user with Edit Item permission" option. This selection means the workflow must be started manually, which gives the writing assignment creator the chance to create the task, verify and otherwise think about it, and later start the workflow that will issue the assignments. Click Next to display the second page for defining this workflow.

Select a workflow template:

Disposition Approval
Three-state
Grading
Collect Feedback - SharePoint 201

Description:
Use this workflow to track items in a list.

Type a unique name for this workflow:

Manage Draft Documents

Select a task list:

Tasks

Description:
Use the Tasks list to keep track of work that you or your team needs to complete.

Select a history list:

Workflow History

Description:
History list for workflow.

☑ Allow this workflow to be manually started by an authenticated user with Edit Item permission
  ☐ Require Manage Lists Permissions to start the workflow.

☐ Start this workflow to approve publishing a major version of an item.

☐ Start this workflow when a new item is created.

☐ Start this workflow when an item is changed.

FIGURE 9-22: Defining the Three-State Workflow

Figure 9-23 shows the top of the second Three-state workflow creation page. SharePoint code examined the list and selected Status because it was the only choice column in the list. If more than one such column existed, you would need to select the one you want.

5. Select which choice values correspond to the first, second, and third states.

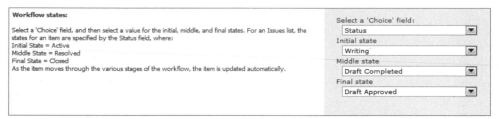

FIGURE 9-23: Setting Workflow States

6. Use the next set of choices to indicate what should happen when the workflow is started. Figure 9-24 shows that SharePoint should create a task with the Title and Description indicated. You could also include a Task Due Date, but do not do that here because you didn't create such a column earlier in your custom list. SharePoint is suggesting the column Modified because it is as close to Task Due Date as it can come. As shown in this example, deselect that check box. Finally, assign the task by choosing the Author column from the Include list field drop-down list.

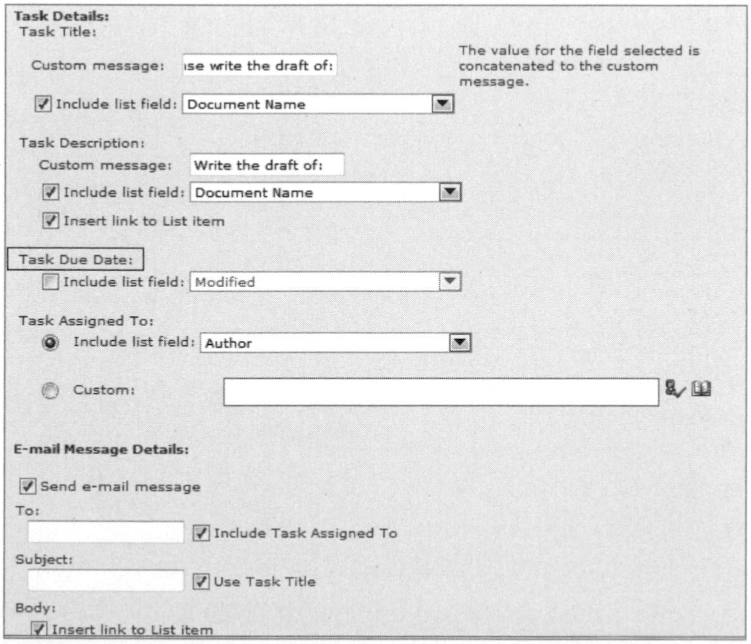

FIGURE 9-24: Specifying Action When the Task Is Created

Emails will be sent, by default, to the Task Assigned To person (Author) and will include the subject and body as shown in Figure 9-24. You could also include other names in the To text box.

7. You use the last part of the Three-state definition page to specify what should happen when the task status becomes Draft Complete. At that point, SharePoint needs to create a Review Draft task for someone. As shown in Figure 9-25, the title of the task will be "Please review the draft of:" followed by the value of Document Name. Task Description will be similar.

The review task will be assigned to the value of Created By in the list, which is the name of the person who created the Writing Assignment item. If you had created a column, such as Reviewer, when you created the Writing Assignment custom list, you could have used that value here. For this example, Created By works just fine.

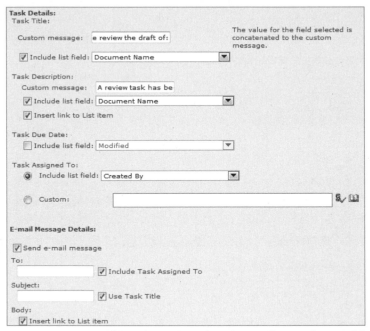

FIGURE 9-25: Specifying the Action When Status Changes from Writing to Draft Complete

As stated, you need not provide instructions to SharePoint about what is to be done when the task status changes from Draft Complete to Draft Approved. That change finishes the workflow, and SharePoint will complete the workflow, change the workflow status to Complete, and send appropriate emails.

Using the Three-State Workflow

So far, you have designed and created the writing assignments workflow. In this section you will see how SharePoint implements it.

The Manage Draft Documents workflow is based on the Writing Assignments list, so the first task is to create an item in that list. In Figure 9-26, the user (who is Katherine Hepburn, though you cannot tell that from this figure), is creating a writing assignment for Joseph Schumpeter. She sets the Status of the task to Writing.

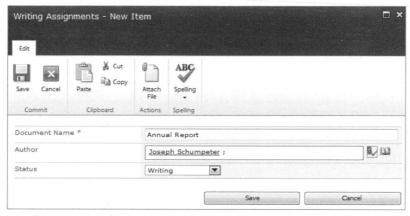

FIGURE 9-26: Creating a New Item in the Writing Assignments List

This workflow does not automatically start with the creation of a list item (it could, but you did not set it up that way). Hence, the workflow must be manually started. To do so, follow these steps:

1. Navigate to the Writing Assignments list and select the check box next to the task for which the workflow is to be started. Figure 9-27 shows Annual Report selected. If you do not select an item, the Workflows icon will be disabled, so be sure to select a task.

2. Click the Workflows icon.

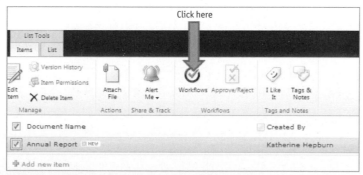

FIGURE 9-27: Manually Starting a Workflow (1)

3. In the page that appears, click the workflow icon next to the workflow that you want to start. In Figure 9-28, there is only one icon to click because this list has only one workflow. However, if there were several workflows, you would click the icon next to the workflow you want to start.

FIGURE 9-28: Manually Starting a Workflow (2)

In response, SharePoint takes the actions specified for the first transition of the workflow from startup to Writing. As shown in Figure 9-29, SharePoint creates a task in the Tasks list for the author, in this case, Joseph Schumpeter.

> **Note** This task will appear in the Tasks list, not in the Writing Assignments list. The Tasks list stores tasks for managing activity in the Writing Assignments list.

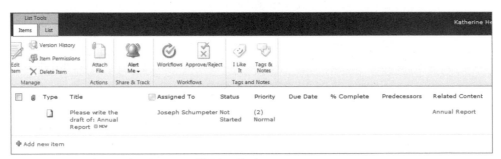

FIGURE 9-29: SharePoint Creates a Writing Task

4. After the person assigned the task creates the draft of the document, he or she can open the task, change its status to Draft Completed as shown in Figure 9-30, and click Save. In response, SharePoint takes the actions defined for the second transition. In this example, SharePoint creates a review task for the person who created the Writing Assignment, who in this case is Katherine Hepburn. That task appears as shown in Figure 9-31.

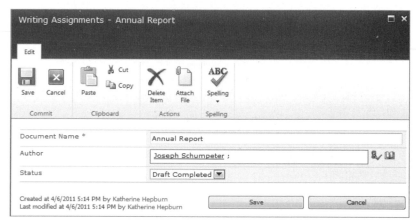

FIGURE 9-30: Writer Changes the Writing Assignment Task Status

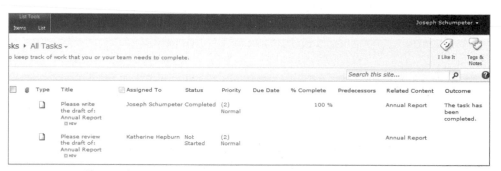

FIGURE 9-31: SharePoint Creates a Review Task

5. The person assigned the next task can now take action. In this example, Katherine will review the document and then change the status of her task in the Tasks list to Draft Approved. At that point, all tasks have been completed, as shown in Figure 9-32.

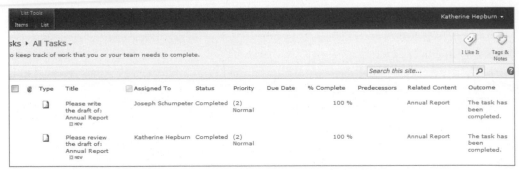

FIGURE 9-32: Task List Tasks Completed

Because the third state has been reached, the workflow is completed. Figure 9-33 shows the Writing Assignments task list. Notice that the Manage Draft Documents workflow is marked as Completed for the Annual Report document.

FIGURE 9-33: Manage Draft Documents Workflow Completed

Before leaving this workflow, reflect for a moment that three-state workflows:

▪ **Can manage any task:** Because this is a general workflow, you could use it to manage any assignment, like asking your spouse to clean the garage. Alas, SharePoint cannot ensure that the work will be done, but it will keep careful records of assignments and what hasn't been done!

▪ **Can pinpoint unfinished tasks:** Unlike with the approval workflow, if the assignment reviewer does not approve the work, SharePoint will not do anything special. However, the workflow will stay open until either the task is deleted or the reviewer finally marks the assignment as completed. So, open workflows are good indicators of unfinished work.

▪ **Can be a great project planning tool:** The ability to create a task but not start the workflow automatically can be very useful. When planning a project, you can create and organize many tasks before making the assignments. Project planners can think through the specified tasks and then start the workflow when appropriate. The assignments will not appear in the task list until that has been done.

Other SharePoint Workflow Possibilities

SharePoint workflows go way beyond the built-in workflows you've learned about here. You can create your own custom workflows that are incredibly useful. Consider that, when using SharePoint, you have access to your team's email accounts, task lists, document libraries, indeed, everything on your site (and if you want, even on other sites that you have permission to access).

Furthermore, you can plug the logic of your process into the middle of SharePoint's processing. You can trap events like posting or changing documents or tasks and then take actions in response. You can also integrate SharePoint columns with Office documents.

Here's a simple example: A professor creates a workflow on a student work submission library that automatically alerts the professor when a student posts a new paper. When the professor opens the document, he or she grades and saves it back. The workflow takes the grade from the paper, stores it in a grade book, and sends an email to the student notifying him or her of the grade received. If the grade is especially high (or low), the workflow can be programmed to take special actions. The only work for the professor is to read the alert email, click the document link in that email, and grade the paper. All the rest is done by SharePoint.

Workflows are the non-programmers business process programming tool. Workflows of simple to moderate complexity are easy to create. To do so, however, you must learn how to use Microsoft SharePoint Designer. The good news is that you can download SharePoint Designer, license free.

Creating basic level workflows in SharePoint Designer is like creating rules for email filters. Workflows consist of sets of steps in the format of "When this occurs, and then do this." Workflows can have logic and looping as well.

If you are involved in designing and implementing business processes, if you have a logical mind, and if you don't mind digging into some detail, consider creating your own workflows.

What You've Learned

In this chapter you learned the basic framework for SharePoint workflows and you learned the purpose of the four built-in workflows. You've learned how the approval workflow works, how to create an approval workflow, and how approval workflows are managed by SharePoint. You've seen the role of task and history lists in approval workflows.

This chapter also presented the generic, three-state workflow. You created a list to base that workflow upon, added the needed Choice column, and then created a three-state workflow to manage the assignment and execution of writing assignments.

With the knowledge of this chapter, you should be able to create and use any of the four built-in SharePoint workflows.

What's Next?

The next three chapters of this book address the sharing of team knowledge. Chapter 10 describes how to set up and use videoconferencing using the Lync component of Office 365. You'll see how to share documents, screens, whiteboards, and other resources with your team in real time. So, read on!

Sharing Knowledge

Of Course, This Would Never Happen in <u>Your</u> Business...

"Adam, I want to get everyone together with that hot new office space consultant." Joe Schumpeter, lead architect for a 1,000 bed hospital design project at Baker, Barker, Bickle, is talking on the phone with Adam Smith, project manager.

"Fine, Joe, let's do it. Who all do you want?"

"Let's see. You, me, Katherine, and that consultant, Teresa Barnsworthy."

"You want to bring everyone here?"

"Sure, why not?"

"I can think of a couple of reasons. One is that it's going to be a week or two before everyone can get together. And the second one, forgive me Mr. Big-deal, internationally award-winning architect, is, well, cost."

"Hmpf. With the fees this project is bringing us in, I think we could pay a few travel expenses."

"Joe, you would be surprised. We have what we like to a call a travel budget and, believe it or not, we're overspent on it."

"Oh, come on..."

"Besides, she's a consultant who lives in Canada, and she's going to bill us, or rather, bill you for her travel time and time here on the job."

"Look, I met her at the Builders Conference in LA. I heard her speak, knew we had to talk to her, so I called her. She has some incredible ideas for making spaces more humane, and I think they're reasonably doable. So, I want to get her on board."

"Okay, Joe, I'll do it. But, first, did you think about a conference call? Just to set it up?"

"Nah, I want us to see what's she's doing and have a chance to brainstorm how we could work some of that into our new children's wing. I want to get her to make a few sketches, or at least show us some of what she's done."

"We could try one of those online video conferencing services. I'd have to open an account with them, get everyone to install their software, and then learn how to use it. I hear that's not so easy."

"Don't know."

"Okay, I'll try to get everyone into Omaha. Early next month, okay?"

"Early next month? You're kidding. I'm supposed to have the concept designs done by May third! Get real."

"Joe, you get real. We won't get everyone together before then."

It Doesn't Have to Be That Way...

Remote Whiteboard Sessions with Lync

YOUR BUSINESS OR WORKGROUP is probably like most. From time to time you need to get in a room with whiteboards on the walls and brainstorm about a problem or an opportunity. If your organization has geographically dispersed locations, you'll also have key people in those locations, making it difficult and expensive, if not impossible, to get people together in the same physical location. Clearly the answer is to use web technology to conduct a virtual meeting. But the solutions generally available are stand-alone solutions that require advanced scheduling, and they can be expensive. With the integrated online meeting capabilities provided by Lync, you can use Office 365 to conduct online meetings with a click of your mouse or you can schedule them in advance if that works better for you. Once you are in the meeting, you can share your desktop with those in attendance, share only a particular program, make an online PowerPoint presentation, or share a virtual whiteboard.

In this chapter you'll learn the basics of how to schedule an online meeting using the integrated features of Lync and Outlook. You'll also see how to share a virtual whiteboard and use the built-in Lync markup tools to annotate it much as you would do if you were in a meeting room with a physical whiteboard.

In Chapter 12, you'll learn some additional details about scheduling a remote PowerPoint presentation and you'll get some tips on how to prepare for and conduct the remote presentation.

Specifically, in this chapter, you'll learn how to

- Use Outlook to schedule an online meeting

- As the meeting organizer, see who is planning to attend the meeting, who will not attend, who may attend, and who has not yet responded

- As an invitee, accept a meeting invitation using Outlook

- As an invitee, accept a meeting invitation using your browser-based email, and, if you have never attended a Lync online meeting, how to make sure your computer is ready.

- Facilitate a brainstorming session using a shared whiteboard

- Use the whiteboard tools during the session

- Save the annotated whiteboard as documentation of the session

Using Outlook to Schedule an Online Meeting

As you learned in Chapter 3, you can initiate an online meeting instantly by a few clicks of your mouse. However, not everyone you want to meet with will be available on the spur of the moment. As a result you'll need to find a time for the meeting that works for everyone. Thanks to the integration of the components of Office 365, scheduling an online Lync meeting is easy using Outlook. Just follow these steps:

1. Open Outlook and click Calendar in the navigation pane.

2. Click the date you want to schedule the meeting (in this example, January 3).

3. To schedule a Lync online meeting, click New Online Meeting, as shown in Figure 10-1.

4. Schedule a time for the meeting by double-clicking the desired time slot. The New Online Meeting window opens. In the chapter example, because Adam wants to schedule the meeting for 10:00 a.m., he selects that time from the Start Time drop-down menu. Adam wants the meeting to last for an hour, but he does not select an end time just yet. You'll see how Adam changes the duration of the meeting in a moment.

5. Click Scheduling Assistant in the Outlook ribbon to add people to be invited to the meeting, as shown in Figure 10-2. Lync (integrating with Outlook) automatically

creates links in the body of the meeting window. Meeting attendees can click the links to join the meeting when the time comes. You'll see this in action next.

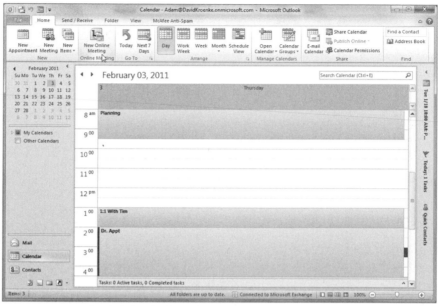

FIGURE 10-1: Adam's Calendar for February 3

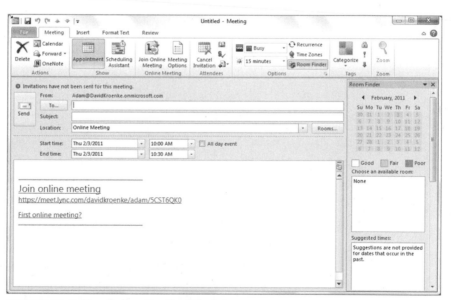

FIGURE 10-2: New Online Meeting Window

One of the challenges of scheduling any meeting is finding a time that works for everyone. Outlook can help with that in a big way with its Scheduling Assistant window, shown in Figure 10-3.

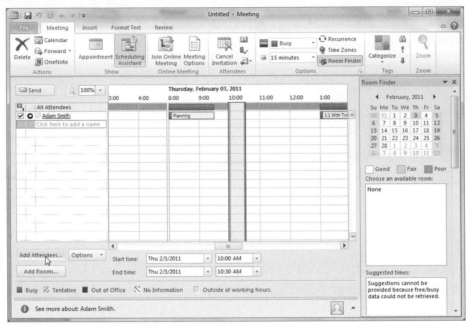

FIGURE 10-3: Scheduling Assistant Window

Outlook displays the current meeting start and end times with two vertical lines across the attendee list. It currently shows the start time on the left (in green) as 10:00 AM, and the end time on the right (in red) as 10:30 AM.

6. To add people from your company to the meeting request, click Add Attendees, as shown in Figure 10-3. In this example, the result is the display of a list of people in Adam's organization, shown in Figure 10-4.

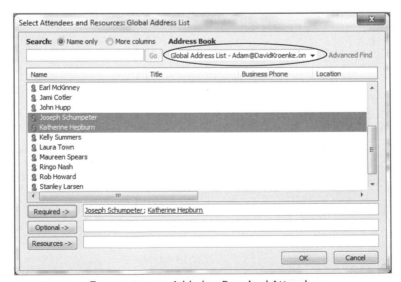

FIGURE 10-4: Teammates are Added as Required Attendees

Note

Note that the Address Book selected in this example (by Adam) is the Global Address List (referred to as the *GAL*) shown at the top right of the dialog in Figure 10-4. You can just as easily select people from your personal Contact list by selecting Contact from the Address Book drop-down menu. This would be how Adam adds Teresa (the outside consultant) as an attendee to this meeting.

7. To select meeting attendees, click the person's name in the main area of the dialog (you can select multiple names by clicking the first name, then holding down the Ctrl key while you click the second name) and then click Required, as shown in Figure 10-4.

8. Click OK. The Address Book disappears and the attendees' names (Joe and Katharine) appear in the Scheduling Assistant window.

Note

Note that the free/busy information for the attendees displays so that the person scheduling the meeting can see at a glance whether any schedule conflicts exist for them at the time of the meeting (10:00 AM and 11:00 AM on January 3). This extremely valuable information is another result of the integration of the components of Office 365!

9. To change the end time of the meeting, click the end time line in the Scheduling Assistant window and drag it to the right to lengthen the meeting or to the left to shorten it. In this example, Adam changes the end time to 11:00 AM, as shown in Figure 10-5.

10. To return to the Appointment window, click Appointment in the ribbon, as shown in Figure 10-5.

11. Add a meeting subject and a comment in the body of the meeting request, then click Send, as shown in Figure 10-6.

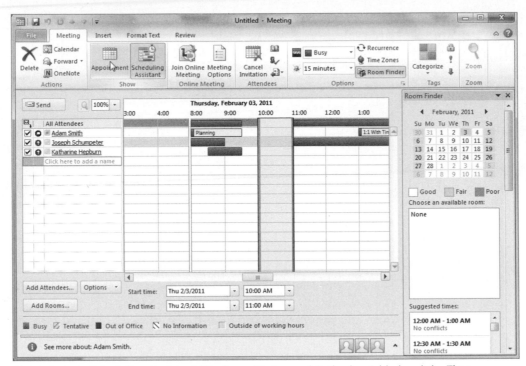

FIGURE 10-5: Scheduling Assistant Window with Joe and Katharine Added and the Time Extended

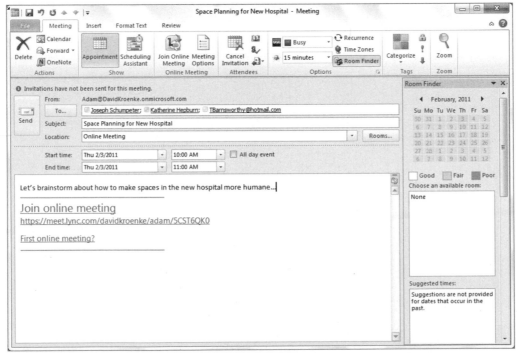

FIGURE 10-6: Completed Meeting Invitation

Accepting a Meeting Request in Outlook

When a meeting attendee (such as Joe) receives the meeting request in Outlook, he or she can click the email to view the request in the reading pane. Note that Outlook shows an excerpt of the attendee's calendar so that the attendee can see at a glance whether he or she can attend the meeting.

To accept the meeting, the attendee clicks Accept → Send the Response Now, as shown in Figure 10-7, if the attendee is not sure whether they can attend he or she can indicate that to the meeting organizer by clicking Tentative. Of course, if the invitee cannot attend they can click Decline. All three primary responses of Accept, Tentative and Decline have the same sub-responses as follows:

- If the invitee simply wants to send the response with no comment, he or she can click Send the Response Now as shown in Figure 10-7.

- If the invitee wants to make a comment to the organizer of the meeting he or she can click Edit the Response before Sending.

- If, for whatever reason the invitee does not want to send a response, he or she can click Do Not Send a Response.

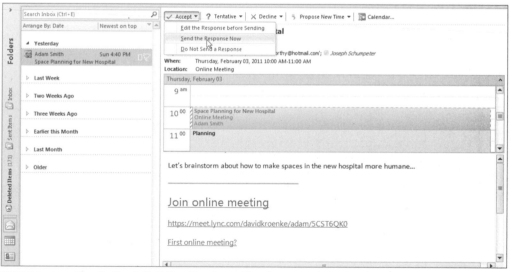

FIGURE 10-7: The Outlook Mail Reading Pane Showing a Partial Calendar

Checking the Status of Meeting Invitations

As the meeting organizer, you'll probably want to know who has accepted your meeting request, who has declined, and who has not yet responded so you can reschedule if you need to. To see who has responded, follow these steps:

1. In the Outlook Calendar, open the meeting by double-clicking it.

2. Click Tracking, as shown in Figure 10-8, to open the tracking window.

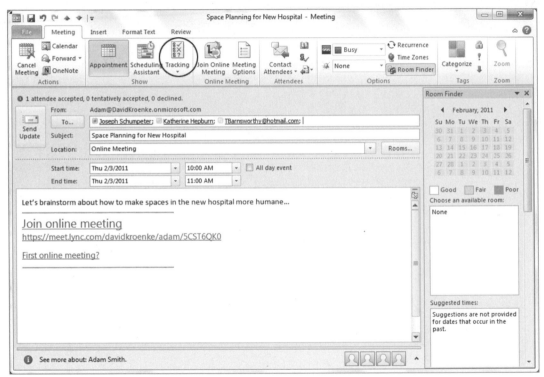

FIGURE 10-8: Clicking the Tracking Button to See Who Has Accepted the Meeting

In the chapter example, the tracking window in Figure 10-9 shows the meeting organizer (Adam) that Joe and Katharine have both accepted the meeting invitation, but Teresa has not yet responded.

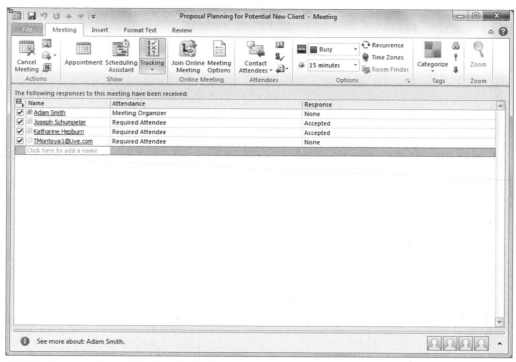

FIGURE 10-9: Status of Meeting Invitations

Accepting a Meeting Request Using a Browser

What if you're outside an organization and you're sent a meeting request? You can use your browser to access your email request and accept it from there. In the chapter example, if Teresa were using Outlook to manage her Windows Live email, her experience in accepting Adam's meeting request would be identical to Joe's and Katharine's.

However, if your meeting attendee uses a browser to manage Windows Live email or Google's gmail, he or she will open the email meeting request and then click the Accept link, as shown in Figure 10-10.

After clicking Calendar in the left navigation pane of the browser, the attendee can view the meeting. To see meeting details, the user can hover over the meeting, as shown in Figure 10-11.

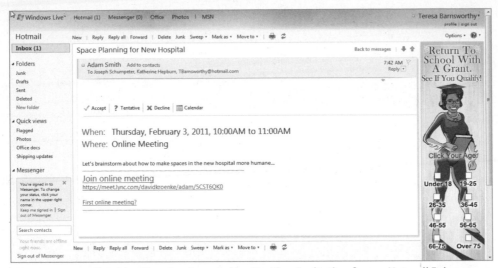

FIGURE 10-10: Outside Attendee Accepts the Meeting Invitation from a Hotmail Inbox

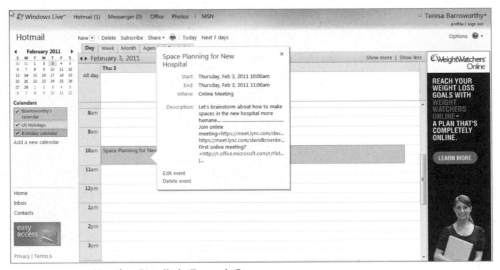

FIGURE 10-11: Meeting Details in Teresa's Browser

Preparing for a First Online Meeting (Attendee)

Meeting attendees who do not have Lync already installed on their computers need to do a little setup work before they can attend a Lync meeting. Thankfully, Office 365 makes this very easy. This process will normally take just a few minutes to complete.

To attend an online meeting when you're an outside (non-company) person, follow these steps:

1. Click the First Online Meeting? link that is included in the meeting invitation. This link takes you to the Lync Online Help and How-to section of the Microsoft Office website. Click Getting Started as shown in Figure 10-12.

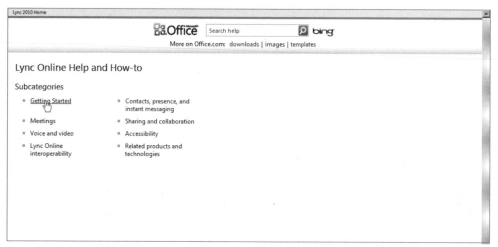

FIGURE 10-12: Lync Online Help and How-to Web Page

2. Click the First Online Meeting link, as shown in Figure 10-13.

FIGURE 10-13: Clicking the First Online Meeting Link

3. In the First Online Meeting window that appears, click the Meeting Readiness link, as shown in Figure 10-14.

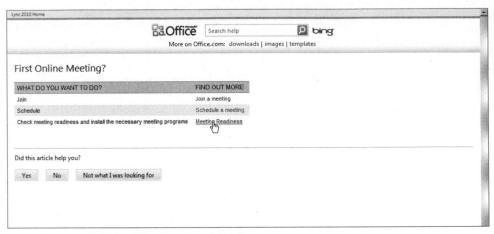

FIGURE 10-14: Clicking "Meeting Readiness"

The message shown in Figure 10-15 should appear. In the chapter example, although Teresa can participate in an online meeting using a browser, this meeting involves sharing a virtual whiteboard, which requires that she install Microsoft Communicator "14" Attendee.

4. To install this program, click the Install Communicator "14" Attendee link (shown in Figure 10-15), and follow the prompts to download and install the required software.

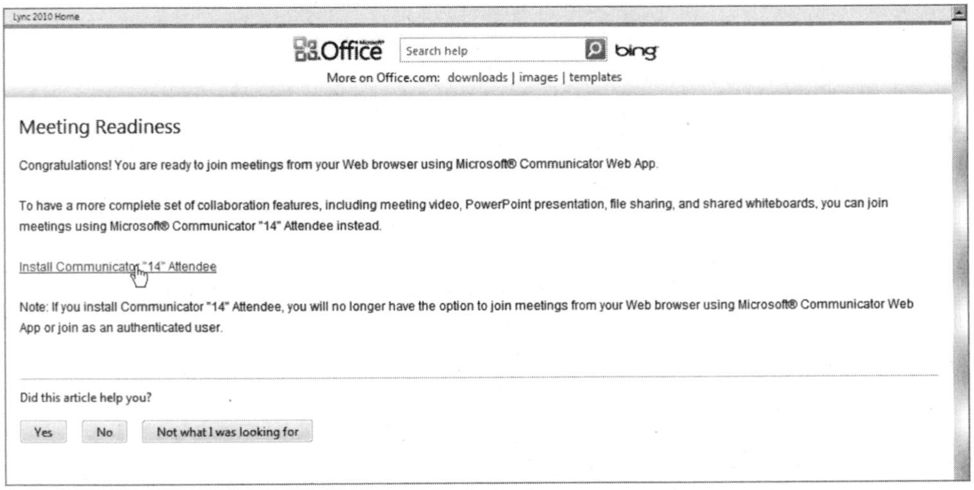

FIGURE 10-15: Install Communicator "14" Attendee to Participate in the Whiteboarding Session

Note If Lync is already installed on your machine, the message shown in Figure 10-16 appears instead of the page shown in Figure 10-15. If you needed to install software as shown in Figure 10-15, you will see the message shown in Figure 10-16 once the installation is complete.

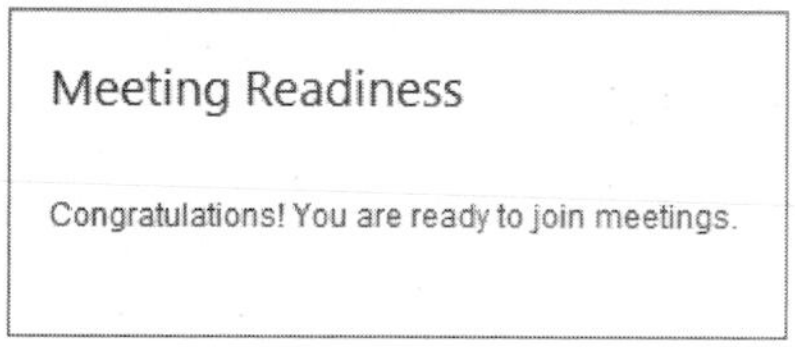

Meeting Readiness

Congratulations! You are ready to join meetings.

FIGURE 10-16: Message Received If You Have the Required Software Installed

Facilitating a Brainstorming Session Using a Shared Whiteboard

At this point, you have learned how to schedule an online meeting with Outlook, how to accept meeting requests in Outlook, and how to accept meeting requests using browser based mail. This section shows you how to set up for your virtual brainstorming session and how to use the whiteboarding tools.

Note By default, scheduling a meeting in the calendar in Outlook means that you will receive a reminder 15 minutes prior to the meeting. However, logging online half an hour before time is a good idea in the event that your attendees log online early.

The following steps assume that the meeting organizer (Adam) decides to join the meeting early and refresh his memory about how the whiteboarding tools work. To do that, follow these steps.

1. In the Outlook calendar, double click the meeting, as shown in Figure 10-17.

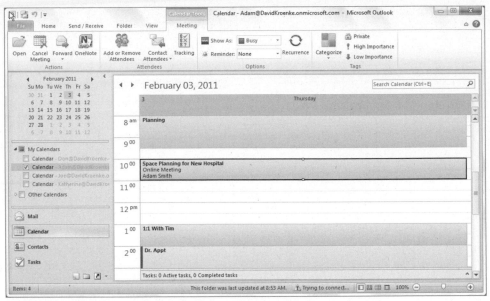

FIGURE 10-17: Opening the Meeting in the Outlook Calendar

2. After the meeting is open, click Join Online Meeting, as shown in Figure 10-18. The Meeting Audio dialog box shown in Figure 10-19 appears.

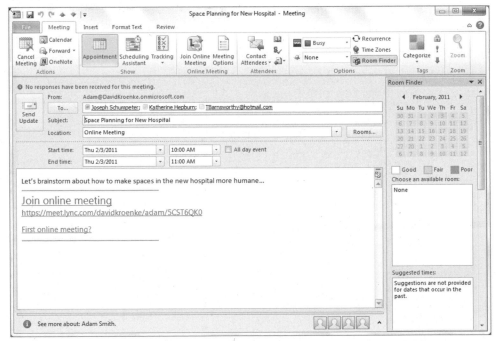

FIGURE 10-18: Clicking the Join Online Meeting Link

FIGURE 10-19: Click OK to Use Lync Integrated Audio and Video

3. To use Lync integrated audio and video, accept the default (Use Lync integrated audio and video) by clicking OK.

> **Note** If your computer is equipped with a speaker and a microphone, it is best to use Lync integrated audio. However, if, for whatever reason, using Lync integrated audio won't work for you, select the Call Me At option and type a phone number in field that follows the option.

After a short delay the Lync meeting window appears, as shown in Figure 10-20. The small box to the left of Adam's name (his presence indicator) automatically turns from green to red indicating that he is no longer available to be contacted by IM (he's in a meeting).

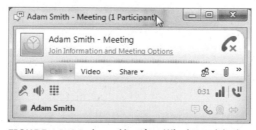

FIGURE 10-20: Lync Meeting Window with the Presence Indicator Automatically Updated

Figure 10-21 shows the Lync window of a meeting attendee (Joe Schumpeter). Although you cannot see the color, the presence indicator for Adam (the small bar on the left side of Adam's picture box) updates to red, and displays a status note saying, "In a conference call."

FIGURE 10-21: The Presence Information as Seen by a Teammate

Because of the integration of the components of Office 365, presence information is automatically updated wherever it appears. For instance, in the chapter example, if Joe wanted to send an email to Adam, he could see that Adam is currently in a conference call by simply hovering his cursor over Adam's name in Outlook, as shown in Figure 10-22.

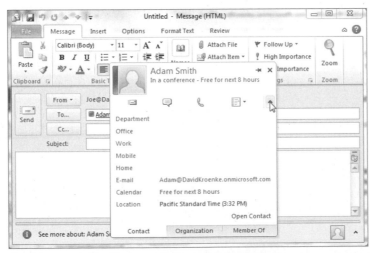

FIGURE 10-22: The Presence Information in Outlook

Facilitate a Brainstorming Session Using a Shared Whiteboard

Now that your meeting is in session, how do you best share the information that the various participants have to offer? Office 365 offers a virtual *whiteboard*, a feature that allows meeting participants to draw as they explain their concepts to each other as if each meeting attendee were in front of the same whiteboard in a conference room. Because the chapter example meeting is a brainstorming session, Adam will share a whiteboard.

You'll want to open the shared whiteboard just prior to the meeting by expanding the Share drop-down menu, clicking the small inverted triangle, and then clicking New Whiteboard, as shown in Figure 10-23.

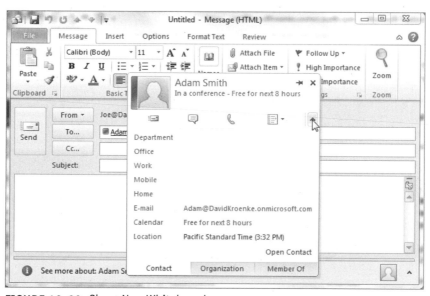

FIGURE 10-23: Share New Whiteboard

The Lync meeting window expands to display the Lync *stage*, which includes a new, blank whiteboard, as shown in Figure 10-24.

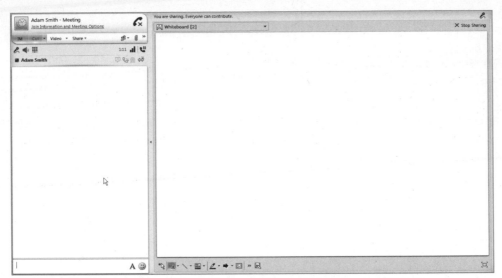

FIGURE 10-24: Expanded Meeting Window with Stage Displaying a New Whiteboard

Several tools are available to use with the whiteboard. The tools are represented by icons at the bottom of the whiteboard, as shown in Figure 10-25.

FIGURE 10-25: The Whiteboard Tools

From left to right, the whiteboard tool icons are Laser Pointer, Select and Type (sometimes referred to as "text tool"), Choose Drawing Tool (sometimes referred to as "drawing tool"), Select a Color, Pen, Stamp, Insert Image, and Save with Annotations.

The Virtual Laser Pointer

During meetings in physical meeting rooms, the participants can stand next to the physical whiteboard and point to areas they are discussing. In a virtual meeting room that becomes a challenge. To help with this conundrum Lync provides the Virtual Laser tool. To activate it, click the Laser Pointer icon as shown in Figure 10-26.

To use the pointer, move the cursor to the whiteboard, click the left mouse button, and hold it down as you move it around the whiteboard, as shown in Figure 10-27. Each participant has a unique color for his or her laser pointer, and their names are displayed so attendees can tell what each participant is pointing to.

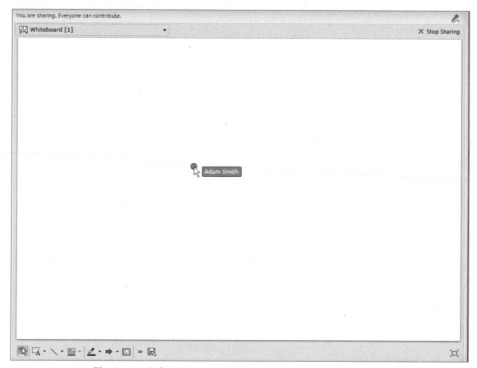

FIGURE 10-26: The Laser Pointer

Annotation Tools

Lync also provides several useful tools that participants can use to make annotations on the whiteboard. After all, that's the whole point of a whiteboarding session. In the next sections of this chapter you will see how to use these tools to:

- Choose a color for your annotations
- Annotate the whiteboard with text
- Add lines, arrows, etc.
- Draw freehand with pens and highlighters
- Add virtual stamps (arrows, checks and "X"s)
- Insert images

Table 10-1 shows only the tools you will use in the following sections as you see the Whiteboard in action. Note that these are similar in function and look to the Lync PowerPoint annotation tools (discussed in Chapter 12), although not quite the same.

TABLE 10-1: Whiteboard Annotation Tools

Icon	Tool name	Description
	Chose a Color	Allows you to choose what color your annotation tool will mark in. During meetings, you can have different teammates chose a color so that each meeting participant as a unique way to identify each other.
	Select and Type	Allows you to add text to the whiteboard.
	Choose Drawing Tool	Clicking this reveals a set of drawing tools which you can use to add shapes and lines to the whiteboard.
	Choose Pen Tool	Allows you to draw freehand on the whiteboard.
	Stamp	Clicking this tool gives you access to three stamps—Arrow, Check, and X—that you can use to mark the presentation slide.
	Insert Image	Allows you to add an image from the folder of your choice to the presentation slide.
	Save with Annotations	Activates a dialog where you can navigate to a folder and save the whiteboard with its various annotations.

Choosing a Color for Your Annotations

The default color for text, stamp and drawing tools is black. To make your annotations stand out from others, you can select a color before using those annotation tools. To select a color, click the Choose a Color icon shown in Table 10-1 to open a color palette appears as shown in Figure 10-27.

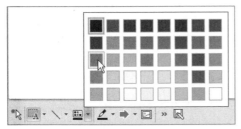

FIGURE 10-27: The Color Palette

In the example used in this chapter, Joe selects red, although you cannot see that in this book.

Annotating the Whiteboard with Text

One of the primary ways people communicate in whiteboard sessions is by writing on the whiteboard, in the case of an in-person session, or by applying text to it in the case of an online session. To apply text to the whiteboard, click the Select and Type icon to select a font and font size. Only selection of the font size is shown in Figure 10-28, but you select the font in the same way.

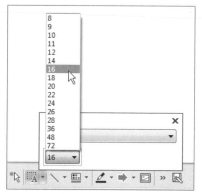

FIGURE 10-28: Selecting a Font Size

To insert text at any location in the whiteboard, simply click in the whiteboard and type the text you want, as shown in Figure 10-29.

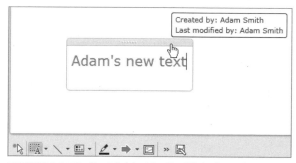

FIGURE 10-29: Text Added to the Whiteboard

Adding Lines, Arrows, etc.

You can add lines, ovals, squares, and rectangles to the whiteboard by clicking on the Choose Drawing Tool icon shown in action in Figure 10-30.

FIGURE 10-30: Choose Drawing Tool for
Selecting a Line, Arrows, Oval, or Rectangle

To add any of the drawing tools to the whiteboard, you simply click and drag in
the whiteboard. Figure 10-33 shows the rectangle drawing tool being used to create
a rectangle around the sample text.

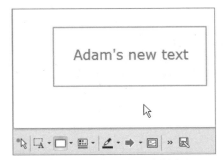

FIGURE 10-31: Whiteboard with a
Rectangle Added

Drawing Freehand

Lync also provides tools for drawing freehand in the whiteboard. Select a specific
one by clicking the Choose Pen Tool icon, as shown in Figure 10-32.

FIGURE 10-32: Pen Selection
in the Choose Pen Tool List

Figure 10-33 shows the sample text underlined with the highlighter tool in the whiteboard.

FIGURE 10-33: Slide Annotated with a Highlighter Tool

Adding Stamps

Lync also offers a choice of three stamps to use with whiteboards. In this example, Adam clicks the Arrow Stamp tool, as shown in Figure 10-34, selects the Arrow stamp, and clicks the whiteboard to place the arrow next to his sample text, as shown in Figure 10-35.

FIGURE 10-34: Selecting the Arrow Stamp

FIGURE 10-35: Arrow Stamp Added

Inserting Images

Lync also provides the ability to add images to a whiteboard. For the example used in the chapter, Teresa might want to add an image of a proposed floor plan. Or, as is done here, someone may want to add a Gantt chart showing the project schedule. To add a picture to the whiteboard, click the Insert Image icon, shown and described in Table 10-1. A Windows Explorer window will open to allow you to navigate to the image you want. Once you've found the image you want click Open. In the example, Adam uses the Insert Image tool to insert a Gantt chart in the whiteboard that the participants can discuss and mark up. See Figure 10-36.

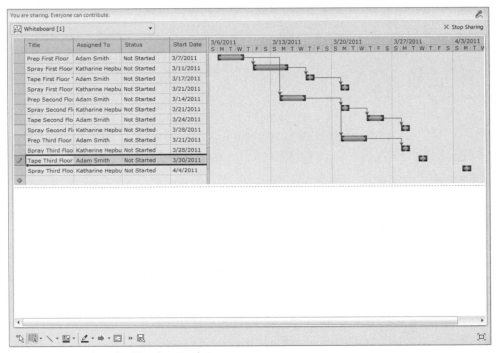

FIGURE 10-36: Let the Meeting Begin!

Saving the Annotated Whiteboard as Meeting Notes

After the meeting is finished, you can save the whiteboard file by clicking the Save with Annotations icon, shown in Table 10-1. You can also add it to the project SharePoint site if you desire. This is a great way to document the meeting!

What You've Learned

Using the power of Office 365, you can obtain the views of the key participants in the project without the time and expense associated with various people from scattered geographical locations traveling to attend an in-person meeting.

Specifically, you've learned how to:

- Use Outlook to schedule an online meeting

- As an invitee, accept a meeting invitation using Outlook

- As the meeting organizer, see who is planning to attend the meeting, who will not attend, who may attend, and who has not yet responded

- As an invitee, accept a meeting invitation using your browser-based email, and, if you have never attended a Lync online meeting, how to make sure your computer is ready

- Facilitate a brainstorming session using a shared whiteboard

- Use the whiteboard tools during the session

- Save the annotated whiteboard as documentation of the session

What's Next?

SharePoint includes numerous features for sharing team knowledge. Chapter 11 considers four of those features:

- **Surveys:** These are the most structured. You use them for obtaining the team's answers to specific questions, in a particular order.

- **Discussion boards:** These are SharePoint lists on which team members can post questions and issues for response by the team. Members can participate in discussion boards according to their interests and expertise.

- **Wiki:** This is a team knowledge base that is created and maintained by team members. Some members of the team create wiki entries, some edit and correct entries, and some just use the knowledge stored in the wiki.

- **Blog:** Team members with special expertise, knowledge, or position on the team can opine to the rest of the team in the form of a blog.

Of Course, This Would Never Happen in <u>Your</u> Business...

Ringo Nash, chief river guide, and Sue Winstrom, owner of Majestic River Ventures (MRV), are sitting in the late afternoon sun at Majestic's annual guide wrap-up. The season has just ended and staff bonuses have just been paid.

"Sue, what a great year! High water late, good clients, and way over our sales goal—we had a lot of great..."

"You know what really bugs me, Ringo?" Sue doesn't usually interrupt, but she's deep in thought.

"No, what?" Ringo is curious at the look on her face.

"Look at those guides."

"Yeah, that's harmless. They're just horsing around."

"Sure, sure. That's not what I mean. What I mean is—well, how many guides did we have, counting the part-timers?"

"Hmm. Maybe 20 or so."

"Right. And how many trips?"

"37?"

"That's my number, too. So now, at the end of the season, off they go with all that experience and knowledge."

"Well, we can hire them back next year!" With a big bonus check in his pocket, Ringo is in no mood to be down.

"Some of them, but they'll forget by then. I just wish there were a way for us to capture what they know—right now." Sue's frustrated.

"You mean a survey or something?"

"Maybe. Did you listen to Kelly telling those stories about the petroglyphs on the canyon walls?"

"Yeah, she knows a lot, but doesn't she major in that stuff at Central State?"

"How do we capture that?"

"A video or something?"

"Nobody's going to remember stuff like that from a video."

"No, probably not."

"Well, anyway, there she goes, and I doubt she'll be back next year. She wants to go to New Zealand. Maybe I'll call her and ask her to tape some of it before she goes."

"Hey, Sue, she's not the only one. I wish I knew half as much as Stanley on running the holes in the Skykomish, or Rob on the brown bears on the Copper."

"You're right. Well, good-bye to another season, anyway."

It Doesn't Have to Be That Way...

Sharing Team Knowledge

SUE'S RIGHT—THOSE 20 OR SO RIVER GUIDES do have knowledge that MRV needs—knowledge about equipment, food, rivers, flora and fauna, river history, and much more. Plus, not every team member has the same knowledge. Majestic needs a way for river guides to share their knowledge and record it for use by guides in the future.

It can be done. SharePoint includes numerous features for sharing team knowledge. This chapter considers four of those features in decreasing order of structure.

- **Surveys:** These are the most structured. Use them for obtaining the team's answers to specific questions, in a particular order.

- **Discussion boards:** These are SharePoint lists on which team members can post questions and issues for response by the team. Members can participate in discussion boards according to their interests and expertise.

- **Wiki:** This is a team knowledge base that is created and maintained by team members. Some members of the team create wiki entries, some edit and correct entries, and some just use the knowledge stored in the wiki.

- **Blog:** Team members with special expertise, knowledge, or position on the team can opine to the rest of the team in the form of a blog.

Specifically, in this chapter you'll learn how to use SharePoint to:

- Create and take a team survey
- Set up and participate in online discussions
- Use wikis to record team knowledge
- Publish personal opinions and knowledge using blogs

These SharePoint features are especially useful for virtual, geographically distributed teams. They enable team members to share opinions, ideas, and knowledge across time zones and geography. These features are especially useful when some team members are less skilled in speaking English (or whatever the team's language is) and struggle to express themselves verbally. These features are also effective for obtaining opinions from soft-spoken or shy team members who may be reluctant to share their considerable knowledge in meetings or conference calls.

Please note that SharePoint provides an industrial-strength version of each of these features. To do full justice to them would require a full chapter for each, or more. Here, you will learn how to use simple versions of them to solve real problems, but you should consider this chapter an introduction, overview, and sampling of how you can use each one. Once you know the nature and basic working of each in this chapter, you can learn more advanced capabilities, if you need them, from the SharePoint help documentation or other sources.

Using Team Surveys

A survey is a list of questions to which team members respond; SharePoint provides an easy way to create them. You can set up surveys so that team members can respond to the survey only once or many times. Members' answers can be anonymous if the survey creator specifies so.

Creating a Survey

A survey is a *list* of questions and you create one using a special type of list. To create the survey, follow these steps:

1. Click Create→ Filter By and then click List. Select Survey, as shown in Figure 11-1. In this example, the user at MRV is creating a list to survey river guides' opinions about camp food named Food Survey.

   In Figure 11-1, if you click the More Options button, you can specify whether survey responses are to be anonymous and whether users can respond to a survey more than once. In Figure 11-2, the survey creator has selected public responses with just one response.

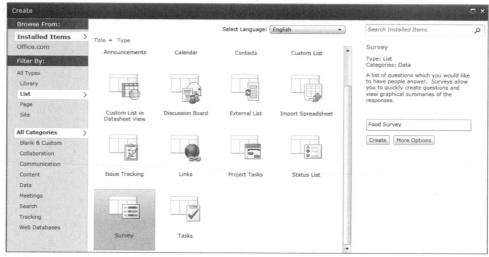

FIGURE 11-1: Creating a Survey List

Note

When setting up a survey, you might want to allow multiple responses so that you can test the survey questions yourself multiple times. When you are satisfied with the survey, you can change to single responses before asking your team members to respond. To change the survey options, go to the survey, select Settings→ Survey Settings, and then click Title, description, and navigation.

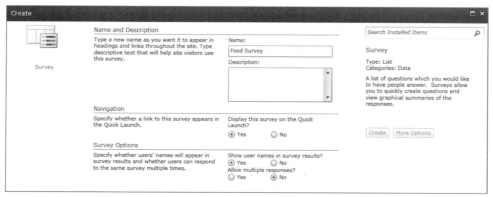

FIGURE 11-2: Specifying Survey Options

2. Click Create, and SharePoint opens a page for creating the first question, as shown in Figure 11-3. In MRV's survey, the response to this question should be a number

between 0 and 15, and the survey creator has set up the options accordingly. Figure 11-4 shows the bottom portion of the question creation page.

3. Click Next Question to add the next question. Click Finish after you have added all the questions.

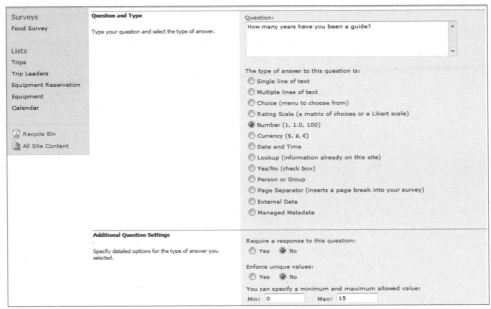

FIGURE 11-3: Creating a Question with a Bounded Numeric Answer

> **Note** Note in Figure 11-4 the comment about branching logic. To create branching logic, you first create all the questions and then specify how answers to one question determine the pathway to other questions. As this page states, you go to the Survey Settings page to define the branching logic. It's easy to do.

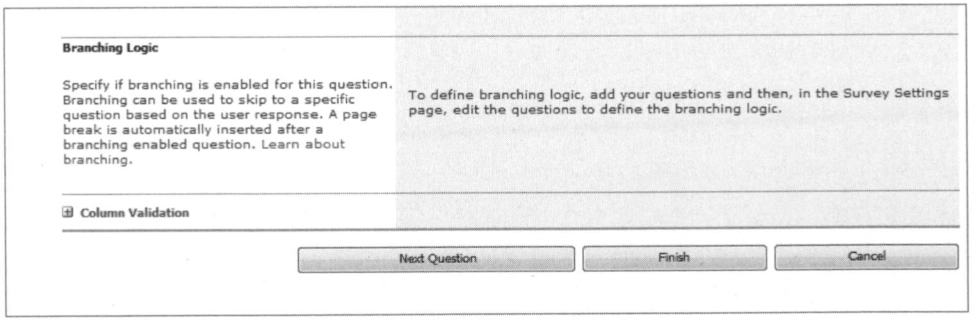

FIGURE 11-4: Remainder of Question Creation Page

Figure 11-5 shows the question creation page for a question that has multiple choices. The text of this question (not shown) is, "Which rivers have you guided?" The choices are the four rivers shown. As specified at the bottom of this figure (via the Checkboxes option), respondents can select more than one option. This makes sense because a guide may have guided several rivers. If the survey creator had selected Radio Buttons to display question choices, then respondents would only have been able to select one river.

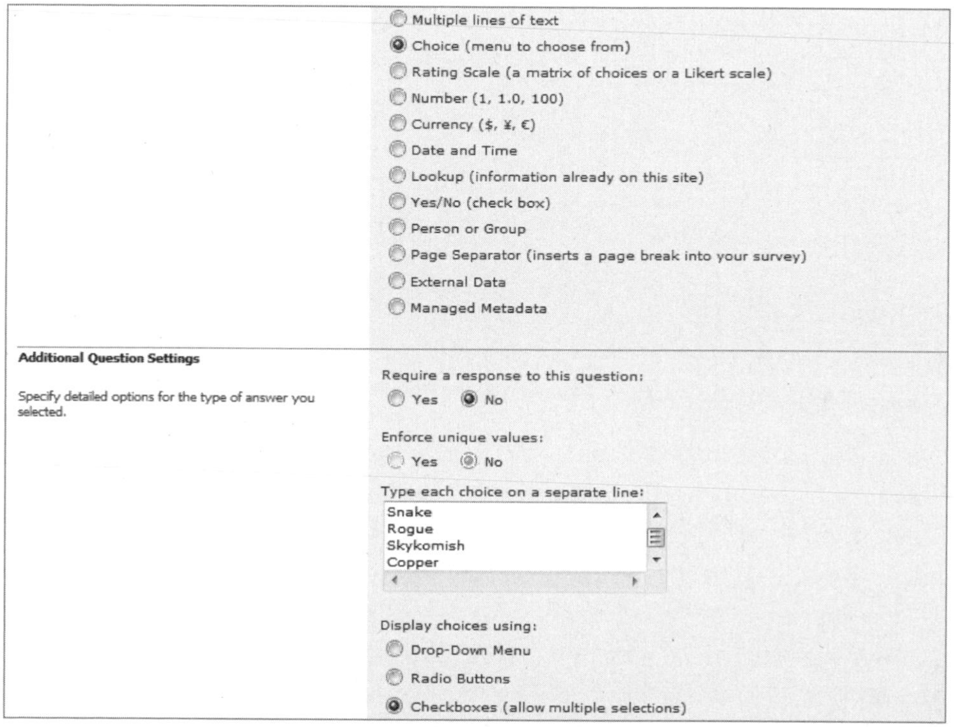

FIGURE 11-5: Creating a Multiple-Answer Choice Question

A rating scale question is one in which the respondents will be shown subquestions and asked to rate each on some scale, say 1 to 5 or 1 to 100. In Figure 11-6, the user is creating a survey question about MRV's food. The question text is not visible in this figure, but it asks the respondent to rate food. As shown, the user has selected Rating Scale and then created the entries to be rated in the sub-question box. The user specified a number range of 5, for 1 to 5, and added text for the minimum, median, and maximum values of Bad, Average, and Great. If you want to see how this question appears to the survey respondents, skip ahead to Figure 11-8.

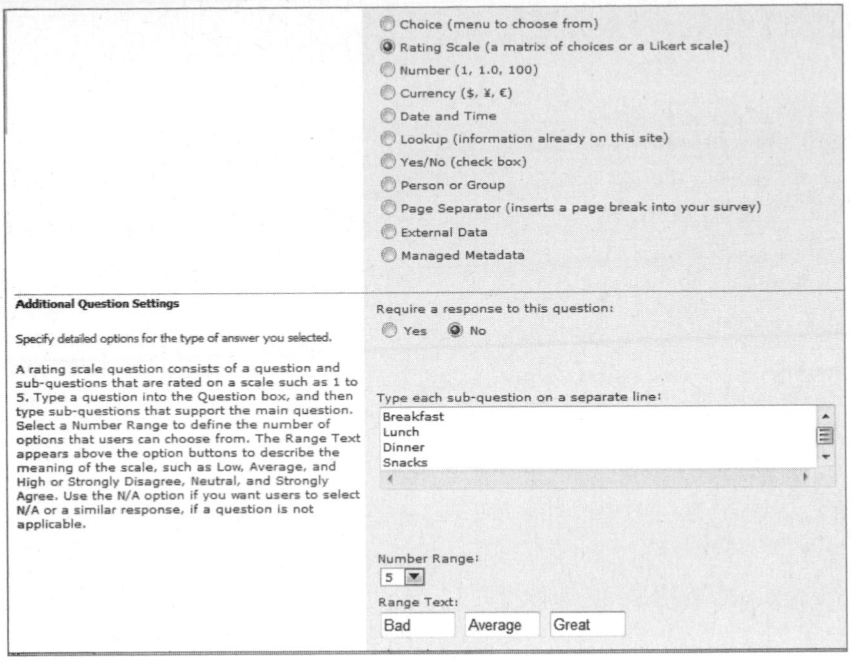

FIGURE 11-6: Creating a Rating Scale Question

Surveys are a great way of "taking the team's temperature." You can use them to find out if the team understands the team's goals, or if the team is satisfied with it's current progress, or if the team believes a certain task is complete. Surveys are also good for detecting changes in team opinions. You can give a survey at the start of a project and again in the middle, and compare results.

Surveys that require more than, say, 10 minutes, are not effective. Survey respondents become bored and answer carelessly. Unless you're a professional survey creator, make it short.

When creating a survey, you also want to keep an important maxim in mind: Never ask a question to which you don't want the answer. If you learn, for example, that the team thinks its management is poor, are you prepared to do something about team management? If not, experience would say: don't ask.

Responding to a Survey

When you click Finish after adding the last question, SharePoint displays the page shown in Figure 11-7. This page also appears whenever a team member clicks the survey name in the Quick Launch or in Lists. Team members take the survey by clicking Respond to the Survey.

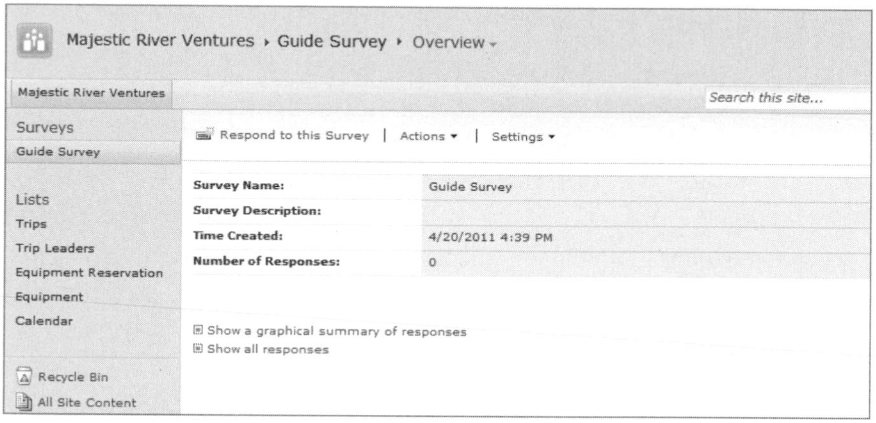

FIGURE 11-7: Default Survey Page

Figure 11-8 shows the page that MRV guides use to respond to this survey. Notice how SharePoint has formatted the answers in accordance with the type of question. The numeric question has a single text box for data entry. The multiple choice question has check boxes, and the rating scale has ratings with the proper labels. Although the preceding section did not show how to make this type of question, the survey also includes two choice-questions that were restricted to a single answer, as shown in Figure 11-8.

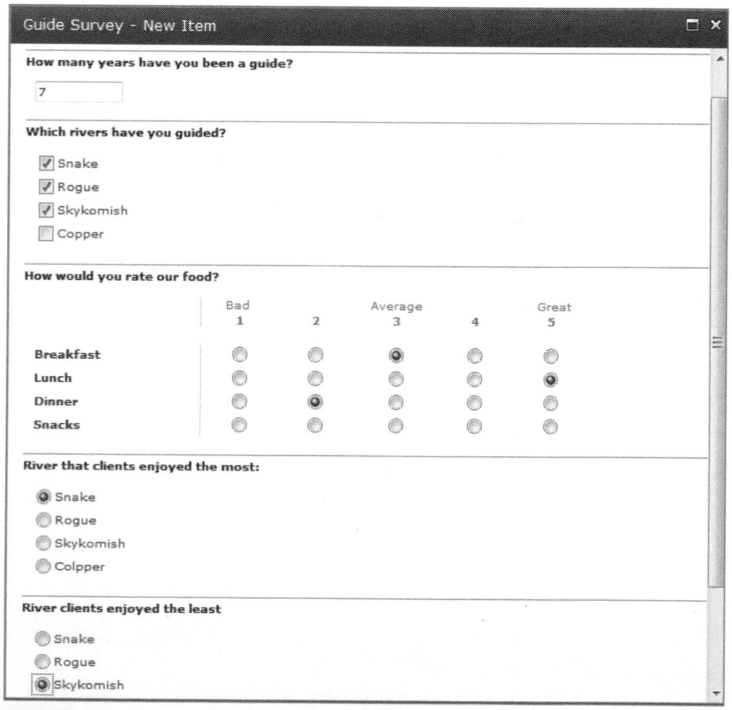

FIGURE 11-8: Page for Taking a Survey

Viewing Survey Results

Now that all your respondents have taken your survey, Office 365 gives you very easy options to view the results. The following list shows the various options:

- **Show a graphical summary of responses:** To best way to view survey results is to click the Show a graphical summary of responses link in the default survey page (refer to Figure 11-7). Again, you can get to this page by clicking the name of the survey in Quick Launch. Anyone with contribute or higher permission on the site can view the results.

Figure 11-9 shows the results of questions 2 and 3 of the MRV survey after it had been taken by four guides. You can see that two guide had guided on just one river, one had guided on three, and one respondent had guided on four. The rivers are named in the summary, as well.

The responses to the rating scale are easily assimilated from this graphical display. In fact, rating scales are one of the best ways of getting the sense of the team on a possibly controversial issue. In this figure, the team views MRV snacks as the best and breakfasts as the worst meal. The responses would likely be more informative if more guides had taken the survey.

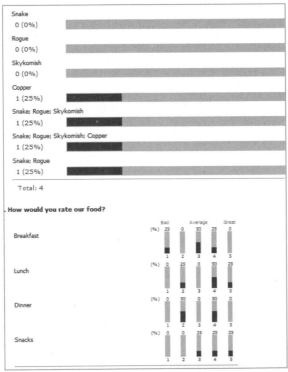

FIGURE 11-9: Graphical Summary of Survey Results

- **Show all responses:** You click this link, shown earlier in Figure 11-7, to see which team members have responded to the survey, as illustrated in Figure 11-10.
- **View Response #:** If you click a specific response number, as shown in Figure 11-10, SharePoint displays that user's answers, as shown in Figure 11-11.

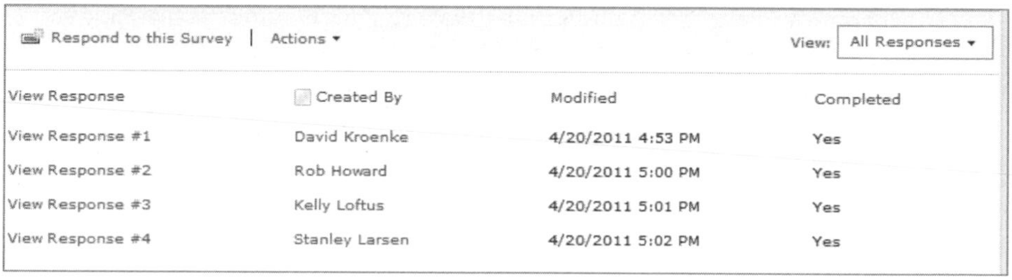

FIGURE 11-10: List of Survey Responses

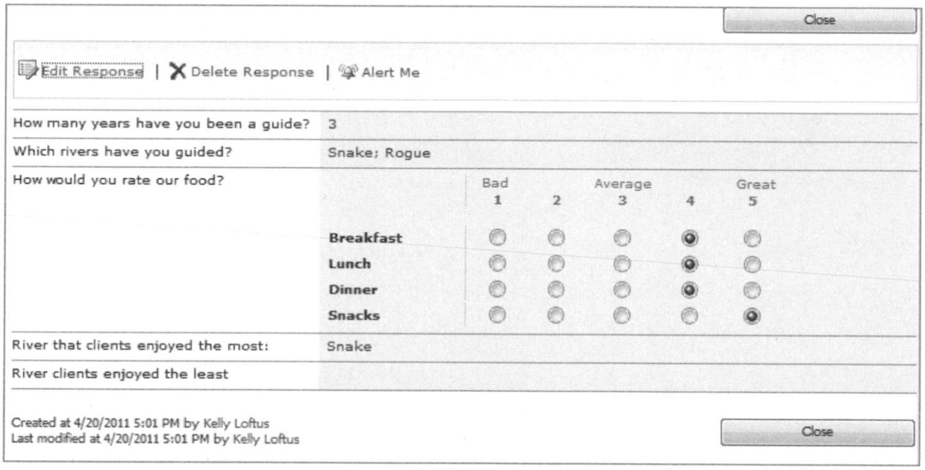

FIGURE 11-11: Question Answers of One Respondent

Creating and Using a Discussion Board

SharePoint provides a forum called a *discussion board* for conducting online discussions as a special type of library. In the forum, team members can post questions or issues and other team members can respond either to the original posting or to responses to that posting. All the postings and responses are stored as library items, but are linked to one another as specified by the users. SharePoint also provides purpose-built pages for viewing postings and responses. You will see how this works in this section.

Using terms from Chapter 1, a *discussion board* facilitates an asynchronous team discussion. Just as in a face-to-face, synchronous meeting, someone says something and others respond, so, too, in a discussion board, one member says something by creating a new entry, and others respond to it by creating responses.

Creating a Discussion Library

As we previously stated, a discussion board is a type of library. To create and use one, follow these steps:

1. Click Create → Filter By Library, and select Discussion Board, as shown in Figure 11-12.

2. Enter a name. In Figure 11-12, the user entered River Evaluations.

3. Click Create and SharePoint will create the library.

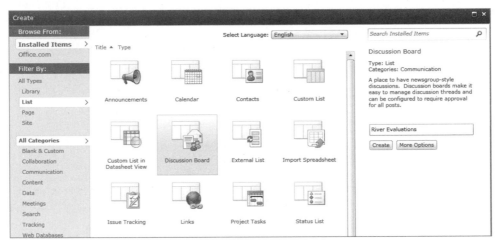

FIGURE 11-12: Creating a Discussion Board

Contributing to the Discussion

Once the discussion board is created, you can start and add to a discussion:

1. Go to that library and click Add new discussion, adding an item as you do in any library. In response, SharePoint displays the page shown in Figure 11-13.

In this example, the user is entering a subject asking MRV team members to offer opinions on why clients don't enjoy a particular river. The post creator adds both a subject and the body of the post.

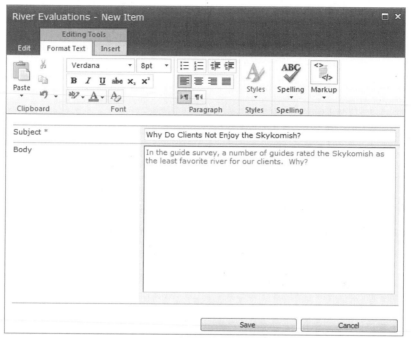

FIGURE 11-13: Starting a New Discussion Item

2. Click Save, the new item is added to the list and SharePoint displays the page shown in Figure 11-14.

FIGURE 11-14: Discussion Board with One Item

3. To view the item, click it in the discussion board library. SharePoint displays the item in a special discussion board page, as shown in Figure 11-15.

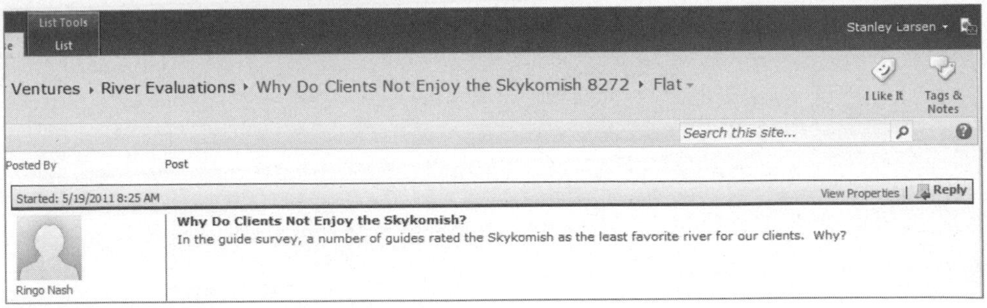

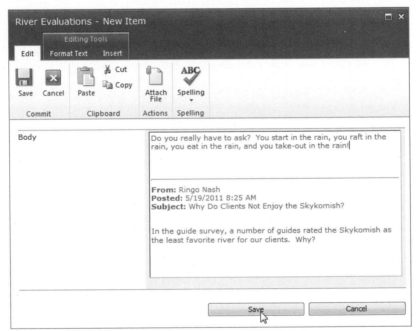

FIGURE 11-15: Discussion Board Item Page

4. To respond to the discussion item, click Reply. SharePoint displays a page for entering the response, like that shown in Figure 11-16. Notice the item to be responded to is at the bottom, and the response is at the top of this page.

FIGURE 11-16: Entering a Response to a Discussion Board Item

5. Click Save. SharePoint displays the page shown in Figure 11-17.

This default format, which is called *Flat*, shows each entry with the same margin, and it is not graphically clear that the second item refers to the first. You can click Show Quoted Messages to see the response. However, an easier-to-interpret display results by using the *Threaded* format.

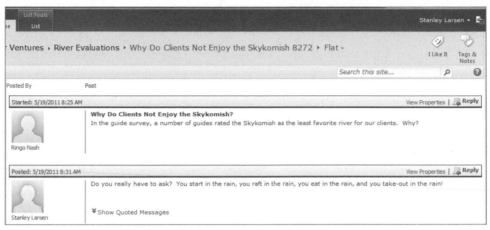

FIGURE 11-17: Discussion Board in Flat Format

To convert a discussion board library display to threaded format, follow these steps:

1. Click the down arrow at the end of the navigation breadcrumbs at the top of the display.

2. Select Threaded. SharePoint opens the page shown in Figure 11-18. Note how the second entry is indented under the first.

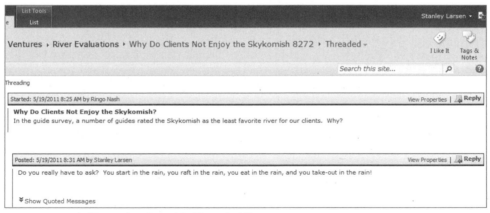

FIGURE 11-18: Discussion Board in Threaded Format

3. To reply to a response, click Reply above the response text. Enter your reply as shown in Figure 11-19. SharePoint displays the reply to the response as indented under the response—in other words, another level of indentation occurs, as shown in Figure 11-20.

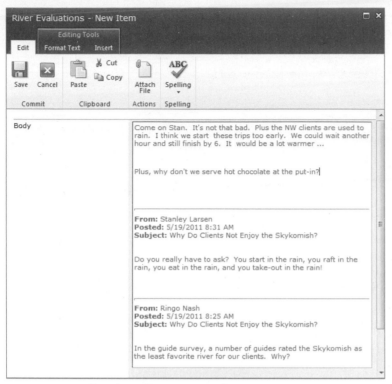

FIGURE 11-19: Entering a Response to a Response

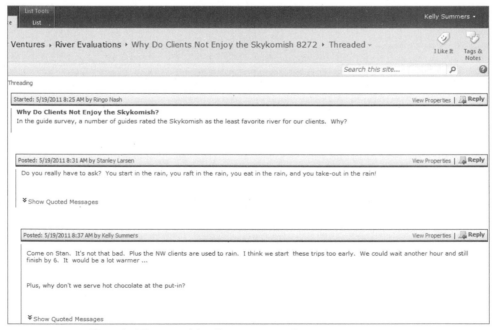

FIGURE 11-20: Threaded Format with a Response to a Response

A discussion board can have many different top-level discussion items, and each of those can have many responses and responses, to responses, as you would expect. Figure 11-21 shows the MRV discussion board with two top-level entries.

By the way, discussion items can include pictures, audio, video, and URL links as well as text.

FIGURE 11-21: Discussion Board with Two Top-level Entries

Storing Team Knowledge with a Wiki

A *wiki* is a SharePoint library that is designed to enable members to document their knowledge in pages and link those pages to other pages in the wiki. Any entry in a wiki can link to many other pages, and any other page can link back to it. Wikis thus have a more flexible structure than discussion boards, which are limited to a hierarchical structure.

Wiki pages can contain text, pictures, audio, and video and can be formatted in rich and interesting ways. Whereas teams use discussion boards for conducing asynchronous discussions, they use wikis more for storing team knowledge. Wikis allow the team to integrate the knowledge they possess as individuals into an integrated team encyclopedia. The Wiki makes that integrated team knowledge available to team members both now and in the future.

Wiki entries can be changed or deleted by anyone with contribute permissions. Team members are usually good at detecting erroneous changes, just like on Wikipedia, but team members need to remember that nothing is cast in stone on a wiki and errors can creep in without careful attention.

Creating a Wiki Library

You have to create a wiki library before anyone can contribute to the wiki. To create a wiki library, follow these steps:

1. Select Create → Filter By Library, and then select Wiki Page Library, as shown in Figure 11-22.

2. Enter a name for the wiki library; here the user entered **River Knowledge**.

3. Click Create and SharePoint creates the wiki.

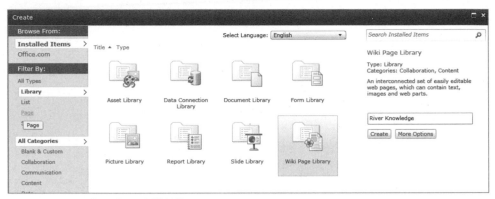

FIGURE 11-22: Creating a Wiki Library

By default, SharePoint creates a wiki with two pages. The first, shown in Figure 11-23, explains what a wiki is and describes potential uses. That first page has a link to a second page that explains how to add and manage wiki entries (inside the circle). You can read that second page to learn more, but you need not read it to continue here.

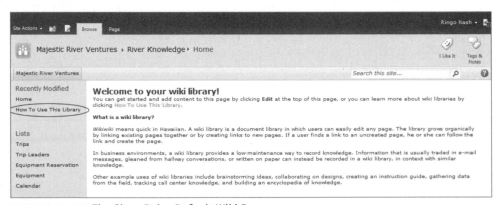

FIGURE 11-23: The SharePoint Default Wiki Page

> **ADVICE** In most cases, teams decide to remove the default pages. To do so, while viewing the top-level wiki entry, click *Page* → *Delete* Page, as shown in Figure 11-24. Delete the How to Use This Library page in the same way as well.

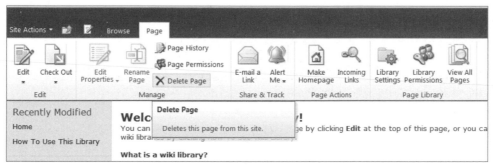

FIGURE 11-24: Deleting a Wiki Page

At this point, the wiki library is empty, as shown in Figure 11-25.

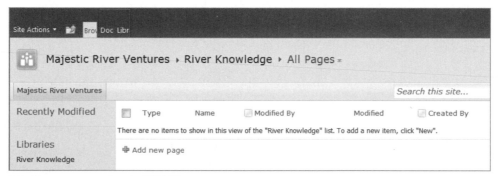

FIGURE 11-25: An Empty Wiki Library

Contributing to the Wiki

Now that you've created the wiki library, everyone with contribute permission on the site can add to it. To contribute to the wiki:

1. Click Add new page in the library's content list (refer to Figure 11-25). SharePoint responds with the dialog box shown in Figure 11-26.

2. Enter the name of the new wiki entry here. Click Create. SharePoint displays the page shown in Figure 11-27 for creating new wiki entries.

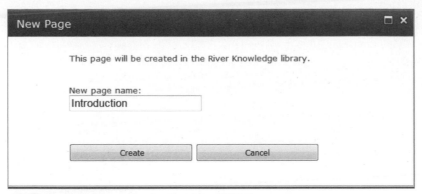

FIGURE 11-26: Dialog Box for Naming a Wiki Entry

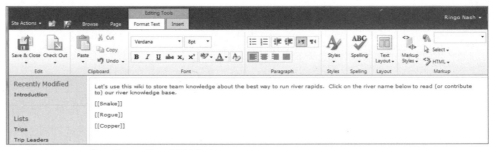

FIGURE 11-27: Creating a New Wiki Entry

3. Add text and other elements to the page as you would for any other document.

4. When you enter text, you can create a link to another page by typing the name of the page you want to link to in double brackets. For example, [[Snake]] tells SharePoint to insert a link to a page named Snake. You can do this even before you've created that linked-to page. In Figure 11-27, the user has created links to three pages for each of the rivers named.

5. Click Save & Close. SharePoint creates the wiki page. See Figure 11-28 for the resulting page. Notice that the links to the three pages have a dashed underline. This notation means that those pages do not yet exist.

6. To create one of those pages, click its link, as shown in Figure 11-28. SharePoint displays the dialog box to create the page, as shown in Figure 11-29. Click Create to create the new page.

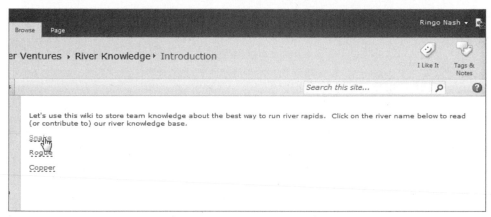

FIGURE 11-28: Wiki Page with Three Links to Nonexistent Pages

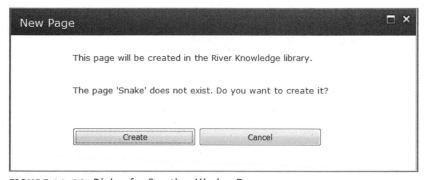

FIGURE 11-29: Dialog for Creating Missing Page

Figure 11-30 shows a user creating the missing page for the Snake River. Notice that the user who created the first page was Ringo Nash, but the user who is creating this page is Rob Howard. Thus, different users can create different pages and link them together. Users can also edit one another's pages in the same way that they would edit their own.

Figure 11-30 shows one other possibility. Examine the last page link. It is a link to the page named Introduction, which already exists. However, the user the user wants SharePoint to name the link something other than Introduction. To do so, the user entered a straight vertical bar after Introduction (the name of the page) and then the words Back to Top. When SharePoint displays the page, it shows the text *Back to Top* rather than the page's name, Introduction, as shown in Figure 11-31.

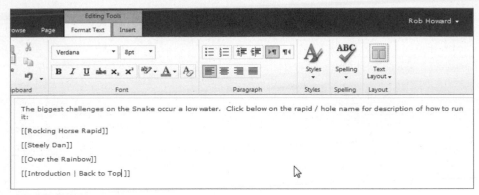

FIGURE 11-30: Creating the Missing Page

Notice in Figure 11-31 that the first three links have a dashed underline, indicating that they do not yet exist. The fourth entry is not underlined because the page to which it refers, the Introduction page, already exists.

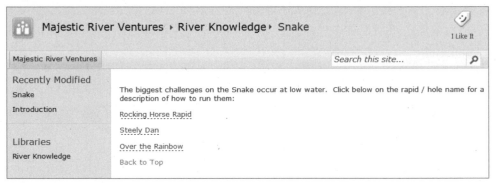

FIGURE 11-31: Wiki Page with Links to Non-existing and Existing Pages

A wiki library is like any SharePoint library, but unlike document libraries, wiki libraries contain wiki pages rather than document names. As shown in Figure 11-32, the pages are listed in the wiki library, just like documents are in any other library. To view the page, click it. From there, you can follow links through the entire library.

Type	Name	Modified By	Modified	Created By	Created
	Rocking Horse Rapid ⬜ NEW	Rob Howard	4/21/2011 11:20 AM	Rob Howard	4/21/2011 11:20 AM
	Snake ⬜ NEW	Rob Howard	4/21/2011 11:19 AM	Rob Howard	4/21/2011 11:17 AM
	Introduction ⬜ NEW	Ringo Nash	4/21/2011 11:13 AM	Ringo Nash	4/21/2011 11:11 AM
➕ Add new page					

FIGURE 11-32: Wiki Library Pages

Cleaning Up the Quick Launch

The top of the Majestic River Ventures SharePoint Quick Launch (the vertical menu on the left part of the screen) looks as shown in Figure 11-33 It has three separate headings, one for the wiki library, one for the discussion board, and one for the survey.

The site will be easier for MRV employees to use if these three headings are consolidated under one heading. Further because these features represent base knowledge and are not used for the operation of the business, MRV decides to put that consolidated heading on the bottom of the Quick Launch menu.

Note   For more information on SharePoint Quick Launch, see Chapters 4 and 5.

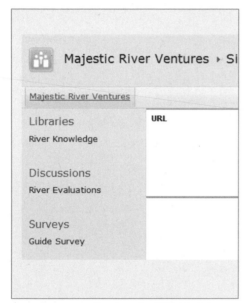

FIGURE 11-33: Top Level of MRV Quick Launch with Too Many Headings

The process of consolidating these entries and moving the consolidation of them to the bottom of Quick Launch is a simple application of skills you already have. Just follow these steps:

1. Go to the home page and, in the lower-left corner, click Customize the Quick Launch.

2. In the page that appears, click the Edit icon next to the word Libraries. In the box labeled Type the description, type in a more informative title—in this example, **Team Knowledge**. Click OK.

3. To move the link to the River Evaluations discussion board under the new Team Knowledge heading, click the Edit icon next to River Evaluations in the page you used in step 2, above. SharePoint opens the page shown in Figure 11-34.

4. In that page, highlight the URL text and copy it to the Clipboard by pressing Ctrl + C.

Alternatively, you can just click River Evaluations, go to that page, and copy the URL from your browser's address bar.

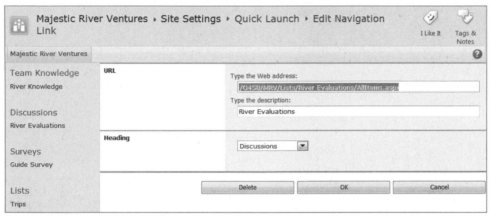

FIGURE 11-34: Obtaining the URL to the River Evaluations Discussion Board

5. Once have the URL, click Cancel in the page that appears like Figure 11-34.

6. Click New Navigation Link in the Quick Launch editing page from step 2, above. In the page that appears (Figure 11-35), press Ctrl+V to paste the URL you just copied into the box labeled Type the Web address.

7. Type in a new name for the discussion board (in this example, **River Evaluations Discussion**) in the second text box, as shown in Figure 11-35.

8. Select Team Knowledge as the heading under which you want to place the new navigation link.

URL	Type the Web address:
	.sharepoint.com/O4SB/MRV/Lists/River%20Evaluations/AllItems.aspx
	Type the description:
	River Evaluations Discussion
Heading	Team Knowledge
	[Heading]
	OK Cancel

FIGURE 11-35: Pasting the URL for the New Navigation Link

9. Follow the process just described to create a link to the Guide Survey and place it under the Team Knowledge heading, as well.

10. Click Change Order in the Quick Launch edit page and change the order of Team Knowledge to 2. The result will appear as shown in Figure 11-36. (The entries under Lists were created for this site in Chapter 8.)

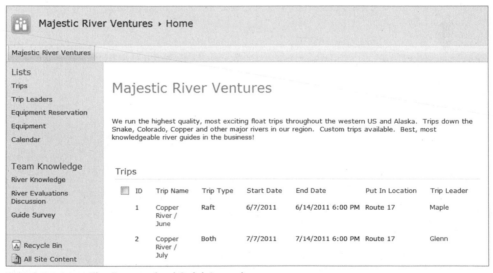

FIGURE 11-36: The Reorganized Quick Launch

Publishing Expertise and Opinions with Blogs

A blog is a SharePoint site that team members can use to publish their personal expertise and to share their own opinions. Unlike surveys, discussion boards, and wikis, which are part of an existing site, a blog is placed into a SharePoint site of its own. Thus, a blog belongs to an individual and not to the team. Because this is so, blogs can be more personal and contain opinions that may not be shared by all team members. At MRV, for example, several of the leaders and experts in the company could have subsites of the primary MRV site for their blogs. This section shows how an MRV employee named Stanley Larsen can publish a blog under the MRV site.

People with ownership permission of the blog site can create new blog entries (called posts) and approve new posts that are submitted by others who do not have ownership permission. People with either ownership or contribute permissions can make comments about blog posts. They can also create new posts for consideration for publishing by owners.

Creating the Blog Site

To create a blog site, follow these steps:

1. Go to the site that will be the parent of the blog. Select Create→ Filter By Sites, and then select Blog Sites. In Figure 11-37, the user is creating a site named Stan's Blog.

2. The creator of this site wants to specify unique site permissions, so, instead of clicking Create, he (here, Stan) clicks More Options to open the page that will enable him to specify unique permissions.

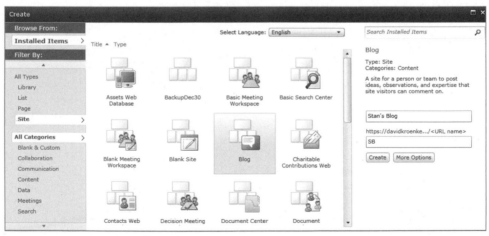

FIGURE 11-37: Creating a Blog Site

3. In the page that appears, select Use unique permissions, as shown in Figure 11-38.

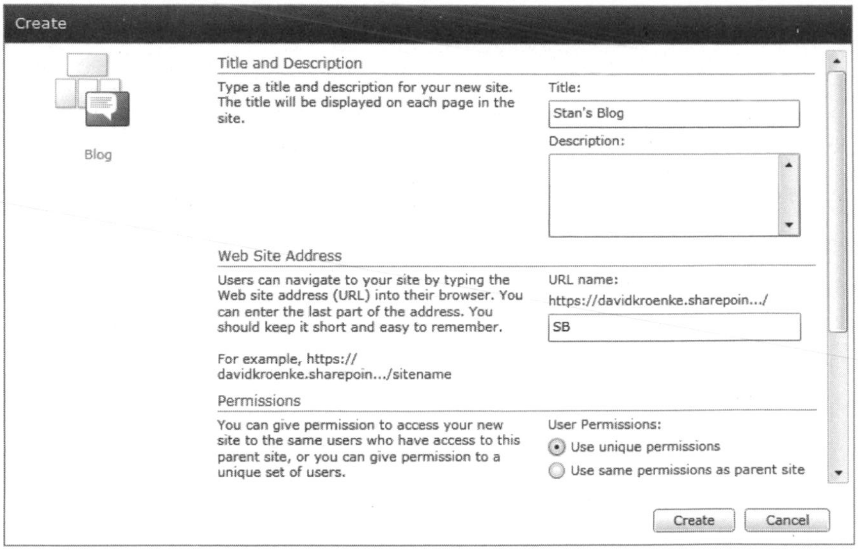

FIGURE 11-38: Setting Unique Permissions for the Blog Site

> **Note**
> Why create unique permissions for a blog? MRV might want some people to be owners of the blog, so they can create entries, but not want them to be owners of the MRV site. Or, MRV might want to restrict the ability to contribute to or read the blog to specified users. Both are possible with unique permissions.

As you can tell from Figure 11-39, Stanley set up the groups so that Stanley, Rob, Kelly, and Joseph Schumpeter can read content on the site, Stanley, Kelly, and Rob can contribute to this site, and Stanley is the sole owner of this site

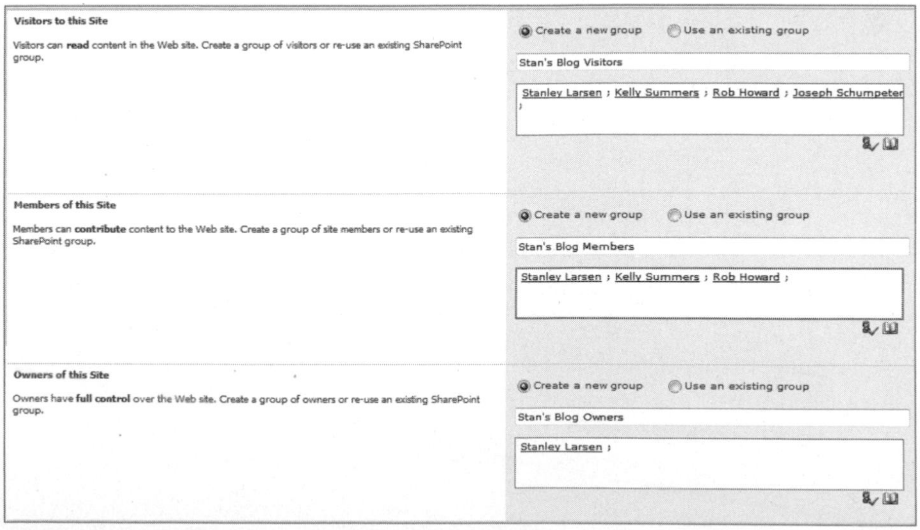

FIGURE 11-39: Setting Up Blog Site Permissions

Blog Post and Comment Permissions

Table 11-1 summarizes blog permissions. As shown, team members with read permission (those in the visitors group) can only read blogs and blog comments. Team members with contribute permissions can create blog posts and submit them for approval / rejection by those with owner permission. Those with contribute permission can also create and publish comments on existing blog entries. Finally, those with owner permission can create and publish both blog entries and comments on existing entries. They also can approve or reject blog entries submitted by contributors.

TABLE 11-1: Blog Post and Comments Permissions

	Read Permission	**Contribute Permission**	**Owner Permission**
Blog posts	Read only	Create and submit for approval / rejection by owners	Create and publish Approve / reject submissions
Comments on blog posts	Read only	Create and publish	Create and publish

These permissions mean that Stanley, as an owner, can create new blog posts and publish them himself. Rob and Kelly, as contributors, can create new posts, but those must be approved by Stanley before SharePoint will publish them on the blog. However, Rob and Kelly can make comments on blog posts that SharePoint will automatically publish. Joe, as visitor, can only read the blog; he can neither create new posts nor can he make comments on existing ones.

Customizing the Blog

Figure 11-40 shows the first page of the blog as created by default by SharePoint. To remove the generic appearance of this site, three elements need to be changed: the categories that appear in the Quick Launch, the text of the first blog entry, and the generic description of the blogger.

Categories are just ways of collecting blog entries. You can have one or three (as shown), twenty-five, or any number. The number doesn't matter. Categories are simply a way of grouping blog posts. By the way, you can place a particular post into multiple categories. You will see how to do that in Figure 11-49.

FIGURE 11-40: Default First Blog Page, Which Needs Three Corrections

To customize your blog, follow these steps:

1. Open the categories list by clicking the Categories heading in the Quick Launch.

2. As shown in Figure 11-41, click the Edit icon next to each category and rename it in the Edit dialog box that SharePoint presents. Figure 11-42 shows the result of the changes that Stanley made. Figure 11-43 shows the appearance of the home page of the blog site after these changes.

FIGURE 11-41: Editing Category Names

FIGURE 11-42: Category Names After Edit

FIGURE 11-43: The Home Page with New Category Names

3. To change the first blog entry, click Manage posts in the menu labeled Blog Tools on the far right of the page.

4. In the page that appears, select the Welcome page and click Edit in the upper-right side of that page. SharePoint produces the dialog shown in Figure 11-44.

Stanley, the user, can delete, add, and edit the blog post in this dialog box. He can also assign that post to one or more categories if he wants.

Figure 11-45 shows the changes that Stanley made to this post. Notice the warning at the top of this form. Because Stan is the owner of this blog site, SharePoint enables the button labeled Publish in the upper left of the ribbon and so the warning is inappropriate. Another non-owner user, however, would not be able to publish. Figure 11-46 shows the first blog post after the change.

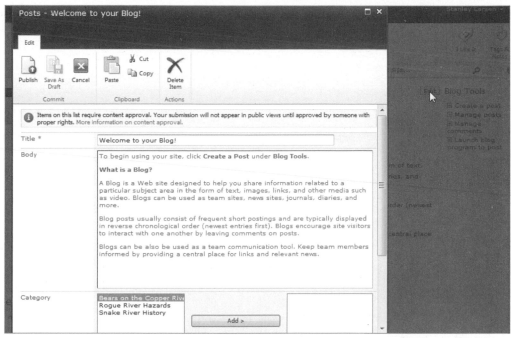

FIGURE 11-44: Editing an Existing Blog Post

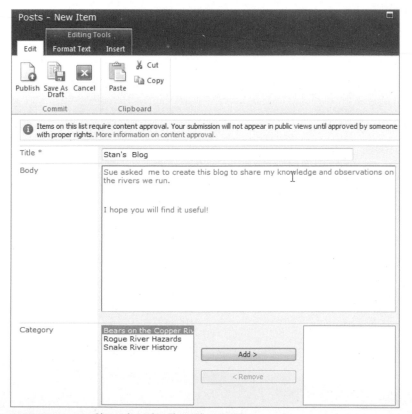

FIGURE 11-45: Changing the First Blog Post

FIGURE 11-46: The Blog with Changed First Post

The final change you need to make is to rewrite the text in the About this blog section of the home page. To do that:

1. Go to the home page, click Site Actions, and then click Edit Page.

2. Edit the text as you desire.

3. Click Save & Close. In Stanley's case, his page appears as shown in Figure 11-47.

FIGURE 11-47: Home Page with a Modified About this blog Text

Creating Blog Posts (Owner)

Team members with owner permission, such as Stanley, can create blog posts as follows:

1. Click Create a post in the menu on the right side of the home page (see Figure 11-47). In response, SharePoint creates the post creation dialog shown in Figure 11-48. Notice the user (again Stanley) added text for Title and Body of this post as shown. He also added it to the Bears on the Copper River. He could have added it to other categories as well.

2. Click Publish. Because Stanley is an owner of this site, the Publish button is enabled. Clicking it posts the blog entry, as shown in Figure 11-49.

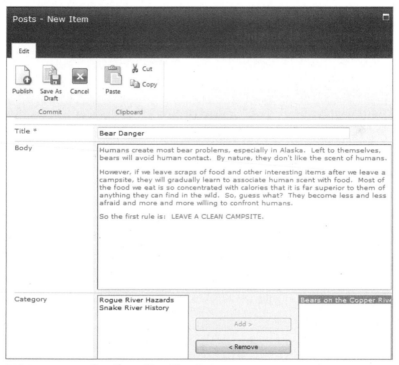

FIGURE 11-48: Creating a New Blog Entry

FIGURE 11-49: Home Page with a New Blog Entry

Creating Comments and Submitting Blog Posts (Contributor)

The new post shown in Figure 11-49 has no comments. However, any user with Contribute permission can create one. In Figure 11-50, a contributor (Rob Howard) clicks the folder icon beside Comments. SharePoint expands the page to include a space for making a comment. In this figure, the contributor adds a comment, which he can then save. Although the contributor is not an owner of this site, his comment is automatically published.

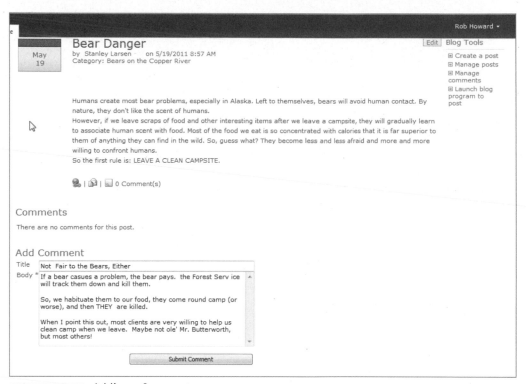

FIGURE 11-50: Adding a Comment

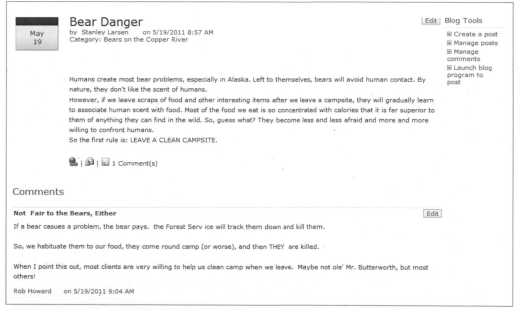

FIGURE 11-51: Post with Comment

As stated, users (like Rob and Kelly), who have contribute permission can create blog posts that will be submitted to the blog owner (Stanley in this case) for approval. In Figure 11-52, Rob is creating a new blog post. Observe that the Publish icon is disabled for him.

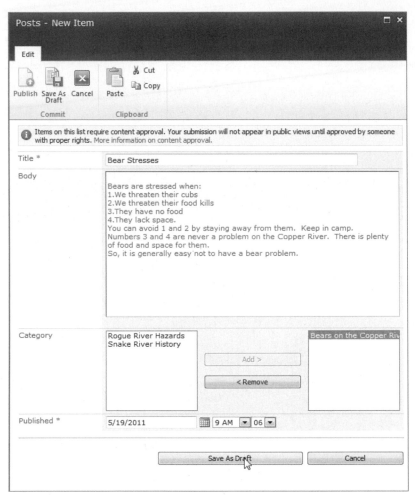

FIGURE 11-52: Creating a New Blog Post without Publish Permission

Approving Blog Posts (Owners)

To publish the post, a site owner (in this case, Stanley), can go to the Posts list that SharePoint uses to manage blog posts, and select Edit Item from the drop-down menu, as shown in Figure 11-53. (Other approval methods exist as well.) In response SharePoint produces the dialog shown in Figure 11-54.

FIGURE 11-53: Approving a Post Using the Posts List Items

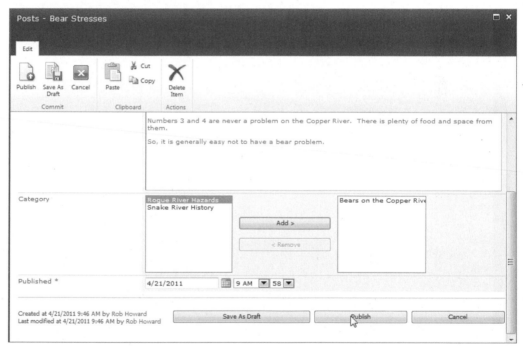

FIGURE 11-54: Publishing a Post Submitted by Non-Owner

Because Stanley is an owner of this site, the Publish icon is enabled and the Publish button appears. When Stanley clicks Publish, Rob's blog post is published to the blog, as shown in Figure 11-55.

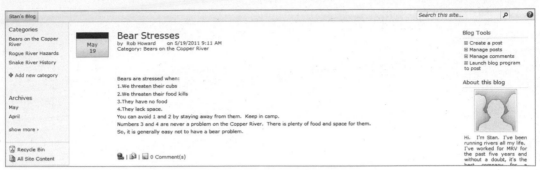

FIGURE 11-55: The Blog with Rob's Post Published

This discussion might make this process seem more complicated than it is. The best way to learn how to use the blogging feature of SharePoint is to create a test site and experiment with it. Using a blog is actually quite easy and a great way for team experts and managers to share their knowledge, thoughts, and opinions—and for others to comment upon them.

What You've Learned

In this chapter you learned about four SharePoint facilities for sharing team knowledge. Surveys are the most structured and are best used for 'taking the team's temperature' on some topic of importance to the team.

Discussion boards are a facility for conducting asynchronous conversations. Someone makes a statement or asks a question and other team members respond to that statement or question. Wiki's are repositories of team knowledge. Any wiki entry can link to many other entries and can be linked to by many other entries.

Finally, blogs are sites in which team members can post their own opinions. Unlike wikis, which represent the team's understanding and knowledge, a blog publishes the thoughts and opinions of an individual within the team.

As you have seen, SharePoint provides a useful array of facilities for teams and individuals to share their knowledge.

What's Next?

The next chapter returns to Lync meetings and shows you how to conduct a public webinar. You will learn how to extend the skills you learned in Chapter 10 to conduct a more formal and controlled virtual presentation.

Of Course, This Would Never Happen in <u>Your</u> Business...

Joe Schumpeter is on a Lync call with Laura Larsen, owner of Larsen Painting:

"Laura, I'm really sorry. We spent weeks planning this presentation, and we received confirmations from everyone that they would attend."

"Well, Joe, there's not much we can do about it now. The money's gone." Laura doesn't sound happy.

"I just can't believe it. I called everyone yesterday, as in Thursday, and they all said they'd be coming."

"How many did come?"

"Of the 23 confirmed attendees? Ah, 4," Misery creeps out of Joe's voice.

Laura is truly puzzled. "Did you talk with any of those who didn't come?"

"I called a half a dozen...they all said they really wanted to attend, but couldn't for various logistical reasons. It could have been GREAT. Sam and Eleanore from the Glacier Peak Lodge project were there. They were going on and on about how much they like us. So why couldn't those people from the city hear that? Or the project managers of the big harbor renewal project? They said they'd be there and we'd have had the best possible word-of-mouth—we just need to get them in the same room."

"Joe, I know you feel badly, but I have to ask. How much did it cost us?"

"About $2,600." Joe is embarrassed—and worried.

"$650 each for the four who showed?"

"Yup."

"Joe, do something else, and ask me before you spend any more money."

"Okay, Laura. I'm on it."

It Doesn't Have to Be That Way...

Remote Presentations Using Lync

IN-PERSON, FACE-TO-FACE SALES SEMINARS are always a risk. As happened to Larsen Painting, people do commit to meetings and then not show, and it's expensive and embarrassing when they don't. Such attendance has always been a problem, but lately, with the frantic 24/7 pace of the professional business world, the problem is worse.

Even when you can get many to attend, what happens? If you have the real decision-makers, the people you want, their phones start to ring. You're lucky if you can get half the attendees to pay attention to half the presentation.

Webinars are the answer. You probably have attended or conducted WebEx events, or other forms of webinar. The good news for Office 365 users is that you can do it with Lync at a fraction of the cost. Plus, Lync provides great integration with Office as you've seen, and particularly great integration with PowerPoint, as you're about to learn.

Specifically, in this chapter, you'll learn how to:

- Use Outlook to schedule an online meeting (brief summary and reference to Chapter 10)
- Use Online Meeting Options to control who has access to the meeting and who can serve as presenters
- Use the special tools built into Lync to conduct an online SharePoint presentation
- Save the marked-up presentation

Using Outlook to Schedule an Online Meeting

Chapter 10 shows how to schedule on online meeting primarily attended by people inside the organization using Office 365. However, in this section, you learn how to schedule a meeting with potential customers—in Joe's case, with people outside of Larsen Printing.

PAUSE AND REFLECT: LET'S DEFINE A FEW BASIC TERMS

The following are a list of terms that you need to know as you're reading through this chapter.

- **Attendee:** An attendee is anyone who is able to join a meeting. Whether attendees automatically join the meeting or they are required to wait in the virtual lobby until admitted by a presenter depends on the meeting options set by the meeting organizer or a presenter. Attendees may also be granted either or both of the following privileges:

  - **Annotate presentation:** Anyone with this privilege can use Lync's annotation tools to annotate the slides in a PowerPoint presentation. Any participant can annotate a shared whiteboard.

  - **View privately:** Those who have this privilege can view content other than what the presenter is showing.

- **Lobby:** Depending on the meeting options set by the meeting organizer or a presenter, some people are not allowed immediately to join a meeting, but are required to wait in a virtual lobby until admitted by a presenter.

- **Meeting Organizer:** The person who sets up the meeting, determines the initial meeting options, and invites people to the meeting. This chapter shows how to do that using Outlook 2010—the most convenient way to organize a meeting. The organizer does not have to join the meeting before anyone else can join. However, if the organizer set the meeting option such that only the organizer can initially be a presenter, then none of the participants can share anything (desktop, application, whiteboard, PowerPoint, etc.). In such a case once the Organizer joins the meeting he or she can promote one or more of the other attendees to be presenters and the meeting can continue.

- **Presenter:** Only presenters can share their desktop and applications, present files, and manage meeting options. Presenters are also the only ones who can admit people into the meeting from the lobby, and promote attendees to be presenters and vice versa. The meeting organizer is a presenter by default.

To schedule an online meeting, follow these steps:

1. Open the Outlook calendar and click the date you want for your meeting. In this example, Joe selects February 16.

2. Because this meeting is a Lync online meeting, click New Online Meeting in the Outlook ribbon, as shown in Figure 12-1.

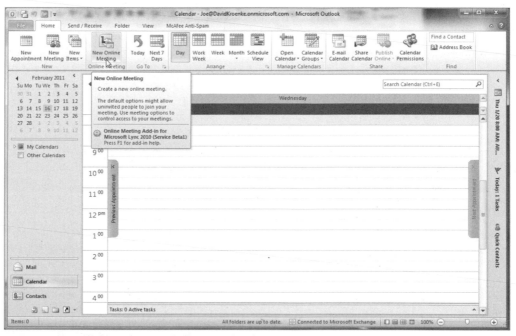

FIGURE 12-1: Clicking the New Online Meeting button

3. Add Attendees to the meeting request. To do this, click Scheduling Assistant in the Outlook ribbon, as shown in Figure 12-2.

4. When the Scheduling Assistant window opens, click Add Attendees, and a window opens with a list of people from the Global Address List (GAL). In this example, this includes only people from Larsen Painting, as shown in Figure 12-3.

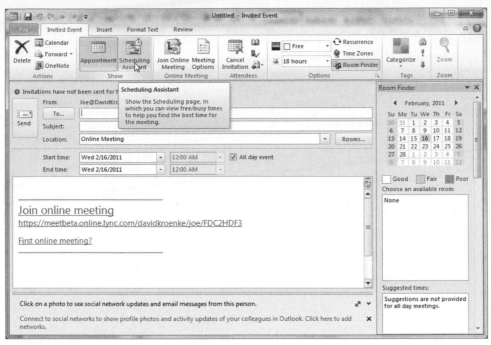

FIGURE 12-2: Clicking the Scheduling Assistant to Add Attendees

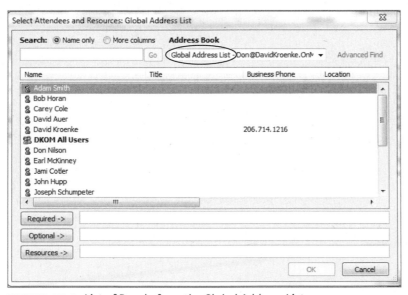

FIGURE 12-3: List of People from the Global Address List

5. To see a list of people not from your Global Address List, expand the Address Book drop-down list, and select Contacts, as shown in Figure 12-4.

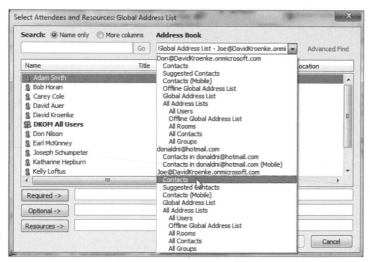

FIGURE 12-4: Select Contacts to See a List of Contacts Outside of Your Company

6. To select people to invite, press and hold the Ctrl key and select people from your list. In this example, Joe selects seven people from his Contacts list to invite to the meeting. When you're done selecting people, release the Ctrl key, click Required, and then click OK, as shown in Figure 12-5.

Note

> By using the Required and Optional boxes in the Add Attendees window, the meeting organizer can indicate to the invitees which ones the organizer feels are essential participants and which are optional so the invitees can make decisions about which meetings they absolutely have to attend.

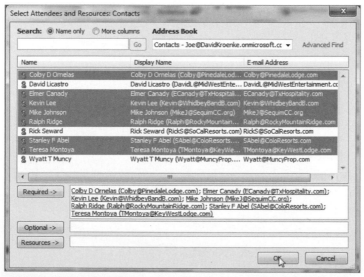

FIGURE 12-5: Adding Seven People from a Contact List as Required Attendees

Figure 12-6 shows the Scheduling Assistant window with the seven attendees added. Notice the slash marks across the calendar for those seven people. That's because those people are outside of Larsen Painting and Outlook is unable to retrieve their free/busy information.

7. Return to the Appointment window by clicking Appointment as shown in Figure 12-6.

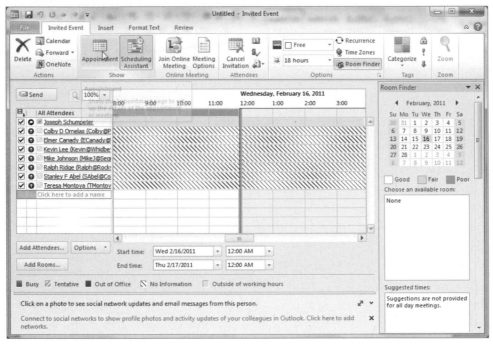

FIGURE 12-6: New Attendees Added

8. Now, select meeting specifics:

   ▪ Add a Subject of the meeting.

   ▪ If this isn't an all-day event, deselect the All day event check box and select a Start time and End time.

   ▪ Enter some text to the body of the meeting request inviting the attendees to join you for an online presentation.

   ▪ You can also add a reminder for those who have not previously attended a Lync online meeting to click the "First online meeting?" link to make sure their computers are all set.

9. Perhaps the default meeting options won't work for your meeting. To change them, click Meeting Options in the Outlook ribbon as shown in Figure 12-7.

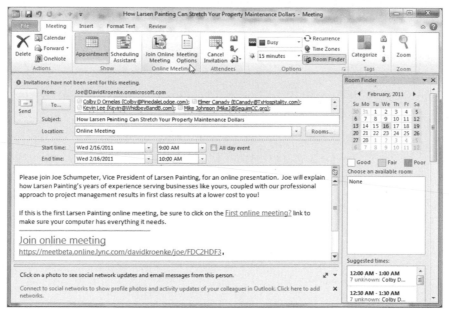

FIGURE 12-7: Meeting Subject, Start and End Times Set, and Invitation Language Added

The Meeting Options dialog has two sections: Access and Presenters, which are discussed in the next two sections.

Access Options

The Access option selected determines which attendees can join the meeting directly, and which ones have to wait in the "lobby" until a presenter admits them. The Access options are:

- **Organizer only (locked):** If this option is chosen, the only one allowed to join the meeting directly is the meeting organizer. Everyone else will have to be admitted by the organizer, who is a presenter by default, or someone admitted by the organizer, then promoted to presenter.

- **People I invite from my company:** Only those from the company who receive invitations are admitted automatically. Others from the company and those outside the company will have to be admitted by a presenter.

- **People from my company:** Anyone from the company, invited or not, is admitted automatically. Those from outside the company must be admitted by a presenter. *This is the default access option.*

- **Everyone including people outside my company (there are no restrictions):** Anyone with a link to the meeting may join and will be automatically admitted.

Presenter Options

The Presenter option selected determines which attendees are granted presenter privileges. The presenter options are:

- **Organizer only:** Obviously this option means that only the meeting organizer can serve as a presenter.

- **People from my company:** Anyone from the company, invited to the meeting or not, can exercise presenter privileges with no further action by the meeting organizer or another presenter. *This is the default presenter option.*

- **Everyone including people outside my company (there are no restrictions):** After admitted to the meeting anyone may serve as a presenter.

- **People I choose:** Joe can select from a list of meeting attendees by clicking the Manage Presenters link. The dialog box used for selecting specific attendees to be presenters is shown in Figure 12-8.

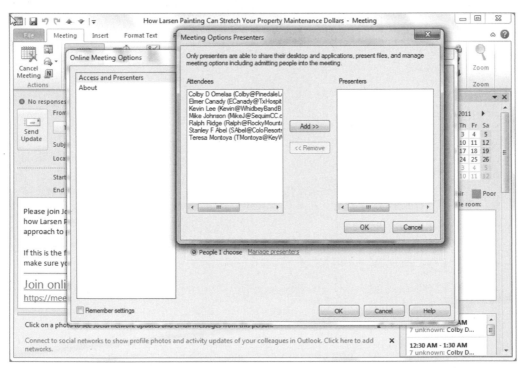

FIGURE 12-8: Selecting Specific Presenters

Joe is fine with the default presenter option of People from my company. Although he intends to do the presentation himself, the possibility exists that an associate may decide to join the meeting, and having them able to pitch in as needed would be useful.

However, Joe is not happy with the default access option. Only people from Larsen Painting are automatically admitted to the meeting, which means Joe may need to interrupt his presentation to admit the people he's invited. That would not only be frustrating for Joe, but, more importantly, to the potential customers that Joe is trying to land. What's more, if someone emails a meeting link to a friend, Joe would love to have that person hear his presentation. The more the merrier!

If you need different meeting options as well, do the following:

1. Click the Customize access and presenters for the meeting check box as shown in Figure 12-9.

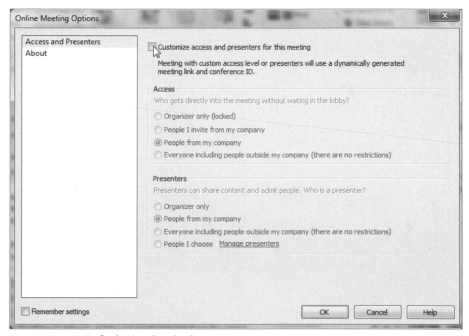

FIGURE 12-9: Default Meeting Options

2. Select the Access option of Everyone including people outside your company, and then click OK as shown in Figure 12-10.

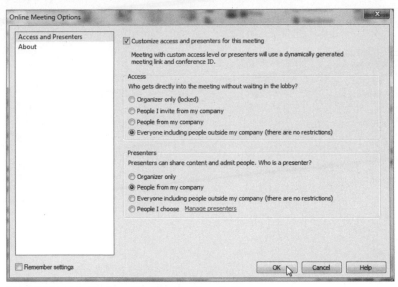

FIGURE 12-10: Custom Meeting Options Set

The meeting request is now ready to go.

Joe looks it over one more time to verify that the meeting date and time are what he wants, the attendee list is correct, the meeting options he wants have been set, there's an appropriate subject line, and the text in the body of the meeting request looks good. Joe clicks Send, as shown in Figure 12-11.

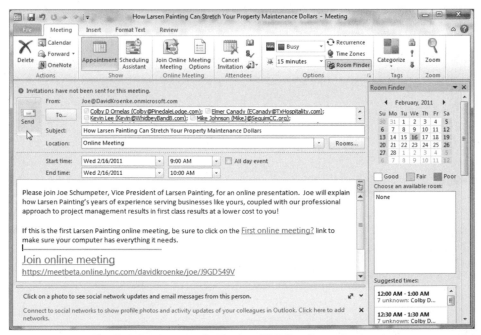

FIGURE 12-11: The Meeting Request Is Ready—Click Send

Preparing for an Online PowerPoint Presentation

Once the meeting invitations have been sent as discussed in the preceding section, you'll want to do some advanced preparation by uploading the PowerPoint file and verifying that the meeting options are set the way you want them. To do that you will "join" the meeting in advance of the scheduled time and follow the steps outlined in the sections that follow.

Verifying the Meeting Options and Uploading the PowerPoint File

PowerPoint files are large, and there will be a substantial delay at the beginning of your meeting if you wait until the meeting is underway before uploading your file. Also you should verify that the meeting options are set the way you want them. To do these two things, follow these steps:

1. Open the meeting in your Outlook calendar, and click Join Online Meeting in the Outlook ribbon, as shown in Figure 12-12.

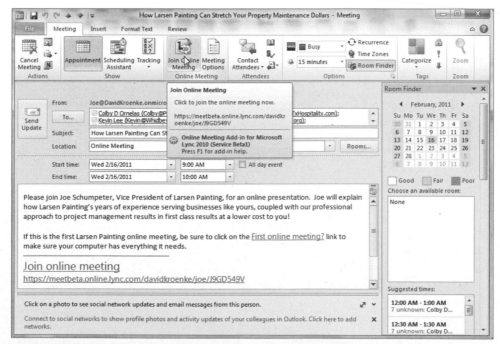

FIGURE 12-12: Meeting Information from Joe's Outlook Calendar

2. When presented with the Join Online Audio dialog box, accept the default choice of Use Lync (integrated audio and video) by clicking OK.

> **Note**
>
> Remember, Joe is "joining" the meeting in advance of the scheduled time to upload his PowerPoint file and to verify that the meeting options are set the way he wants them. When the meeting time comes, the attendees will be presented with this same Join Online Audio dialog box. Most attendees will choose to use Lync integrated audio and video since the audio and video are handled automatically by Lync. If the attendee doesn't want audio for whatever reason, he or she could choose *Do not join audio*. If the attendee is using a device that doesn't have a microphone or speakers she could choose to have Lync call her so she can use her telephone for meeting audio.

FIGURE 12-13: Join Meeting Audio Dialog Box

3. After a few seconds, you'll see the Lync meeting window in Figure 12-14. To make sure the meeting options are set as you intended, click the Join Information and Meeting Options link as shown.

FIGURE 12-14: Lync Meeting Window

You'll see the dialog box shown in Figure 12-15. Note that it contains the meeting link. You can use this link to invite a last minute attendee to the meeting via email or instant messaging.

Confirming Meeting Options

As you learned earlier in the chapter, you can select a number of meeting options when you prepare the meeting invitations. However, it's a good idea to confirm that those options are set as you intended. To do that, click the Meeting Options button as shown in Figure 12-15.

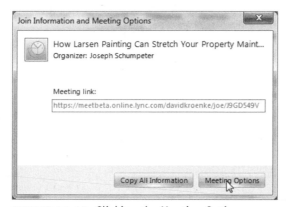

FIGURE 12-15: Clicking the Meeting Options

As you can see, the Online Meeting Options dialog box contains the same Meeting access and Presenters sections that Joe had access to when he prepared the meeting invitation in Outlook. However, notice the additional section, Privileges. You can grant two privileges:

- **View privately:** This option determines who can view slides other than the one the presenter is showing. Meeting attendees can privately look ahead in the presentation or review a slide they've already seen. The View privately options are:

    - Presenters only

    - Everyone

    - None

    In this example, Joe is happy with the default of Presenters only because he would prefer the attendees concentrate on what he's saying and not get distracted by scanning ahead in the deck.

- **Annotate Presentations:** This option controls who can use the various tools available in Lync to annotate the PowerPoint deck. The Annotate presentations options are again:

  - Presenters only

  - Everyone

  - None

Joe does not want attendees marking up his deck as he presents, so he changes the Annotate presentations option to Presenters only, as shown in Figure 12-16.

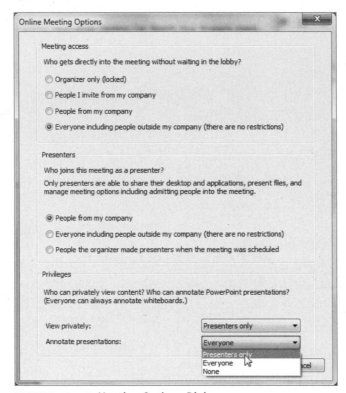

FIGURE 12-16: Meeting Options Dialog

After you have the meeting options the way you want, click OK as shown in Figure 12-17.

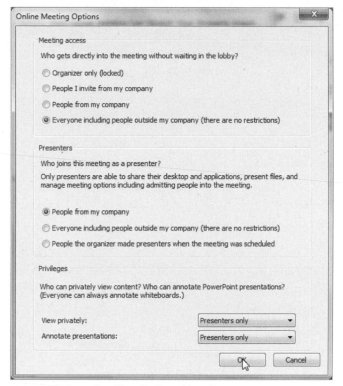

FIGURE 12-17: Meeting Options Now Set

Uploading a PowerPoint File

Now that you have the presentation scheduled and you have verified the meeting options, you must upload the PowerPoint file so you can share it with the attendees of the meeting.

To upload your PowerPoint file, follow these steps:

1. Click Share → PowerPoint Presentation as shown in Figure 12-18. You'll see a Windows Explorer window.

FIGURE 12-18: Selecting PowerPoint Presentation

2. Navigate to the location where your PowerPoint deck is stored and select it. Naturally, for this example, the file is stored in the Larsen Painting Office 365 SharePoint site. Another example of the integration of SharePoint is the SharePoint Sites option as shown in Figure 12-19.

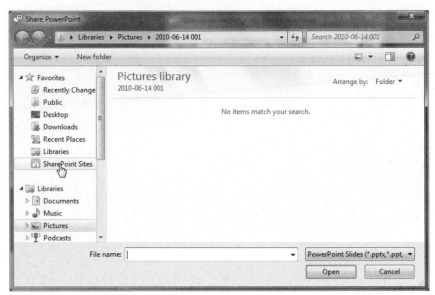

FIGURE 12-19: SharePoint Sites as an Option in Windows Explorer

For this example, Joe navigates to the Shared Documents library in the Larsen Painting SharePoint site, and selects his PowerPoint file as shown in Figure 12-20.

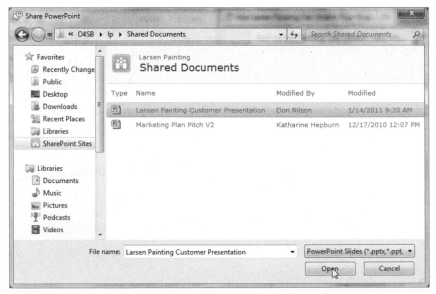

FIGURE 12-20: Selecting the PowerPoint Deck from SharePoint

3. Click Open. The Lync stage appears, with two indications that the PowerPoint file is being uploaded as shown in Figure 12-21.

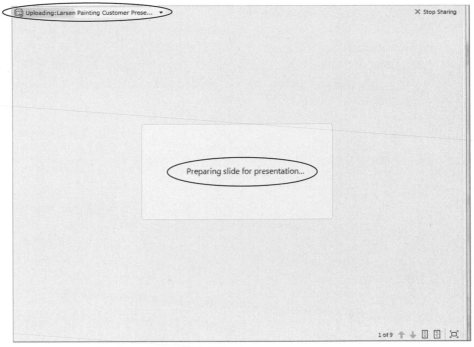

FIGURE 12-21: The PowerPoint Deck Uploads

After the PowerPoint file is uploaded, the first slide appears in the Lync stage as shown in Figure 12-22.

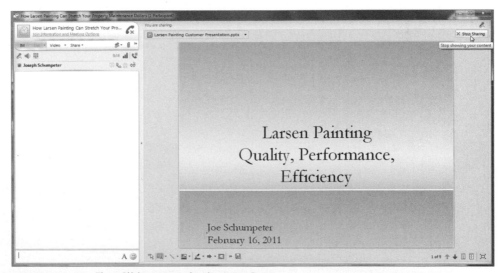

FIGURE 12-22: First Slide Appear in the Lync Stage

4. Now that the file is uploaded to Lync in preparation for the meeting, you can click the People Options icon, and then click Remove Everyone and End Meeting, as shown in Figure 12-23, which closes the Lync meeting window.

 Note Remember that a separate copy of Joe's PowerPoint presentation now exists on the Lync Online server. Any changes Joe makes to the presentation will not appear in the Lync copy. Joe will need to remove the old version from the Lync meeting, and upload the new one.

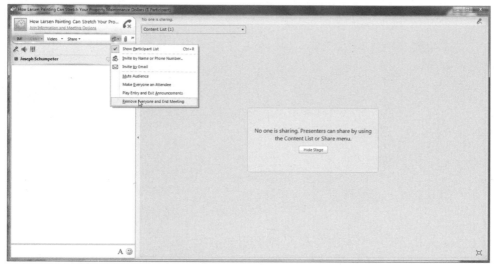

FIGURE 12-23: Closing the Meeting Session

Delivering the Online PowerPoint Presentation

Now that your meeting has been scheduled, you have verified the meeting options, and you uploaded your PowerPoint deck in advance by using a preview session of the meeting, you are ready to deliver the presentation. In this section you will learn how to use Lync and the special presentation tools to do just that.

Sharing the PowerPoint Presentation

On the day of the meeting, Outlook sends you a reminder a few minutes before the meeting is scheduled to start. The same is true for all the attendees who have accepted the meeting invitation. As the presenter, you will need to join the meeting. To join the meeting and make the presentation follow these steps:

1. Click the Join Online button as shown in Figure 12-24.

FIGURE 12-24: Click Join Online When the Outlook Reminder Pops Up

2. To display the first slide of the presentation so people joining the meeting will see that, click Share → Recent Content, and then the name of the PowerPoint file, as shown in Figure 12-25.

FIGURE 12-25: Selecting the Saved PowerPoint Presentation to Share

The first slide appears on the Lync stage as shown in Figure 12-26, and you're ready for the attendees to join the meeting.

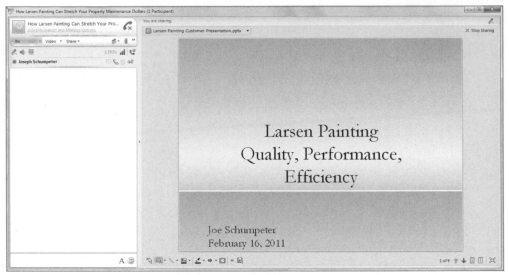

FIGURE 12-26: The First Slide Is Displayed Waiting for the Attendees to Join the Meeting

Using the Lync PowerPoint Presentation Tools

After the meeting is underway, a number of tools are available to assist you with your presentation. These are shown in Figure 12-27. They include:

- **Navigation tools:** These help you move one slide at a time or help you locate a specific slide.

- **Laser pointer:** Allows you to draw the audience's attention to a specific area of a slide.

- **Annotation tools:** Allows you to electronically mark slides as you present them to the audience.

The following sections discuss each set of tools in full detail.

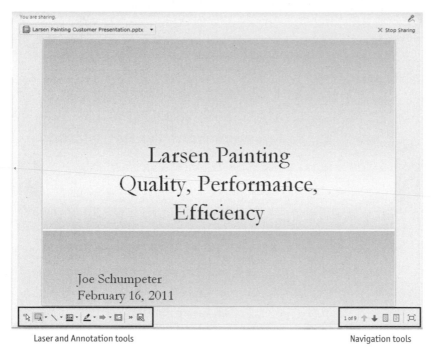

Laser and Annotation tools   Navigation tools

FIGURE 12-27: Location of the Navigation, Laser, and Annotation Tools

Navigation Tools

The navigation tools are located at the bottom right of the Lync stage as shown in Figure 12-27 and described in Table 12-1. These tools allow the presenter to move from one slide to another, to display thumbnail versions of the slides so you can select a particular slide if you want, and to display presenter's notes to remind you of the points you might want to emphasize for the slide. These notes are part of the PowerPoint file.

TABLE 12-1: PowerPoint Navigation Tools (provided by Lync)

Icon	Navigation Tool	Description
↑	Up arrow	Moves you backward one slide at a time.
↓	Down arrow	Moves you forward one slide at a time.
▤	Show thumbnails	Enables you to move to any slide in the presentation with one click by clicking on the thumbnail of the slide you want, as shown in Figure 12-28. This is only visible to the presenter.
▤	Show presenter notes	Displays the presenter notes under each slide, as shown in Figure 12-29. This is only visible to the presenter.

FIGURE 12-28: Thumbnails Displayed

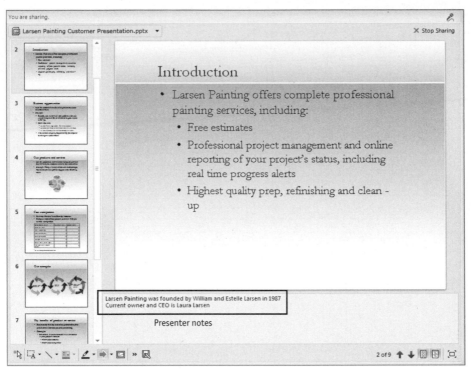

FIGURE 12-29: Presenter Notes Displayed to the Presenter Beneath Each Slide

The Virtual Laser Pointer

Anyone who has done PowerPoint presentations knows how useful a laser pointer can be. Lync provides one for each presenter to use during online PowerPoint presentations. This feature comes in handy when multiple presenters are at the meeting. Each has a unique color laser pointer, labeled with that presenter's name so attendees can determine which presenter is pointing to what area of the slide.

To activate it, follow these steps:

1. Click the laser pointer icon located on the right bottom of the Lync stage. The tool location is shown in Figure 12-27. Figure 12-30 shows the actual Laser pointer tool.

FIGURE 12-30: The Laser Pointer Icon

2. You display the laser pointer by clicking and dragging in the slide as shown in Figure 12-31. (The black box in the figure is not part of the laser pointer.) Note that Joe's name is displayed next to the laser pointer.

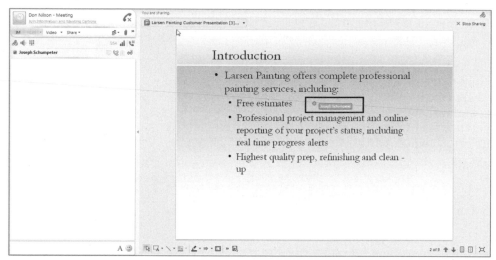

FIGURE 12-31: Joe's Laser Pointer

Annotation Tools

Lync also provides several useful tools that presenters and, if authorized, attendees can use to make annotations on the slides. The default color of the annotation tools is black, but you can change their color to make your annotations stand out. You learn more about that shortly, but first, Table 12-2 shows all the annotation tools and describes what they do.

TABLE 12-2: Annotation Tools

Icon	Tool name	Description
	Text	Adds text to the presentation slide on display. Clicking the icon gives you access to a dialog where you can select a font and font size for your text.
	Choose Drawing Tool	Adds shapes to your presentation. Clicking the icon reveals a dialog where you can select a line, a single or double arrow line, an oval or a rectangle.
	Choose a Color	Allows you to choose what color your annotation tool will mark in.

continues

TABLE 12-2: Annotation Tools *(continued)*

Icon	Tool name	Description
✎ ▾	Choose a Pen	Clicking this reveals various colored pens and highlighters that you can use to mark the presentation slide.
➡ ▾	Check Stamp	Clicking this tool gives you access to three stamps—Arrow, Check, and X—that you can use to mark the presentation slide.
▣	Insert Image	Allows you to add an image from the folder of your choice to the presentation slide.
▧	Additional tools	Provides access to commands including Undo, Redo, Cut, Copy, Paste, Paste as Image, Delete Selected Annotations, and Delete All Annotations from This Page
»	Save with Annotations	Activates a dialog where you can navigate to a folder and save the PowerPoint presentation with the annotations made to the various slides.

To see annotation tools in action, follow these steps:

1. **Choosing a color:** Click the Choose a Color icon. The default color is black. However, you can choose whatever color you want (in this example, Joe selects dark green from the palette shown in Figure 12-32).

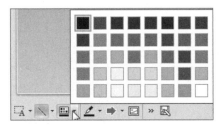

FIGURE 12-32: The Color Palette

2. **Adding text:** Click the Text icon, and select a font and font size as shown in Figure 12-33. To annotate a slide with text, simply click in the slide and type the text you want, as shown in Figure 12-34.

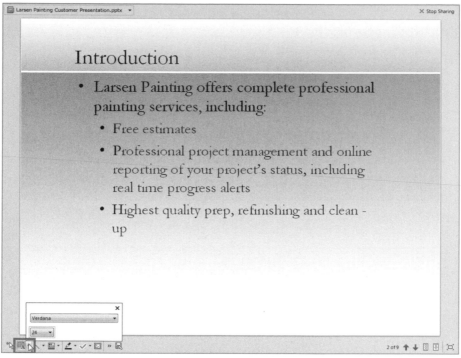

FIGURE 12-33: Selecting a Font and Font Size

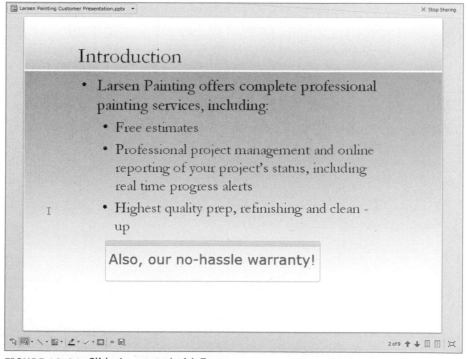

FIGURE 12-34: Slide Annotated with Text

3. **Add a shape:** You can annotate slides with lines, ovals, squares, and rectangles. Click the Choose Drawing Tool icon to access a window with variously shaped tools that you can select, as shown in Figure 12-35. Move your cursor to draw your shape.

FIGURE 12-35: Icon for Selecting Line, Arrows, Oval, or Rectangle

In this example, Joe selects the rectangle and uses the tool to create a rectangle around the second bullet, as shown in Figure 12-36. Although you can't see it, the rectangle is dark green because that was the color Joe chose previously.

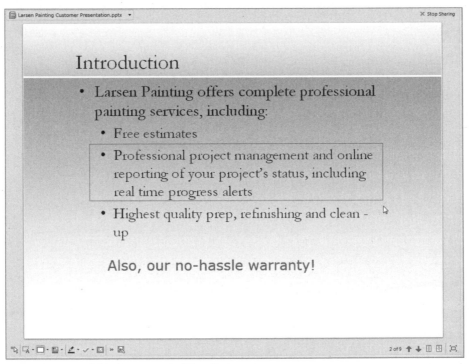

FIGURE 12-36: Slide Annotated with a Rectangle

4. **Mark with Pens and Highlighters:** You can also draw freehand in the slides. You select a specific one by clicking the Choose a Pen Tool icon, which reveals different colored pens and highlighters, as shown in Figure 12-37.

FIGURE 12-37: Pen Selection in the Choose a Pen Tool List

In this example, Joe selects the yellow highlighter and highlights "Free esti-mates" in the slide, as shown in Figure 12-38.

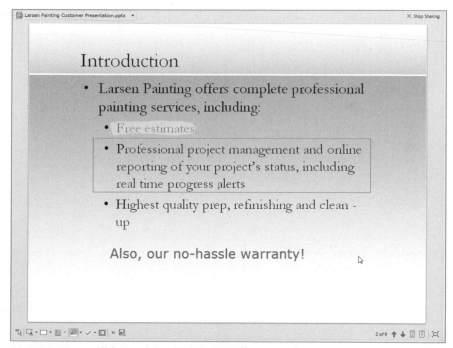

FIGURE 12-38: Slide Annotated with a Highlighter Tool

5. **Stamp the slide:** Lync also offers a choice of three stamps—Arrow, Check, and X—to use in annotating slides. In this example, Joe chooses the Check Stamp, as shown in Figure 12-39. As Joe covers each bullet in the slide, he places a check next to it, as shown in Figure 12-40.

FIGURE 12-39: Selecting the Check Stamp

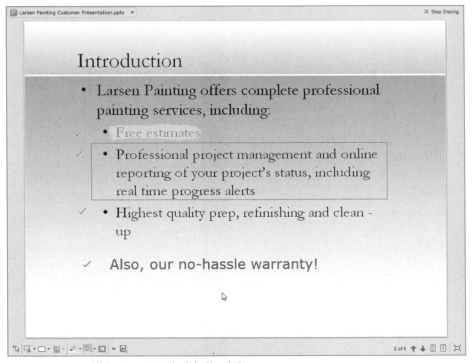

FIGURE 12-40: Slide Annotated with Check Stamps

6. **Add images to the slide:** Lync also provides the ability to add images to slides. You just click the Insert Image icon, and you're presented with a Windows Explorer window that you use to navigate to the image you want to add to the slide, as shown in Figure 12-41.

Figure 12-42 shows the slide after Joe adds an image.

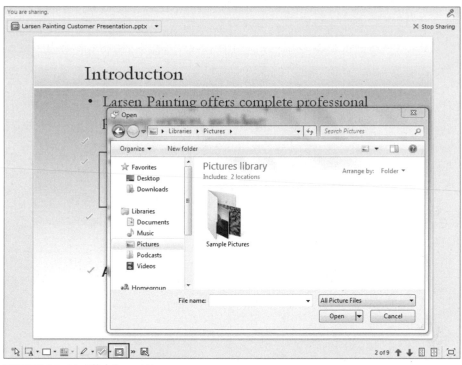

FIGURE 12-41: Click Insert Image

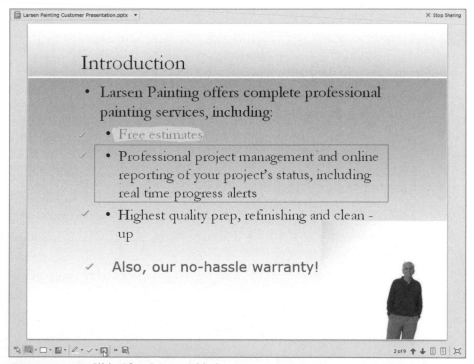

FIGURE 12-42: Slide After Image Added

7. **Save annotations:** When the presentation is finished, the presenter can save the annotated file. To do this, you click the Save with Annotations icon, which opens a Windows Save As dialog box. Navigate to the location where you want to save the annotated file, and click Save. In this example, Joe decides to add the annotated file to the Larsen Painting SharePoint site (shown in Figure 12-43).

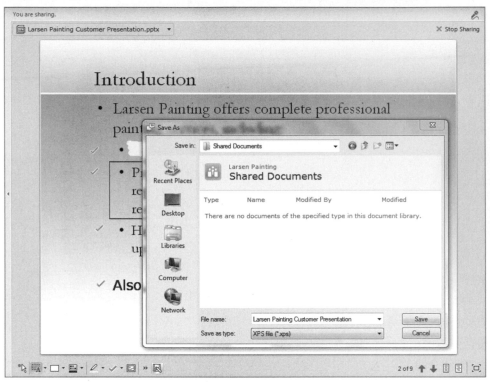

FIGURE 12-43: Save with Annotations

8. **Delete Annotations:** If you choose, you can remove the annotations from the PowerPoint deck by selecting the Delete All Annotations from This Page item, shown in Figure 12-44, which you access by clicking the Additional Tools icon (the right double chevron).

Figure 12-45 shows the slide with all annotations removed.

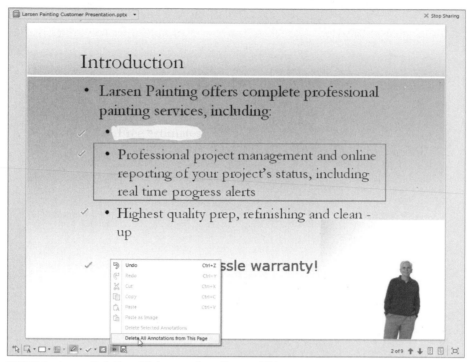

FIGURE 12-44: Deleting All Annotations from a Slide

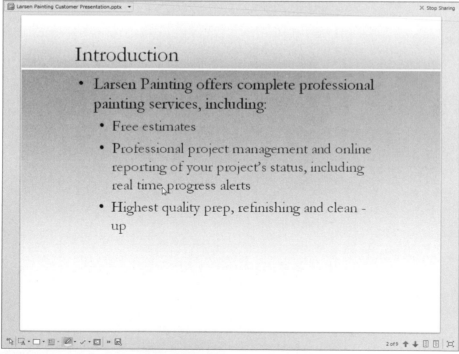

FIGURE 12-45: All Annotations Removed

What You've Learned

In this chapter, you've learned that Lync provides great integration with Microsoft PowerPoint, which allows you to make PowerPoint slide presentations over the Internet.

Specifically, you've learned how to:

- Use Outlook to schedule an online meeting
- Use Online Meeting Options to control who has access to the meeting and who can serve as presenters
- Use the special tools built into Lync to conduct an online SharePoint presentation
- Save the marked-up presentation

What's Next?

In the last ten chapters, you've seen common business challenges and you've learned how you can use Office 365 to get the job done better, improve your team, create a rich and rewarding experience, and facilitate critical feedback and effective iteration because of two critical facts:

- Office 365 makes it easier to communicate, both synchronously and asynchronously
- Office 365 makes it easy to share

Then next step depends on you, your organization and its particular circumstances.

Glossary

Annotate Presentation A privilege that may be granted to an attendee of a meeting where a PowerPoint presentation is made. An attendee with this privilege can use Lync's annotation tools to annotate the slides used in the presentation. Any attendee can annotate a shared whiteboard.

Approval Workflow Used to obtain approval over something: a document, a proposal, a problem definition, and so on. The item that is being approved can be stored within the SharePoint site, but it need not be.

Attendee Anyone who is able to join a meeting. Whether attendees automatically join the meeting or they are required to wait in the virtual lobby until admitted by a presenter depends on the meeting options set by the meeting organizer or a presenter. See Chapter 12 for details.

Blog A website or portion of a website where an individual or team posts periodic, sometimes daily, comments and updates about a particular topic. A blog

in SharePoint is a SharePoint site that team members can use to publish their expertise and share opinions.

Calendar View A view that displays a task list in the form of a calendar. See also *View*. See Chapter 6 for details.

Choice Column A column in a SharePoint list that provides a list of valid values that the user can choose from. Choice columns can either restrict the user to selecting one of the values presented or allow the user to enter a value not in the list of values. See Chapter 8 for details.

Cloud The term *cloud* comes from the symbol that computer professionals use to designate the Internet on diagrams during whiteboard sessions. The principle behind the cloud is that instead of running powerful server programs such as Microsoft SharePoint Server, Microsoft Lync Server, and Microsoft Exchange Server in your company's expensive data centers (and what small business can afford such things?), those server programs run on computers housed in remote data centers, and you access them over the Internet. Thus, it is said that those server programs are "hosted" by a third party (see also *host/hosting*). In the case of Office 365, that third party is Microsoft Corporation, which has sophisticated data centers located in several locations around the world.

Document Properties Data items that describe a document. Some of the properties are Type, Name, Modified (the date and time the document was last modified), and Modified By (the person who made the most recent change).

Exchange Online The online version of Microsoft Exchange Server 2010, which is the latest version of Microsoft's messaging platform. Exchange Online provides the background infrastructure that allows users to manage their email, maintain appointment calendars, store contact information, and manage their daily task lists all with Microsoft Outlook or the browser version, Outlook Web Access.

Gantt Chart View A view that displays a task list in the form of a Gantt Chart. A Gantt Chart is a graphical display that places tasks on a timeline and shows dependencies among those tasks. See *Task Predecessor* and *View*. Also, see Chapter 6 for details.

Host/Hosting To host a service means to provide the computer hardware and software, other computer infrastructure, and the IT staff and the buildings that house them that are necessary for making access to the service available over the Internet.

Internet The public worldwide computer network system made up of a network of networks. It consists of millions of private, public, academic, business, and government networks providing a vast range of information resources and services, such as the interlinked documents of the World Wide Web and the infrastructure to support electronic mail.

IM Instant messaging. A feature in Lync that allows you to "chat" with an individual or group of people by typing messages in the instant messaging window. Although not nearly as useful as starting an audio or, better yet, a video conversation, it serves a purpose when, for whatever reason, audio or video is not an option at the moment.

Inheritance See *Permission Inheritance*.

IT Staff Information Technology professionals including system administrators, network technicians, and help-desk personnel responsible for designing, equipping, and maintaining a data center within which the computer programs run that make up a service such as Microsoft Exchange Server, Microsoft Lync Server, or Microsoft SharePoint Server.

Lobby Depending on the meeting options set by the meeting organizer or a presenter, some people may not be allowed immediately to join a meeting, but will be required to wait in a virtual lobby until admitted by a presenter.

Lync Client The program that users interact with on their computers to utilize the powerful communications capabilities of Office

365, which are provided by Lync Online. In addition to the full-featured Lync 2010 client, there is also Microsoft Lync 2010 Attendee, which is a conferencing client that allows users without the full version of Lync 2010 installed to participate in online meetings. Those who prefer, or must, use a browser to participate in online meetings, can use Lync Web App, which provides most of the Lync 2010 features in an online meeting, including viewing and presenting PowerPoint slides, meeting-wide IM, file distribution, and application and desktop sharing. One limitation with Lync Web App is that you must use phone-based audio instead of the integrated Lync audio. Lync audio is handled by the Lync Online server instead of the outside phone network, which will involve separate fees from the service provider.

Lync Online Provides a virtual connection between you and your colleagues through instant messaging; audio/video calling; and conducting online meetings during which you can do PowerPoint presentations, share your computer desktop and applications, share whiteboards, conduct online polls, and collaborate in real time from practically anywhere.

Meeting Organizer The person who sets up the meeting, determines the initial meeting options, and invites people to the meeting.

Metadata Data about data. For example, document properties represent data about a document.

Microsoft Excel Part of Microsoft's Office Suite used for creating and editing electronic spreadsheets used for a variety of things, including budgets, financial models, scientific and mathematical models, and so on.

Microsoft Outlook Part of Microsoft's Office Suite used for managing business and personal email, calendars, contacts, and tasks. Most business people spend a big part of their workday using Microsoft Outlook.

Microsoft Powerpoint Part of Microsoft's Office Suite used for preparing, displaying, and/or printing slides for presentations.

Microsoft SharePoint SharePoint is a rich, web-based platform with lots of capabilities, which are summarized in Chapter 2. In addition, Chapters 4, 5, 6, 8, 9, and 11 of this book illustrate how SharePoint can be used for effective collaboration.

Overlay Mode A display mode in Microsoft Outlook by which several calendars can be combined to show a single calendar.

Permission Inheritance By default, SharePoint subsites have the same groups and permissions as the parent site. This can be convenient if you are using subsites to control complexity of your site, but can be dangerous if you are using subsites to provide privacy for what is stored in the subsite. See Chapter 5 for details.

Personal Task List View A view that displays a task list showing only those tasks assigned to whomever is signed into SharePoint when the task list view is accessed. See Chapter 6 for details.

Predecessor See *Task Predecessor*.

Presence Information A status indicator that conveys the ability and willingness of a potential communication partner to communicate. In Microsoft Office applications this information is shown in a small square immediately to the left of the contact's name. The color of the square indicates whether the person is available (green), away (yellow), or busy (red). A gray square indicates that presence information for the contact is not currently available. In the Lync client, presence information is displayed as a small bar along the left side of the contact's picture.

Presenter Only presenters are able to share their desktop and applications, present files, and manage meeting options. Presenters are also the only ones who can admit people into the meeting from the Lobby, and promote attendees to be presenters and vice versa. Presenters may be designated by the meeting organizer at the time the meeting invitations are created, or they may be designated during the online session. Meeting organizers are presenters by default. See also *Attendee* and *Lobby*.

Quick Launch See *SharePoint Quick Launch*.

Ribbon A tabbed toolbar displayed at the top of Microsoft Office applications and organized in a task-oriented fashion. The ribbon, which is part of what Microsoft calls its Fluent User Interface, replaced the menus and toolbars used in Microsoft Office applications prior to Office 2007.

Security Group Used by SharePoint, and widely in other areas of computing, to manage who can do what within a SharePoint site or subsite. Instead of granting permissions to individual users, you grant permissions to groups, and then add users to the groups that have the permissions you want those users to have.

Share In Lync online video meetings you can display (share) various things from your computer screen so that the other participants in the meeting can see them. If you choose, you can share your desktop, which means that everyone in the meeting can see, in real time, everything that is displayed on your computer screen. This is often not a prudent choice. Alternatively, you can share only, say, the Excel workbook you are working on currently, or the browser session you have going, or the accounting application you are using. In addition, you can create a virtual whiteboard and share that with the meeting attendees so the group can capture their thoughts from a brain-storming session. You can also use the built in Lync tools to share a PointPoint file and make an online presentation.

SharePoint Designer A large sophisticated desktop application that you can use for customizing SharePoint sites.

SharePoint Online The online version of Microsoft's SharePoint Server 2010. With

SharePoint Online you can create sites to collaborate with colleagues, partners, and customers. SharePoint is a rich, web-based platform with lots of capabilities, which are summarized in Chapter 2. In addition, Chapters 4, 5, 6, 8, 9, and 11 of this book illustrate how you can use SharePoint for effective collaboration.

SharePoint Quick Launch A vertical menu on the left side of a SharePoint page. This menu is a list of links that point to resources in the SharePoint site. By default, the Quick Launch has Libraries (Site Pages, Shared Documents), Lists (Calendar, Tasks), and Discussion (Team Discussion).

SharePoint Site A collection of libraries, lists, calendars, tasks, and other resources. SharePoint sites can have one or more children sites, called subsites.

SharePoint Team Site The most common SharePoint site. As with all SharePoint sites, you can customize Team Sites to suit the specific needs of your team. See Chapter 4 for details.

SharePoint Workflow A sequence of steps involving tasks that SharePoint assigns to those who are responsible for them in the order specified by the creator of the workflow. At the completion of each step in the workflow, SharePoint closes the task, generates optional emails to specified personnel that the task has been completed, and then creates tasks for the next step in the workflow. SharePoint enforces the rules specified for the

workflow by the workflow creator. See also *Three-state Workflow*. See Chapter 9 for details.

Shared Documents The default SharePoint document library used to store documents.

Site Columns Built-in column definitions that you can use to create your own custom lists in SharePoint.

Site Theme A graphic design that includes typefaces, sizes, and colors, as well as screen background colors.

Subsite A SharePoint site that is a child of another (parent) SharePoint site. See *SharePoint Site*. See Chapter 5 for how to use subsites to reduce complexity and provide privacy for a SharePoint site.

Task Predecessor A task that must be completed before another task. For example, "Prep First Floor" must be completed before the task "Paint First Floor Walls" can be started.

Three-state Workflow A generalized SharePoint workflow that deals only with tasks. In creating a three-state workflow, you specify exactly three stages that the task can have, and instruct SharePoint what action to take when the workflow is started and when a user marks the task as having moved from the initial state to the second state. See Chapter 9 for details.

View A presentation of a library or list. A SharePoint view can contain items from multiple libraries and lists. Views give incredible power and flexibility to

SharePoint. See Chapters 4 and 8 for details.

View Privately A privilege that may be granted to an attendee of a meeting where a PowerPoint presentation is made. Those who have this privilege can view content other than what the presenter is showing.

Wiki A wiki is a website, or portion of a website that allows multiple people to post content. It is an effective way to gather views from various people and make them available on the Internet or within a company intranet. A Share-Point wiki is a SharePoint library that is designed to allow members to document their knowledge in page displays and link those pages to other pages in the wiki. Any entry in a wiki can link to many other pages, and any other page can link back to it.

Workflow History List A list in which SharePoint stores the workflow history log.

Index